Ghosts, Spirits & Angels

Thomas Lee Freese

A͞P™
Acclaim Press
MORLEY, MISSOURI

Acclaim Press
— Your Next Great Book —

P.O. Box 238
Morley, Missouri 63767
(573) 472-9800
www.acclaimpress.com

Library of Congress Cataloging-in-Publication Data

Freese, Thomas Lee.
  Ghosts, spirits, and angels: true tales from Kentucky and beyond
/ by Thomas Lee Freese.
      p. cm.
  Includes bibliographical references.
  ISBN-13: 978-1-935001-25-6
  ISBN-10: 1-935001-25-6
  1. Ghosts. 2. Spirits. 3. Angels. 4. Kentucky--Miscellanea. I.
Title.
  BF1461.F74 2009
  133.1--dc22

                              2009030444

First Printing 2009
Printed in the United States of America
10 9 8 7 6 5 4 3 2 1

Table of Contents

Foreword

As you will see, the amount of information varies from one story to the next. I decided to include many stories, despite their having but a few paragraphs. Collectively, these mini-tales add to the body of the book, providing more than an assembled verbiage. Each story importantly adds to the variety and pulls from different sources, different locations and families. Not every tale is the *Legend of Sleepy Hollow*.

A certain percentage of the stories are told by the person who either experienced the ghost, or received some or all of the tales from a family member. These accounts are faithful to the style and substance of that person's way of telling; I made minor editorial corrections to basic standards.

I heard a few good stories which didn't make it into the book, because, whenever possible, I attempted to reach the person who had told the story. If they declined to have the story published, I honored that request. A few stories, though experienced and reported to me as true, were so amazingly bizarre that I decided to withhold them. In some tales, the names or other identifying information was changed.

Acknowledgments

I previously wrote some stories, published in the *Chevy Chaser* and *Southsider* Magazines, (Lexington, Kentucky). I am grateful to all the individuals who shared their stories, many of them personal events and most involving family members.

Introduction

Why are ghosts a powerful force in our experience and imagination? What role do spirits play in our lives, as we so often insist that life consists only of provable empirical reality? Where do we place angels in our modern narrative, so many years past Biblical folklore? The answers may be found in these simple stories from my friends, family and acquaintances.

Our minds hold vast potential. From babies to young adolescents, the plasticity of the brain organism expands and creates new neural circuits with mere imaginative exercise, let alone with each interactive life experience. Children find or create imaginary friends, and the quality of their adult life might be determined by the reaction of family and of other significant adults, as they talk about how they see ghosts, spirits and angels. Do we allow or expect our children to express a mindset that sees fairies, walks with angels, or converses with deceased spirits? If our rational mind cannot conceive of metaphysical possibility superimposed on a mechanistic universe, then we may miss the very miracles that we ask for in our hearts and prayers.

To bravely set aside primitive fears or dismissive religious rigid conceptualism may allow us freedom to hear and see the unusual, the odd and that which otherwise does not fit into our commonplace thinking. Even the ghost story itself has become a ghost wandering in a library of literary stereotypes. Must we only see a ghost in a rundown Victorian mansion, in the month of October, while the wind blows screeching branches against an antique window pane? That's a good story, a modus of creating fearful metaphor, but it doesn't represent the variety of true tales I have heard. The real stories are immediate, accessible to every person. Ghosts are everywhere, in new homes, in a Walgreens®, in daylight and in spring as well as fall. A whole host of people, poised as investigators, examined their photographs and electronic records, seeking the Holy Grail of proof of life on the other side. Their efforts have merit yet miss the point. A spirit encounter represents a grace, a gift from one dimension to another. While flashing camera lights, I might miss the nuance of communication, or the essential who, what and why.

One familiar method of contacting spirits and angels stretches our notion of existential separation; how can a psychic talk to my grandmother or receive an angelic message? We doubt, we question and we insist in front of others that impossible things do not happen in our rational world. But wasn't the alternative world always with us, not far away, in backyards where children play, in quiet dreamy predawn moments in our beds, and in hospital rooms when the soul of a beloved passes?

Here are the stories of real people. The character of ghosts and creativity of interaction correspond to the range of personalities we experience in normal life. The relationships with the living and those on the other side are comforting or troubled, or negotiable. Frustrated mortals shout to ghosts to "shut up" or "move out of my home." What separates the characteristics of ghosts compared to spirits may not be so great, and yet again, another step into mystery and the spirit is called an angel. What defines each grouping may not be shrouds versus wings, but rather the intent or level of intervention. Thus, a spirit might save a life but be considered an angel. Or, a ghost may keep a protective presence in force for decades and in so doing increase status as a spirit.

Ghost stories are a growth industry, as we are all pushed through time to return to spirit; we all have potential to continue our work on the other side, as kindred spirits. We see ghosts in dreams, cars, bedrooms, hallways, outside, public places, post offices, graveyards, floating in the air, historic old homes, basements, closets, barns, front yards, pictures, on TV, bathroom, attics, floating over streams and in all the places we go and see. When the near-inevitable encounter comes our way, we cannot deny the intimate communication or connection of their mind with ours. I think of Grandpa, and his picture falls off the shelf. I remember my deceased friend, and her favorite song plays on the radio. The many seeming coincidences accumulate into anecdotal experiential evidence. You may deny whatever you wish, but I know what I have seen, heard and felt.

Thus, the stories of ghosts, spirits and angels are so personally meaningful, and putting them in this book will encourage still others to 'fess up. Our brief lives may come and go with scant material wealth or fame, but we all have our narrative, our story and our belief in the other world.

Ghosts, Spirits & Angels

True Tales from Kentucky and Beyond

Ghosts

GHOST, n. The outward and visible sign of an inward fear. (From The Devil's Dictionary, Ambrose Bierce).

Non-believers of ghosts seem as amused by the faithful, as believers are astounded by the doubtful. There are those who never will believe (so they say) and yet again there are rational skeptics, dubious of photographic orbs and house sounds easily explained away. In fact, the proposed errors in perceiving ghosts make a fascinating list. Ghostly experiences are denied in favor of insect sounds, houses settling, pipes moaning, wind, mist, smoke, incorrect visual interpretation (such as labeling the scene of a dog running by as a ghost), psychological projection, rowdy cats, wishful thinking, imagination, and more.

In strictly logical terms, we cannot presume to call phenomenon real based solely upon the frequency of anecdotal evidence. So what if people, rich and poor, old and young, wise and foolish, contemporary and ancient, from all over the world claim to have seen ghosts? Does that prove they exist?

On the other hand, it is indeed difficult to deny our senses. I asked someone why her religion tells her that ghosts aren't real.

Puzzled, I asked her, "If the figure by your bed at night looks like your grandma, smells like your grandma, and talks like your grandma, why wouldn't the most obvious explanation be true – that this is the ghost of your grandma?"

She replied, "It is the devil."

I was amazed. I heard over 200 ghost stories over the years from many persons. She assured me that there are no ghosts, but rather in each instance the devil takes the form of our loved ones. I asked her one more question.

"If the devil may appear as anyone he wishes, then how do you know whether or not you're now talking to me or to the devil?" She had no reply.

Obviously, ghosts are a dynamic part of our folklore and popular culture. It's difficult to say if the fantastic, fabricated stories inoculate the skeptics from opening their mind to humble and near spirits. Does the overriding fear of the devil preclude the perception of benign ghostly interaction in our mortal lives? Can skeptics prove that the soul does not survive death and can they give evidence that ghosts are <u>not</u> present? Hans Holzer, ghost investigator, noted that, "The human mind is as clever of inventing away as it is as hallucinating."

It is my understanding that a ghost is the spirit or soul remnant of a person who lived and died. In some accounts, it seems that the person saw a visual reenactment of trauma or death, but that the real soul has flown away. But in other stories, it appears that person's soul is very present, interacting and giving full evidence of their typical character, foibles and personality attributes. The names for ghosts are many – earthbound spirits, stay-behinds, others, entities, apparition, specter, wraith, revenant, and shade. Despite our efforts to hold the ghost at arm's length, to distance ourselves from the dead, the spirits seem to insist on entering our world, speaking to us, and sitting at our bedside, bringing help or hindrance, touching our shoulder, teasing and pleasing us.

Ghosts are not going away.

Someone Who Is Not There

When I was a child, I suppose I saw movies with ghosts, and I certainly appreciated a good Halloween tale, too. I don't recall experiencing ghosts until one night when I was about twelve years old. I heard a loud thump in the middle of the night. I awoke, startled and frozen in fear. I lay quietly in the bottom bunk bed, and after being quiet for a few seconds, spoke to my unseen older brother in the top bunk.

"Did you hear that?"

"Yes," was his simple answer, and he said no more.

My rational mind, quick to supply good excuses, thought that it might have been my father, coming down the hallway, and bumping into our wall as he walked back to my parents' bedroom. But the next day, I questioned my mother who said that my father hadn't been up.

I asked her, "Have you ever seen or heard a ghost?"

She said "No," but after a few moments passed, and I looked at her eyes, I could see that she was scanning her memory.

She said, "There was one time, when I was coming back from Barbie's place, at Byrnes Mill, (my great aunt's farm). I looked over on the hill, where the old sea captain had a house, near the old graveyard, and I saw a man dressed in old-time clothes. When I went through the field gate, turning back to close the gate, he was gone." (For my Mother's own version see, "Old Man on Gravestone below").

That was it. No moaning, no chains, no old house, just one odd thing that happened, like my hearing a noise at night that woke me up but yet had no explanation. Perhaps that story fueled my desire to hear more, although I'm not sure that hearing hundreds of other ghost stories has answered any questions. But over the decades, when I wasn't really looking for a ghost, they appeared. I visited a friend in Indianapolis to stay overnight and market my jewelry. We talked, and she said she worked a split shift. She said when she returned after several hours we'd go out for dinner, and invited me to nap on the sofa, which I did. When I awoke, I had that disorienting feeling one has having slept and awakened in a different home. Plus, it was daytime when I lay down, and the September day had turned to night. (Added to that, I feel that upon awakening, our mind and body take a few moments to look around and determine, who am I, where am I?)

As I lay on my left side, I saw, as much in my mind's eye, an older woman across the living room, sitting in the old wooden rocking chair. I noticed that her bearing was erect, not stiff, but rather good posture for an older woman. The image faded away, and once again my rational mind caught up with my sight of the ghost.

"You didn't really see that," I told myself. But I wasn't convinced. When Myra returned, I asked her about her home.

"Well, I got a good price on the home, as an elderly friend of the family passed away. The family gave me a good price on a lot of the furniture."

"What did the elderly woman look like?" I asked.

Myra gave a brief description, and it matched the figure I saw. I slowly realized that I saw her ghost. Maybe she watched over me, kept me company, as I napped. Or she was simply hanging out in her home. I didn't have a fear, or fascination, really; it was just something odd that happened.

Old Man on Gravestone
Joan Freese, Chesterfield, Missouri

There were a couple of incidents that I can't forget. One of them happened when I was 18 years old. I was at my grandfather's farm out in the country, in Byrnes Mill, Missouri. I spent my vacation at the farm. One of my chief pleasures was riding whatever current horse they had. I don't know where they got those horses, but it seemed like every horse had some kind of quirk.

There was Dolly, the white horse that balked like a mule unless you had a stick. It could be just a ten-inch stick in your hand, a twig, and then she would go for you, because she thought you were going to beat her up. When we held a stick in hand she would behave fine. That was the only quirk she had.

But this particular time I was riding Babe. He was fine, but had a trick knee and stumbled once in a while. He was kind of a dumb horse. Anyway, I enjoyed riding him because I liked to ride the horses, and I went out into the pastures. In one of the pastures near their barn there was a little cemetery. Near it was an old log cabin house that was built around the time of the Civil War by a Doctor Smith. Legend had it (from my aunts) that when the Yankees were coming, Dr. Smith buried his gold, but nobody found it.

I still remember my Aunt Rose saying, "Someday I'm going to look for that gold."

Nobody ever found it. The house unfortunately is all torn down now and the cemetery is in pretty bad condition. But at the time I'm talking about it was not in too bad of a state. The stones were still standing and there was a big tree in the middle of it.

As I approached down the lane where the cows used to come in I saw a man sitting on one of the gravestones. I was about thirty yards away from him. And I thought, "*I don't recognize him.*" He was an older gentleman just sitting there, looking out toward me. I wasn't close enough to actually see who he was. But I thought, "*I wonder who that is?*" He had on a light color top and gray pants. I rode a little further and the dumb horse stumbled a bit. I looked up again and there was absolutely <u>no one there</u>.

This was out in the middle of a field. There was really no place he could go. And I have no idea if he was a ghost or not. But I couldn't explain it and I still remember it to this day.

Flapping Curtains With No Breeze
Joan Freese, Chesterfield, Missouri

The other incident I remember happened when we were in Ireland. Our oldest daughter, Jane, worked for TWA, so we took a few trips without having to spend a lot of money on airfare. It was nice when it lasted. We rented a car at the airport and drove off, taking our chances on places to stay. At that time – I don't know how things are now, because this was about 1990, '91, people weren't too leery about letting folks stay at their places.

This was in Navan. We came in Dublin the night before and drove up a little north of Dublin. That's where my grandfather came from, in that general area. Another thing that was funny, in Dublin my grandfather's name was Byrne. So I looked in the Dublin phone book and there were pages and pages of Byrnes! We drove up to the house and rang the doorbell. And it was a young girl that let us in.

And she said, "Oh we've got a room but my mom and dad are down in Dublin. But come in."

I imagine you don't do that as freely now. But it was a nice, interesting old house. She put us in a room upstairs. It wasn't a big room or anything.

It was getting chilly outside so the windows were shut. There wasn't a lot of heat but it was comfortable. We were really tired so we both fell asleep pretty easily. I woke up in the middle of the night. <u>It had gotten so cold</u>. I looked for my coat to put it over me because I was so cold! When I was up, I looked at the window. The window curtains were flapping but when I walked over to the window I saw that it was shut tight. I thought, *"woo, that gives me a creepy feeling!"*

Weird Photos

Many people take photographs that show odd images within the composition. There can be whispy shapes, unexplained fog, phantom lights, circular orbs, faces or figures, and more. While it is true that camera straps, equipment malfunction, genuine fog, ambient reflected light, and other false anomalies can be eagerly but wrongly labeled as evidence of spirit activity, there are many occasions when photos bring evidence of another dimension.

I travel about Kentucky to perform as a storyteller, often going to libraries and schools. I went last fall to Warsaw, Kentucky,

Slave quarters Warsaw, Gallatin County, Kentucky.

to tell ghost stories at their public library. Locals there encouraged me to go a block away to an historic house. The historical society had an open house and allowed me to walk about and take pictures. The story goes that a bride, dressed for her wedding on the very day of the celebration, fell and broke her neck on the inside stairs. While I didn't find anything unusual in pictures of the stairs, I also took pictures outside of the brick slave quarters.

When I returned home, and transferred the digital pictures to my computer, I was amazed to find a whispy shape in front of the door, and a photograph that had many orbs floating around, and more whispy fog around the upper section of the image. One wonders if a long ago slave still guards the entrance to his home; the hazy shape almost appears to be bent at the knees, head hanging down…as if suspended from shackles tied to his hands.

The General's Cabin

I write travel articles for Lexington's *Chevy Chaser Magazine*, and received a generous offer of a complementary weekend stay at a lovely, rustic hand-built cabin in Lee County, not far from Natural Bridge State Park. I invited friends to join me for the weekend, and one friend met me off the Parkway, and we drove together to the cabin. We came to Peddler's Fork, not far from Beattyville, Kentucky. This is where the General built a cabin, and where his wife and he ran a restaurant. We stayed at the General's Cabin, she was able to stay one night and I left the next day to hike in Natural Bridge State Resort Park.

Joy Massey, the General's daughter from Lexington, operates the General's Cabin. It is available year-round, sleeps six, and has every modern convenience except cable TV. It's less than a 30-minute drive to trailheads in the Red River Gorge and Natural Bridge. It sits on a ridge north of Beattyville, and overlooks wooded hills and hollows of native tulip poplar, oak, and hemlock. It is quiet, and that is good.

The cabin's builder was born in 1920, just a few miles from where the General's Cabin now stands. James Little attended and graduated from the University of Kentucky; he studied engineering and worked shoveling coal for the college's physical plant's boiler room. He also enrolled in the ROTC, and in 1941, Jim Little was selected for pilot's training; he first served overseas with the 56th Fighter Group in Egypt. In 1942, Lieutenant Little was reassigned to the 23rd Fighter Group in China, which replaced the American Volunteer Group, known as the Flying Tigers. James Little earned the reputation as an ace pilot; after bailing out during one mission, he survived partial parachute deployment and was rescued and protected by friendly Chinese forces. The pilots of the Flying Tigers had safe conduct letters from Chinese Nationalist Leader Chiang-Kai-Shek sown into the insides of their flight jackets. These letters with the American and Chinese flag symbols, provided instructions written in Chinese characters; they were called "blood chits."

Jim Little recovered from his leg injury, and also dysentery, and returned to his Flight Group. From 1943 to 1946, Lt. – later Captain – Little worked as a test pilot at Eglin Field, Florida, where he flew early model jets. He married Jane Keith, of Rock Springs, Wyoming, in 1943, and his assignments led them to Spokane, Washington, Japan and Korea. As a squadron commander, Capt. Little saw combat during the first year of the Korean War, again earning the five confirmed kills of an ace pilot. Subsequent positions in Japan, Germany, Vietnam and the U.S. brought James Little to the level of Brigadier General. He retired from active duty in 1969, and settled with his wife and daughters in Lexington.

General's Cabin front detail unexplained haze.

General Little purchased a little over 160 acres in Lee County, and called it Peddler's Fork Farm. He built his cabin out of timber from the property, using poplar for the posts, piers and most of the exterior, and using oak for the cabin's interior. He completed the house in 1977, and Mr. and Mrs. Little stayed there until the General's death in 1995. His industrious wife encouraged General Little to build a restaurant, which was erected in 1979-80 and became Peddler's Fork Inn. Jane served dinner on Friday and Saturday nights, using locally grown produce and the finest meats from Lexington. Though successful, the couple reluctantly closed the Inn after a few years, deciding to curtail ambitious projects in favor of genuine retirement. The cabin and restaurant eventually fell into disuse, but the Masseys began a renovation of the General's Cabin in 2001.

As Samara and I sat outside in the late afternoon, we talked about how she senses spirits. I had already read about the history of the cabin, and I stayed overnight by myself once before. I definitely felt a presence, even though there was no one around for some distance. There were lush potted ferns outside, on the long and welcoming porch. Inside the massive walnut doors, there were lots of windows; the windows were recycled from an old school on the property and are set in at creative angles. As we talked, it crossed my mind to ask Samara if she sensed a spirit with the cabin. She told me there was a male behind me, up in the air a bit, toward the end of the driveway. This fairly confirmed my notion that the General still stays about his cabin. But little did I know that his hazy form would show up in one of my digital photos of the front porch, (previous page).

The Evil Ones Draw Nigh

I met Anne at a Christmas party in 1993, and we enjoyed becoming friends and started dating that following year. I enjoyed her wit, and being a Kentucky native, she had wonderful stories that fascinated me. With her folksy sayings, and down-home cooking, she provided a welcome home for me during my days of working around the state, teaching as an artist-in-residence. I would travel for weeks or months at a time, coming back to Lexington, not having a home. Anne was creative, doing collages, gardening and cleaning homes to help support herself and children. Some fair weather nights, we went outside and lay on her car's front hood, to look at the stars.

Anne told me that she lived in New York City, and worked as an entertainer, playing guitar and singing. She had a clear singing voice with good projection. She stayed at an apartment, returning each night to climb several flights of stairs. An older man, who lived at the bottom of the stairs, would hear her footsteps, and often come out of his apartment, saying,

"How ya doing, baby?"

Sometime later, the older gentleman passed away. Anne returned home one night, put her hand on the banister to climb the stairs, and, yes, she heard one more time,

"How ya doing baby?"

Anne told a few stories of family challenges, growing up. She talked about, as a teenager, experimenting with Ouija board communication. She grew up on a farm near Nicholasville, Kentucky. She said it was the old Hoover place. Evidently there had been a massacre of people there during the Civil War, by Confederate independents. She said the massacre was covered up by Governor Crittenden's administration. I have not tracked down the historical information to verify this story.

But what interested me more was when Anne told about her and her friend's Ouija communication with Mary Hoover, the family matriarch. She said they carried the board out to the black wooden burley barn, plying the hundred-year-old ghost with silly questions. One night, while in the midst of a session, she said the planchette suddenly stopped, and then moved again, spelling out this message, "I have to go now. The evil ones draw nigh."

Anne said that the weather was totally calm that night, but as soon as Mary Hoover sounded her alarm, a strange wind descended upon their Jessamine County farm. The wind whipped the trees, and she and her friend looked at each other with eyes widened by fear. They threw down the Ouija board and ran for safety in the farmhouse.

Anne did not use the Ouija board again. When I dated her, she was in her late 40's, and she studied the Bible and belonged to a fundamental-style Christian church. She seemed to have no trouble acknowledging the existence of ghosts, spirits or angels.

Good Knight

Some houses have more history than haunting, and perhaps that is true of the 222-year-old John Knight home in western Shelby County, near Finchville. A walk into the hallway past the "newer" (19th century) front rooms takes visitors to a view of large, squared logs cut from virgin timber just after the American colonies won independence from Britain. The Knight home has over 3,600 square feet; the original log structure had four rooms that were 18 x 18 feet square. There is a large cellar that, up until the 1970's, still had a running spring. To the west of the home, away from KY 55 in what was likely once the front yard, there is a cistern and earth-sunken icehouse. Owner Kathy Nash showed me an attic door, which has ax marks said to be evidence of Civil War guerrillas trying to find valuables.

Cathy gave me a tour of the house and nearby grounds. She did some research on her old home, and loaned to me a copy of *That Dark and Bloody River: Chronicles of the Ohio River Valley* by Allan W. Eckert. Later, I read the amazing tale of Dr. Knight, who served as a military physician during the French and Indian wars. Additional information about Dr. Knight is in *Historic Families of Kentucky* by Thomas Marshall Green.

Dr. Knight studied medicine at the University of Aberdeen, Scotland. He came to America as a stowaway. He worked off his passage as an indentured servant to Colonel William Crawford through tutoring his children. He served at Fort Pitt as a surgeon's mate. He tried to save the Indian chief Anacota, who was unarmed and mortally wounded by a pioneer. Dr. Knight was later named chief surgeon at Ft. Pitt through Col. William Crawford's

Dr. John Knight home, Shelby County, Kentucky.

recommendations. He was the brigade surgeon on the march against the Indian town of Sandusky in June of 1782. Dr. John Knight carried his array of surgical instruments in saddlebags, and skillfully treated wounded during that battle. On retreating, he left behind his trunk full of surgical tools and met up with Col. Crawford. They rode their horses until their horses gave out some 20 miles northeast of the battle. They found another party of four men retreating, with Capt. John Biggs. All the men were recaptured by the Indians, and Col. Crawford was marked for death as the Delaware Indians blamed him for not stopping a previous massacre by whites. They apportioned Knight to be executed by the Shawnees. Both were held captive, along with nine other soldiers. Knight and four others were painted black in preparation for their execution. Crawford and Knight watched as four of the men were tomahawked and scalped. The Indians slapped the bloody scalps on their captives' faces. Then both were forced to run the gauntlet. Crawford and Knight were taken to the Indian council where charges were brought against them. Despite the effort by the Indian's ally, white man Indian agent Simon Girty, the men were taken out to be repainted black for execution. They both refused food and waited for their gruesome end.

On the next day Knight witnessed the terrible torture and killing of Col. Crawford. The day after that Knight was given a Shawnee guard, Tutelu, who marched him toward Wapatomica to again run the gauntlet and be burned at the stake. Knight's hands were bound behind his back and he was made to walk past Crawford's remains. Then Tutelu forced Knight to carry his pack and they walked 15 miles before camping. Knight convinced Tutelu to free his hands when Tutelu couldn't start a flint for their fire. He picked up a large stick and knocked him on the head, then grabbed Tutelu's rifle and pointed it at him. The rifle was actually damaged and Knight, with no weapons or tools, survived three weeks of hiding and making his way back to Wheeling. While recovering, novelist Hugh Henry Brackenridge interviewed Knight, later publishing an account that was not fully true; it was called *Dr. Knight's Narrative.*

Tutelu survived later battles, and told Indians and whites who teased him about Dr. Knight's escape. He commented, "Dr. Knight was a good man. He cured sick folks and I did not want to hurt him." Dr. Knight survived at Ft. Pitt until the end of the revolution and then married a niece of Col. William Crawford. He served in Wayne's campaign in the Northwest in 1793-95. After that, he and his wife moved to Shelby County, Kentucky, where he became widely esteemed for his medical skill, and prior to 1820, he performed successful cancer surgery. He served in the Kentucky State Legislature in 1796. He died in 1838. (Another account of Dr. Knight's escape is also given in *Historical Collections of Ohio, Volume I,* by Henry Howe, Hardin County).

It was interesting that, since Dr. Knight was a "good man", the only reported tale from that house was from someone who was working on the remodeling for Mr. and Mrs. Nash. Through a third party, Kathy Nash was told that that the workman, finished for the day, was preparing for bed in a room in the northeast corner of the house, when he heard a sweet female voice tell him, "Good Night"!

The Ghosts of La Grange

La Grange is a small town in Oldham County northeast of Louisville off Interstate 71. It was incorporated in 1827 and named after the Marquis de Lafayette's French farm. The area was first called The Crossroads, centered on a wagon path from Shelbyville to Westport and from New Castle to Louisville. I have enjoyed a number of trips to La Grange to shop, enjoy small town quiet, dine and hunt for ghosts!

Both the historical tours, which run year-round and the Spirits of La Grange ghost tour, which is available from September 5th through the end of October, begin at the Oldham County History Center. Of the three buildings located on the History Center property, the ghost tour assembles in the J.C. Barnett Archives and Library, erected in 1840.

I went with a friend to hear about the Spirits of La Grange. We gathered in the History Center Archives, milled around looking at the gift shop while a man wearing a black bowler hat prepared to take us walking through history. I kept my digital camera ready for catching orbs or other photographic anomalies. The tour guide, Bill Lammlein, took us walking down Main Street and talked about a dozen homes, giving history and haunting details. Some houses we were allowed into and others he could only regale us with information. All of the ghost tour guides are volunteers. This will be

The Rob Morris Home is on the Ghost Tour.

the sixth year for the Spirits of La Grange tour and the organizers are adding events and additional stops. Each stop and story is fully researched.

At the circa 1830 William T. Barbour House off Main, on Washington Street, the tour guide informed us that it is listed on the National Register of Historic Places. This brick building sure felt like it was inhabited by a number of spirits. In 1846 it was transferred from a private residence to a girl's dormitory for Funk Seminary. Now it is lived in by Linda Foster who runs it as a shop called *Christmas in Kentucky*. Linda was present in period dress and told us about some curious happenings with a large mirror, saved from the Red Cross building in Louisville. Linda also reported her hand being held at night in bed and a powerful odor emanating from the downstairs storage closet.

At our next stop, outside only, we looked at the First Baptist Church. I was pleased to find a small orb showing on my digital picture. We walked back to Main Street to hear stories about the Ballard House. The owner at this 1840 home reports a fair amount of spirit activity, including a woman called Dottie and sightings of a little girl. Other odd occurrences include disturbed or disappearing objects in the office section. At another stop on 300 East Main we gazed at a lovely Italianate mansion, which we heard was built in 1870. Here folks report a restless cellar door, doorknobs which self-turn and evidence of a ghost who ran the calculator machine through all of its paper.

The Irish Rover restaurant takes up two address numbers on the other side of Main Street. A shop previously located there often found dolls and toys moved around. When it was a dance studio the record player sometimes changed speeds when playing. In 1988 the space was converted to offices where the resident ghost shocked one of the owners by wildly spinning a wall-mounted picture. At another haunted site on Main Street we walked inside the former Central Hotel and Peak Funeral Home. What is now the Sweet Ice Cream Shop was formerly the harness shop and post office. Inside, I definitely felt heebie-jeebies. *There has to be a ghost here!*

This location is said to be haunted by Julia. She was a nanny for the Peak family during the 1920's. She lived upstairs with the family. When Mayor Carter lived upstairs, Julia often spooked the Mayor's cat. One night the Mayor retired for bed only to discover her clock hands were running backwards. In addition, a woman dressed in pink has been seen in the evenings in the Ice Cream Shop. The Mayor also saw the spirit of a man who in mortal life was a prominent La Grange businessman.

Our other stops included the former McDowell Pharmacy, Kenyon Hotel, Pete's Pool Hall and DeHaven Baptist Church. The latter has a story of an organist who practiced when the church was empty…except for the sounds of phantom feet shuffling down the aisles and creaking wooden seats from invisible derrieres.

Barbara Manley Edds spoke of strange happenings during the tours.

"Something actually happened tonight. I went into Elsie's with some paranormal investigators. One of the EMF meters worked just fine outside but when we got inside, it just stopped working. After we left the house it began working again. That is typical of the sort of things that happen. Some of the investigators find that the camera, cell phones and flashlights do not properly work in there.

"The Campbell Studio house has the cellar door that will not stay closed. The man dug the cellar by hand, after the house was built and carried all the dirt out bucket by bucket. He was hit by a train there in front of the house and thrown into the yard. He died inside that house, I believe in the room to the far right.

"There have been several things recently. The little girl at The Irish Rover Two was in rare form last Friday night. I was photographing a rehearsal dinner for a wedding party and the groom took a short cut behind the wall separating the waiter's station from the dining area. He didn't know the stories about the little girl but he said that when he walked back there, a booster seat just jumped off the table in front of him. There was no one else there. Then a bit later in that same area, we all heard a tremendous crash and a whole tub of silverware that had been sitting there for weeks suddenly hit the floor. The waitresses said it was the ghost of the little girl. There was not a soul visible nearby when we heard the crash.

"As I was writing you to tell you about some La Grange ghost stories I heard my oldest granddaughter's bus out front. Then I heard her running across the room downstairs and the door slam as she ran out of the house. I got up and went to my front bedroom window and saw the bus, but did not see her.

"I went downstairs and asked my daughter, who was getting ready for work, 'Did Rooie make the bus? I heard her run out but did not see her run to the bus.'

"She told me that Caitlin had gone out early to catch the bus. So then I asked my daughter if she ran across the floor, and she assured me that it was definitely not her."

With the Eyes of a Child

A number of ghost stories from this book and other books highlight a frequent theme of ghosts being invisible to grownups, yet very real to children. When I was in graduate school at the University of Louisville, studying to get my Masters Degree in Expressive Therapies, I met Jennifer Beasley. My classmates quickly discovered that I was a storyteller, and that I particularly liked to hear and tell ghost stories. Jennifer told a story that happened when she was young. It often seems that innocent eyes can be the only ones to see the ghosts in a house. Jennifer relates her tale...

Overhearing me telling ghost stories with my high school buddies, my mother said, "Do you remember the house we visited on Church Street? They always said that one was haunted."

"Do you mean the one with the nice old man?" I replied.

"Old man?" my mother asked.

"You know, he was up in the attic next to the pot bellied stove smoking a pipe. He was wearing a red flannel shirt and overalls. He had eye trouble. He was so nice - remember?" I smiled at the memory of my conversation with the kind old man.

My mother looked confused and said, "There was no one else in the house that day, Jennifer."

Goosebumps erupted all over me, and I quickly told her the story. I just knew she'd remember him if I told her more details. I reminded her of the game my sister and I played. My parents were dreamers, and their idea of a good time was to visit houses they could never afford. My sister and I played a game where we'd race to check out the house to lay claim to our bedrooms. One beautiful day we visited a three story tall Victorian in the oldest part of our town. It was a fine house with a wrap-around porch, and outbuildings. I raced to the top floor to find my "bedroom" and instead found an old man sitting there smoking a pipe. He sat next to an old wood-burning stove. I was young, and talkative, so I greeted him and struck up a conversation. His eyes were strange, they looked clouded over and I talked to him about cataracts.

I was about seven or eight and I said, "Do you have cataracts?"

"No," said he.

"Well, my grandfather does, and that means that there's skin growing on top of his eye. He had an operation and they cut it off and now he can see. Maybe you can get an operation."

The old man laughed at this, and asked me what I was doing in the house. I explained my parents were downstairs and that they were thinking about buying the house, but let him in on the secret that we probably really wouldn't buy it. He seemed to think this was funny too, and soon I heard my mother calling me. I said goodbye and ran back down the stairs. After I finished my story, my mother repeated that there was no one in the house that day other than my family and the real estate agent. My high school buddies sat speechless and saucer-eyed as my mother and I tried to think up an explanation for the man. We couldn't think of anything, unless he was the ghost that was said to have lived there.

Harbeson House

I worked in Flemingsburg, Kentucky as a visiting artist in the later 1990s. After the local folks heard I collected ghost stories, they told me about the Harbeson House. I interviewed the house's owner, Larry Johnson. The Harbeson House is located on Main Street near the Fleming County Courthouse in "downtown" Flemingsburg. It is a large house built circa 1812, with three major architectural styles, Federal, a Greek revival renovation. In the 1860's it underwent another renovation in Italian Gothic style. Larry occasionally opens his house for the Historic Homes Holiday Tours, which raises funds for scholarships. Mr. Johnson was generous with his time for my visit. Since it was dinnertime, he graciously offered to fix me dinner and we talked about his haunted house over soup and sandwiches.

Harbeson House, Flemingsburg, Kentucky.

A young Judge Harbeson had, prior to the outbreak of the Civil War, retired from the Army. But when the conflict began, he felt compelled to join the Confederate Army. His father locked him in the cellar until he cooled off, deciding to join neither army. Larry believes that Judge Harbeson's daughter Amie could be one of the haunting spirits in the Harbeson House. Amie was married in the Harbeson home and eventually moved away with her husband. He showed me the ground floor parlor window where Amie and other family members had diamond-scratched their names many years ago. Amazingly, Larry inherited, with the house, a complete family scrapbook. It's large, perhaps a foot and half square when closed and contains not only newspaper clippings but also family photos. With the family album and his additional research, Larry has pieced together the family's story. Family-owned antiques seemed to magically return to the mansion. A crystal decanter with silver top once owned by Amie and her husband was sent back to the Harbeson House from Charlotte, West Virginia. Larry often feels Amie's presence and so do others.

Early in the period of his ownership, Larry had apartments within the house. Many of the tenants had unusual experiences. One renter, Rocky, disappeared one morning. Rocky later told Larry his reason for quickly vacating his apartment. While in bed, Rocky heard footsteps advance to his bed. He watched in amazement as the bed pressed down as if someone had sat near him. Then the bed lifted up and the sound of footsteps walked away and down the stairs. Larry had another houseguest stay once. He was a hospital administrator. This man reported having a female ghost visit his bed. It happened as he was getting ready to go to sleep. He reported hearing the rustling sound of starchy petticoats approaching his bed. He heard some more footsteps and then the light fixture started to swing.

He pulled the bed sheets back and said aloud, "Come on, honey, get in bed with me!"

Then there was silence.

Larry notes that the ghostly occurrences can happen at any time of the year, although they seem to increase with the full moon. He often realizes that things that he has placed in a specific spot will later not be found there or anywhere at all. Later, after searching the house, Larry discovers the item returned to its original place. This has happened with postage stamps, wallet, checkbook and house keys. Also, a dining room china cabinet would inexplicably open when he or another person would leave the room. Larry and his friend tested the floorboards near the cabinet, trying to see if their foot pressure would open the cabinet, but to no avail.

There is often movement seen, just out of the corner of one's eyes. And once when Larry was in bed with his wife, they heard footsteps dramatically descend the stairs and stop right outside their bedroom door. When his wife suggested that he investigate, Larry replied, "Why bother? They know where we are."

Another time Larry was awakened by the call of his name. He promptly went to open the front door but no one was there. About three years ago, Larry's basset hound saw a ghost. His dog normally was a slow walker with a generally quiet disposition. But on this occasion, his dog became very agitated, barking and looking intently at a spot in the room.

One of Larry's nephews, less than one year old at the time, was found to be awake in his crib. He was standing up and pointing to an empty space.

The Haunted Harbeson House.

And at a family event, a photo was taken which revealed something curious. The Harbeson House was the site of his niece's honeymoon reception. One picture showed something hazy hovering over the punchbowl and cake, behind the mother-in-law. Another photo showed a saber pointing at one of the guest's shoulders. The local photo lab later declared that their picture processing had not produced these anomalies.

When Larry traveled in Europe another renter had a dramatic experience. This man was studying to be a minister at Kentucky Christian College in Grayson. He was married while Larry was away and he and his wife were once sleeping together at the Harbeson House. Perhaps his wife aroused some jealousy in Amie. She awoke to find invisible fingers around her throat. Caught in fear and unable to talk, she was barely able to communicate her distress to her husband. They then became additional tenants who quickly sought other living arrangements.

Larry taught art in the nearby middle school for many years. One of his former students was visiting the Harbeson House and he experienced some vibes on the stairway. He got the strong impression that someone had flung himself off the banister. The odd thing was his father later reported that exactly when his son was at the Harbeson House, two plates had flown off the wall and shattered on their kitchen floor. Larry also had a flying plate at the Harbeson House. But this plate, which had fallen five feet off the wall, didn't break. Instead, it rolled off into the adjacent room and was found to have neither nick nor scratch on it.

Larry Johnson lived in his haunted house for thirty years. He has slowly been renovating rooms. When he was cleaning out a closet, he removed the shelves to find few things stashed in the shelf bracket. There was an oak darning pin and a rolled up newspaper. As he carefully unrolled the yellowed paper, he was startled to find that the old newspaper's date, February 16, 1909, was eighty years to the day before his discovery. And Larry's sister, who lives in Knoxville, Tennessee, has reported some strange things happening in her home after she visits the Harbeson House. Larry and she have jokingly referred to their trading the ghost back and forth.

She has called Larry to say, "Well, we brought the ghost back with us!"

Larry was hosting the Holiday Home Tour when an older woman came up to him and commented that she used to live right across the street. She clearly recalled, after fifty years, how she and her brother would stare at the then vacant Harbeson House, watching a ghostly white figure as it walked back and forth across the second floor porch.

Hospital Ghost

Grace lives in Jeffersonville, Indiana.

Aaron was a baby that started out in our unit (NICU) and ended up a very sick little boy, ventilator dependent, cerebral palsy, etc. He never went home, but was sent to a long-term facility at a couple years of age. He came back to the hospital many times over the next several years and was always admitted to the PICU. That area has since been converted to a part of the NICU and is separated from the main unit at the end of a long hallway. It's an isolated area and usually only has three nurses working in it at a time. The room that was usually Aaron's when he was there is now used as a spare room in that area. The call light system is still intact.

Aaron passed away when he was seven years old. He had a nasty little habit of disconnecting his vent tubing so that the alarms would sound and the nurses would come running. He was quite the practical joker apparently. The story (and no one really knows if it is true or not) is that he did that in his new home one day and the alarms didn't sound properly, leading to his death. We all just felt like Aaron's spirit came back to the place where he felt the most love and felt the most like home.

One night, I was working down in that section and the other two nurses had gone to lunch, leaving me alone (not uncommon for that section). My patient was a baby that had a history of major gut issues and those babies tend to be highly irritable. I had worked with this child for hours, listening to him scream. I finally got him to sleep, tiptoed to his bed and laid him down, still sound asleep. I turned and walked out of the room and to the nurse's station. No sooner had my bottom hit a seat, when this baby let out a scream like someone had pinched him. I went flying back in there and just as I picked him up, I swear I heard a child laugh right in my ear. Keep in mind that this was about midnight, I was in a closed unit alone with 12 infants, all of the lights in that room were turned down and only the glow of the cardiac monitors were lighting the area. I went straight to the light switch, turned on every light in that unit, took the baby and sat out at the station with him until the other nurses came back. Luckily, none of the other babies sounded any alarms, because I wasn't going back in there alone!

On other occasions, we had the sinks turn on by themselves, a whole rack of charts go flying onto the floor, monitors turn off by themselves, and the call light in Aaron's old room would routinely go off when no one was in there.

My last ghost story about that unit happened on a night when I and one other nurse, who had only been off orientation for one night, were alone when a baby coded. We had a code button on the wall to push that called a whole backup team to the room immediately. We pushed it and were doing compressions and face-bagging the baby, whose heart rate was in the 30's and oxygen level was in the teens. The code team came running and couldn't get in the door. They said it was like someone held the door shut. Finally, it just swung open and they made it into the room. Yes, we saved the baby, but barely.

Aaron was a practical joker, but not a malevolent child. I can't see him doing something that dangerous. Twice, nurses had spotted a figure of a young man, 20-ish or so, in the halls of that area and he disappeared without a trace. So I think there were more ghosts than just Aaron hanging around there.

Nighttime Warnings

Thelma Melton, Asher, Kentucky.

There are several incidents that happened in the house that we lived in while we were growing up. We didn't stay in that house very long. My sister and her friend tried to sneak out of the house one night. They thought that our mom was about to catch them, because it seemed they heard her walking through the house. They noticed a light came on, so they slowly went back into the house. But they were surprised to find Mom sound asleep in her bed. They started to go back out and when my sister heard someone coming. Whatever it was walked by them. They actually felt the wind as it passed by! By this time they actually woke Mom up and she heard the same thing. My sister stated that it wouldn't stop moving around until they went back to bed.

I had a rocking chair in my room. One night I woke up and the chair was rocking with no one in it. Let me tell you, I couldn't move. But when I got up and turned on the light it was still moving. My sister's room was next to mine so I ran into her room. She made fun of me so I went back to bed. Then all of a sudden I heard her scream, "Mom!" We all jumped up and went to her room. She told us that after I left the room, someone picked up her mattress and almost flipped her out into the floor.

Another time we had a sleepover with a bunch of our friends. As kids often do, we were sitting up when we were supposed to be in the bed. Suddenly we heard someone in the kitchen, opening cabinet doors and shutting them back. They were banging together pots and pans. But every time we got up and turned on the kitchen light the noise quit.

One time our cousin spent the night, and she slept in my mom's room. Her baby, who was about three months old, slept in my room in a crib. In the morning, my cousin told us that something kept waking her up. She didn't know what it was, but after being awakened, she always went back to sleep. Then once she felt someone touch her. When she opened her eyes, there was a woman dressed in black, standing above her. The woman told her to go check on her son – that he was about to die – so she came running out of Mom's room headed toward mine. About the time she got there, my bedroom door shut hard. Well, she banged on my door until I finally heard her. I got up and opened the door and she ran to the crib, where the baby had gotten strangled and wasn't breathing. I am not sure what she did; I don't remember since he is okay now. We later found out that five babies died in that room – with no explanation.

Deceased House Owner Still Around

I met Sarah Thomas through the Pleasant Hill Singers. Sarah was friendly and very much down-home country. She seemed interested in talking about the Shaker ghost stories and, as she worked at Shakertown for a short time, had a story to share for that book. One of her aunt's was actually one of the three women who claimed to be abducted by a UFO in the 1970's. Sarah seemed nonplussed while telling about their resident ghost…

Sarah:
"Robert" built and owned this house in Lincoln County prior to my mother owning it. My mom moved in after he passed away in 1998. I moved in with her a year later. I didn't know the ghost was there when I moved into the house. I returned from a trip to the ocean and brought back tiny seashells, putting them in a brandy glass on my dresser in the bedroom. In the middle of the night I woke up. I like my room extremely dark when I sleep – but I could feel there was someone in the room. I heard what sounded like somebody looking at the seashells. The seashells sounded like they were being moved, clicking together. Not long after the noise stopped and the feeling of someone being there went away. I went back to sleep. When I woke up, there were three seashells lying on the dresser that had been in the bowl. That was my first experience with Robert.

Sometimes we're sitting in one room and hear him walking in another room. He likes to lock us out of the house. We went to the mailbox or watered the flowers outside, and the door was locked. The screen door cannot be locked from outside, only from the inside. He's not a mean person, but one of the things he thought was funny, when he was alive, was holding the door so people couldn't pull it open. For him it was a big joke.

My dog Lucky knows when he is there. Lucky's dad was a twelve-pound Daschund and his mom was a black Labrador retriever. She wakes up and barks happily, knowing he is present. Robert had a favorite chair in the corner of the living room. Lucky will perk up, looking at that area, when no one else is there, and bark, wagging her tail. It's as if she's saying, "Oh, yippee, Robert is here!" We feel and hear him a lot.

We usually hear him a few times a week. But my mom went away for a week and Robert was extremely active; it was a constant presence. Then when she returned, the activity died down, as if he thought *she's back, everything is fine.*

Family Ghost

I met Cindy when I was working at a psychic fair in Lexington. She and her daughters both enjoy ghost stories and she purchased my two books. She told me she had some ghost stories from Madison County, and she came through with not one, but many amazing stories.

Cindy Savey, Madison County
I lived with a ghost for over twenty years – and he was not always a nice one at that. I really would have loved to have known who it was, just to give it a proper name. It did seem in a strange way to protect us and I would even say that it cared about us all. Several people had experiences with it and believed it to be my mother, but she was living when we began to have our

visits. Lamps turned on and off by themselves. An old mantle clock struck the hour, even though it had not been used since I was a baby. The striking bothered my dad so much he took the weights out and still it sounded. My sister has the clock now, but it has not chimed since it left the house. She even took it to be restored and the man told her that it would never work again. In fact, he told her that there was no way it could possibly have done the things she said.

The ghost threw a royal fit when my parents sold the house. It went on a rage that lasted for months. It was so mad that my stepmother asked it to go with them just to try to stop it from driving everyone crazy. I believe it is still there because the present owner asked me if it was true that my mother had died there. They also asked the neighbors about strange things happening. My mother did not die there, but someone stayed behind. It sounds strange to say this, but it was like losing a family member.

Of all the years with our family ghost, I don't believe that anyone ever got a picture. It did like the answering machine though. We moved to Richmond from Taylorsville, Kentucky, in the mid 1970's. My parents bought the house in a foreclosure from the bank. Shortly after we moved in, we began to hear what sounded like someone walking around upstairs and at times there was a knocking on the walls in the basement. My dad had to take a trip to Louisville one week and I remember my mother waking us up in the middle of the night because she thought someone was in the house. My dad thought that since we had a new house, it was settling. After that we began to have pretty regular occurrences. Then around the holidays in 1978, my mother said that she thought that she could hear someone talking. A few months later she was diagnosed with a brain tumor and all of this was supposed to be in her head. She died the following October. During that summer she spent time with my aunt in Radcliff while she took treatments in Louisville. The ghost stayed here with my dad.

About a month later my dad started dating a woman and things were difficult for a while. In March he started dating my stepmother, whom the ghost seemed to enjoy aggravating. Needless to say, my sisters and I got the blame until one day, when she was at the house alone and told us that she felt like she had been followed around all day long. Apparently, she mopped the floor in the kitchen and went to clean the den in the basement. When she came back upstairs, my dad's pipe was on the kitchen floor. She swore she knew the pipe was in an ashtray in the basement. She said she knew then that a ghost was there.

It really didn't seem to matter who was in the house, as it was just part of the family. I got a chair that hung from the ceiling for Christmas one year. The ghost seemed to like it because it would spin like someone was sitting in it. It liked the light fixture in the hall, which would swing sometimes for no reason. The only person that I know who saw what we thought to be a ghost was my little sister. She came home one Sunday from church and she said she saw a woman in a black dress who was sitting on the sofa, crying. She just said that she didn't have a face. Then it dawned on her that there was someone in the house. She thought someone died or there was some family crisis. She went back to ask the woman what was wrong and she just disappeared. My parents came home to find my sister on the front porch half-hysterical crying that she would never stay by herself again.

My dad bought my stepmother a microwave oven for Christmas one year. One of the first times that she used it, she placed a Corning dish containing corn in it. When she put the dish on the table and tried to take the cover off, the dish slid across the table. When she reached for the dish, it again slid away from her. She grabbed a potholder and took the cover from the dish, which broke in her hand from the heat. We all sat dumbfounded; no one knew what to think or say.

Before my parents moved, they had a china cabinet, which was going to be sent out to be refinished. My stepmother asked if I would help my little sister pack the china so that the cabinet could be picked up. My sister told me about the ghost acting up. Almost from the time that we came home, the ghost began its activities. We felt the anger in the air. It would play the answering machine and open the cabinet doors. If we closed the doors, it would just open them again. This went on for five hours. If we left them open or attempted to talk to it, it would slam the doors closed – not just one door either, but all of the cabinet doors. Later, the man arrived to pick up the cabinet, and he felt the anger, too.

It went on like this for several weeks and got to the point that my stepmother told it, "Look, we have sold the house and we are moving. You can go with us if you want to, but you have to stop this." I think it did go away for a while. They had a cat that played with the air and a rocking chair that rocked on its own, but this was all at the new house. There were the familiar footsteps and knocking on the walls. The new house is quiet now. There are no more footsteps or knocking. So for all we know, it went back to the old house.

Car Accident

When I was a child I remember my father telling a strange story about a car accident that happened in Louisville about 1972. He had a friend who witnessed a horrible accident. His friend saw the accident and stopped to help the victims. Apparently, a truck carrying glass crashed into a car. The glass fell on a convertible that a lady was driving. The man stopped to ask the lady if she was all right. The lady told him that she was fine and the man went on to help the other people involved in the accident. The lady got out of the car and went to see if she could help. The man said that the lady was as pale as ash and that he thought that she was in shock. When he began to look closely at her, he noticed that she had a trickle of blood which ran down her neck. He asked her if she was sure that she was all right and asked if she knew she had been cut. She said that she was all right, only that she had a chill. She then took her scarf off and her head came off with it.

Somehow the glass decapitated the lady without anyone realizing that it happened. My father's friend worked quite a few accident situations, but always told that single accident was his worst he'd seen, and that he would never get over it.

Cursed White Mink Stole

When I was little my mother had a white mink stole. It was so elegant that my sister and I always wanted to wear it. My mother would not let us because it held sentimental value to her. The stole was given to my mother by the husband of her best friend after her death. The mink came from a cousin of my mother's best friend. The cousin was killed in a car accident as a result of having her head cut off. My mother's best friend committed suicide by shooting herself in the head. A few years later my mother attended a function with my father and wore the mink stole. About a week later my mother was diagnosed with a brain tumor and died that year.

My father swore that the stole was cursed because everyone who had worn it had died from some sort of injury or problem with their heads and he destroyed the stole so that nothing would happen to anyone else who owned or wore it.

Miss Sally the Witch

Miss Sally was a spinster in a small community in eastern Kentucky. She socialized with very few people and had a reputation of being a witch. She had a very unusual personality. Miss Sally drove a carriage long after automobiles had become commonplace.

One afternoon my grandmother had a chance meeting with Miss Sally. My grandmother was a very pretty young lady who had been plagued by having warts on her hands for most of her life. Such was the case that she wore gloves to hide her hands. On meeting my grandmother, Miss Sally asked her quite sharply to see her hands. My grandmother was very embarrassed and said that because her hands looked so bad she did not want to show them to her. Again Miss Sally demanded to see her hands. Out of fear of Miss Sally, my grandmother removed her gloves.

Miss Sally then took her hands in hers and said, "What warts? I don't see any warts."

To my grandmother's shock, the warts were all gone. Miss Sally drove off and my grandmother was never again troubled by warts.

Nightly Visitor

We moved into our home about thirteen years ago. At the beginning everything seemed very normal. I was expecting our first child and had a hard time sleeping. I got up in the middle of the night and tried to occupy my time. I heard little noises and never really thought much about it. After all, I grew up with a ghost, so I knew that anything is possible. One night around 2:00 A.M., I happened to be sitting in the living room, when out of the corner of my eye I saw what appeared to be a man walk from the doorway of the other bedroom into the kitchen. I thought, "*I did not just see that.*" The next night, I was up and this time in the kitchen when something or someone walked into the kitchen.

After the birth of my daughter, I was awake only a few times in the night, but as my daughter grew older she appeared, at times, to be watching someone who was not there. Sometimes when she sat in her swing, she appeared to be interacting with someone. When she was older she was a bit fearful of being left by herself anywhere at all in the house. When I took her for a check up, the doctor said that it was just a normal fear of being separated.

When my daughter was two, we adopted a beautiful red Australian shepherd from the pound. He is named Sunglasses. From time to time, Sunglasses is allowed to stay in the house. On such occasions, usually around two in the morning, Sunglasses will come to me and wake me up. After being reassured that everything is all right, he will lay back down next to me and go back to sleep.

These occurrences seemed to be all for myself, my oldest daughter, and our dog. Until one day my youngest daughter asked who the man was who walked through the kitchen at night. I asked the girls about the man, and they described the same person that I had seen in the house for the last thirteen years.

He really does not do anything accept walk through the kitchen. He is quite peaceful, but does seem to be a little lost. He is tall with blond hair. We really have no idea who it might be, but we do know that there was an old house here before the previous owner built this one. It is, in a way, comforting to think you may have someone looking after you.

Impression of a Murder

Cindy told me this story, and it sounded just a bit like a rural legend…until I found a book by Harry G. Enoch, titled, *In Search of Morgan's Station and "The Last Indian Raid in Kentucky"*. A short time before this, I read about numerous gruesome massacres by Indians and brutal reprisals by white settlers in *That Dark and Bloody River*. The degree of hatred combined with a motivation for blind revenge was frightening. What vaguely seemed like warfare accelerated, in some men, to a lifetime of murderous opportunities. The Indian raid on Morgan's Station in Montgomery County, Kentucky took place in April of 1793, just a year after Kentucky became a state and before the existence of Montgomery County. When I researched the history of the Bourbon Iron Works, I discovered that it was constructed in 1791, and thus, theoretically, the story could have occurred as folklore suggests.

In the raid, Indians killed some pioneers outright, and they fled toward the Ohio River with 19 captives. It was called the Murder Branch Massacre, and Kentucky Historical Marker #189 marks the spot of the massacre, ten miles east of Frenchburg on Kentucky 1274. A sandstone house was built two years after the massacre, in 1795, at the location of Morgan's Station. It is a two-story sandstone Dutch Pennsylvania style house, named after Ralph

Morgan. He was a second cousin to Daniel Boone.

The Bourbon Iron Works stone furnace and historical marker are in Bath County, Kentucky, three miles south of Owingsville, on Kentucky 36/965. Marker #993 notes that, "Jacob Myers from Richmond, Virginia, took up land grants here on Slate Creek, 1782. He built the first iron blast furnace in Kentucky, 1791. John Cokey, Owings and Co. formed to operate (the) furnace." The marker notes that later, in the 1800's, the furnace produced grape shot and cannonballs for the U.S. Navy. Cindy said folks would sometimes find

Old Kentucky Iron Furnace.

cannonballs in the creek below the furnace. History is often found in subtle signs and pieces, just off the highways.

Cindy:

When I was a child my family went on picnics to a small park. The park had a very old iron ore furnace. There was a story about mysterious handprints on one of the steel supports inside the furnace. Legend had it that there was an Indian who murdered people in that area. His punishment was to be burned alive in the furnace. At the time in which he was burned, the steel was so hot that his handprints were melted into the support inside. At the end of our picnics, our father would take us to the furnace. While he held us up, we put our tiny hands in the Indian's handprints. The prints were so large that my hands did not even fill his palms. In some strange way I felt as though there was a bond through time and that the spirit of this Indian protected me from evil.

The Bell Witch Cave

After reading "*The Bell Witch*" by Pat Fitzhugh, I was curious to see the Bell Witch Cave. This book details many varied and puzzling phenomena associated with the Bell Witch, from poltergeist activities to conversations with an invisible, very-knowing spirit.

While the original Bell family home has been razed and the site is now farmland, some of the Bell Witch story involves the cave, which is under private ownership. The Bell Witch Cave is open to visitors. It is located south of Bowling Green, Kentucky, in Robertson County, Tennessee, adjacent to Simpson County, Kentucky. Strange things were seen and heard in this Cave back in the 1800's, and some were witnessed by the Bell Family. Unusual occurrences are still occasionally reported in the cave and on the property above the cave. Oddities show up in photographs taken inside the cave or at its entrance. The spirits seem to reserve some of their manifestations for those who are not believers.

John and Lucy Bell moved to Robertson County from North Carolina in 1804. They brought six of their nine children; Lucy bore three more children at their Tennessee home. Pat Fitzhugh, author of *The Bell Witch*, details a story about the Bell's problem with an evil overseer back in North Carolina. In an argument, John Bell shot and killed that man, John Black. The Bell patriarch would not approve of the overseer's fondness for his daughter, Mary. Unusual troubles with crop failures then plagued the Bell farm, after the killing of John Black. It is perhaps suggested by the author that this prior incident may be connected with the bad luck that followed the Bells into Tennessee.

The Bell family farm was located on Johnston Springs Road. They had access to the adjoining Red River and the Sturgeon Creek, which were important sources of water and transportation. The family worked diligently, with the assistance of African-American slaves, on the thousand-acre farm. Tobacco, corn, and wheat were staple crops. Both slave and master worshipped in the Red River Baptist Church. Betsy Bell was born in 1806; much of the Bell Witch activity centered on Betsy and her choice of a husband. John Bell was particularly cursed with the spirit's hatred. The bizarre manifestations of the Bell Witch seem to outline the often-quoted truism that truth is stranger than fiction. Hollywood's creativity would be challenged to match the variety of ways in which the Bell Witch proved her knowledge of community and world events. Once, the spirit quoted, for two visiting ministers, their sermons word for word and in their own voice and manner of speaking, complete with closing prayer. The ministers had delivered their sermons in two separate churches at the same day and hour. John Bell Jr. was warned by the spirit not to travel to North Carolina to collect his father's share of an estate settlement.

The spirit told him, "Your trip will be a very long and hard one, and you'll return with nothing." When John Bell Jr. argued with and disputed the spirit's prediction, the spirit then added, "A very beautiful and charming lady is on her way from Virginia at this very moment to visit some of your neighbors. You and this woman were meant to be together and have the potential to enjoy a lifetime of happiness together; but if you make that trip to North Carolina, you will never meet her." And it happened just as the spirit had predicted. The spirit was, at various times a disembodied voice, a rabbit, a dog and a bird. This entity made itself known by whipping John Bell with an invisible whip, riding behind on a visitor's horse, manifesting candle-like lights outside of the house, rapidly and perfectly quote Scripture, and playing constant pranks on the family, visitors and slaves.

Although the Bell Witch openly stated her intention to torment John Sr. to death, and delivered much misery to all those who lived there, she was also capable of kindness. When Lucy was ill, she sang sweet hymns to her and once showered her bed with hazelnuts and grapes. She gave a gift of stockings to son Jesse's wife Martha. And when the children were caught out in the country during a thunderstorm, the spirit directed them to safety, just moments before lightning destroyed the large trees where they'd been seeking shelter. There were other voices heard besides Kate's, sometimes the voices of children. And since Indian graves were found on the property, it is hard to define the nature of the haunting and sightings. Most of the spirit's activity occurred between 1817 and 1821. John Bell died in late 1820. Kate predicted her return after a seven-year absence, and did indeed come back and hold lengthy conversations with John Bell, Jr. The Bell Witch haunting was a celebrated case at its time. People came from all over the state, country, and from other countries as well. Both sons, Jesse and John Jr., fought under Major General Andrew Jackson and the prominent figure came on their invitation to visit. The Bell Witch caused his wagon to stop for a time and later subdued one of Jackson's men who brandished a pistol, with the intent to "kill" the witch.

The Bell Witch Cave is on private property, and there is a fee to visit the cave. Call to confirm visiting hours or weather possibilities prior to your trip. Their number is (615) 696-3055. In August of 2001, I drove there with a friend and we toured the cave.

The cave itself is peaceful and has wonderful formations. Our guide pointed out an Indian burial site and some interestingly shaped formations. There are lights installed along the cave. Although we didn't experience any strange occurrences, some shimmery apparitions have been seen. Cameras have broken or film rewound; video cameras had glitches and some visitors have heard noises. A persistent folklore suggests not taking any rock or chunk of cave formation out of the cave unless at your peril.

On our way back, we stopped in nearby Cross Plains, Tennessee, and met a lady who had a few interesting experiences in Bell Witch Cave. Dorothy said she is one quarter Native American.

Dorothy recounts what occurred:

Most of the time, I love being in the cave. It feels like a sacred place to me – I feel safe there. I can't explain why. One time, while I was visiting the cave, the daughter of the guide came up to us, and said the lights in the cave kept going out.

I told them, "That's because there is a skeptic in the group."

When the group came back up, the mom (guide) asked them, "Would you like to see the ghost photos?"

And sure enough, one of the women touring said, "I don't believe in that stuff!" Another time, as I sat in front of the owner's house, and talked with their daughter, I heard a laugh and then a crash inside the house.

I asked her, "Is there anyone inside the house?"

She said there wasn't. Shortly after that, a woman who was touring the cave came back running up the path. She got in her car, terrified, and refused to leave her car or tell anyone what happened.

The first time I visited the cave, I was in the main room where the Indian grave is. I felt a chill down my back. When I turned around, I saw a Native American warrior in full dress, with bone breastplate, feathers and all. He looked at me, then vanished. Next, I felt a chill on my left side, and there I saw three elderly Native Americans sitting on the stone ledge that forms a natural bench, past the main room, on the right side entrance of the hallway beyond that. Then they disappeared. Finally, I heard a woman's cry, as if in childbirth, which came from the second cave area. Since I grew up in a haunted house, I wasn't scared. I was kind of used to it. I felt welcome instead.

The Ghosts of Charit Creek

"Charit Creek Lodge, located deep in the Big South Fork National River and Recreation Area, is only accessible by horseback, foot or mountain bike. Well-maintained hiking and horse trails lead you through interesting and beautiful places on your way to the lodge. It is located where Charit Creek and Station Camp Creek meet; the lodge rests in a beautiful pasture framed by magnificent bluffs. This valley has given shelter to travelers in the Big South Fork since the Indian hunting camps. The structure has evolved through the years of habitation, and on the western end there is a log cabin that may have been built in the early 1800s by long hunter Jonathan Blevins. His log structure still stands as part of the lodge. The house became a hunting lodge known locally as the hog farm due to the Russian boar imported by owner Joe Simpson in the early 1960s. It was also operated as a youth hostel from 1987 to 1989."
(Source: *http://www.tomthallcabin.com/attractions/ attractions%20near%20tth.htm*).

I interviewed Amy when I worked in Leslie County, Kentucky, and I was staying at the Mary Breckenridge Home in Hyden. Amy and her husband were resident managers at Charit Lodge about 15 years ago. Amy knew some of the history and she also heard guests report sights and sounds of ghosts.

Amy:

The Park is on the border between Tennessee and Kentucky, three hours south of Richmond, Kentucky. It's in Jamestown, Tennessee. There is a Jamestown, Kentucky, right there too, so it can be confusing. From Jamestown, it's a 45-minute drive to the trailhead. You can't drive into the Lodge. You can ride horses or hike to it.

The original cabin was built by Jonathan Blevins and then people added to it to make the permanent lodge at Charit Creek. There are two cabins that are separate, and one large lodge. The other cabins were brought in after the loggers had cleared out the trees. This is all new forest. The whole thing was logged clean. So every bit of the forest is new. But it's old enough, that when we were there, the habitat had recovered enough to support bears. They reintroduced bears from the Smokey Mountains. One day we were afraid of the bears smelling our camp food, but I haven't heard report of any bears coming into the camp. After the bear release there was a snowfall and one of the rangers followed some tracks up to Hatfield Ridge. There is a little cemetery down there.

This was during the off-season when we had two young East Indian doctors visiting, and I was asked to fix them vegetarian meals. At the same time, there were two elderly nuns staying at the camp, and nobody else. We didn't know whether to seat the meat eaters with the vegetarians. What ended up happening was so delightful. We sat them at two separate but nearby tables, in case they wanted to visit each other. That evening they ended up at the same table, talking with one another.

So the next night the older women had the young doctors out snipe hunting. We had no idea when we were in our cabin at night that we could hear them that far off. The nuns asked for big garbage bags, in which we figured they needed to place their dirty clothes. The next morning, they were laughing so hard at the snipe hunting they had the night before.

At the end of their visit two new guests, husband and wife, rode up on their horses.

The next morning, the woman asked, "Who would let their children come out here in the middle of the night and play in the yard?" There was a huge weeping willow out in the yard.

She said, "How far away are we from children?"

I answered, "There is no way for children to get down here. It's a forty-five minute drive to the nearest children."

And the woman insisted, "But I heard them. There were children playing down here. They were running and laughing, playing in the yard. They were small children playing happily, giggling."

She asked me if my kids were there, and I told her that they were older.

Charit Creek is named after a girl who drowned in the 1920s when trying to cross the rain-swollen stream. There are many accounts of people who say that they saw Charity down there at the stream. Lots of folks asked about her.

"Who was that little girl with? Which family does she belong to?"

I know there were no little girls down there, because people who come to stay at the lodge and cabins have to check in with us. People would also see her walking around on the porches at the main lodge.

People reported seeing an older and smaller man. He's not a very happy ghost. It's supposed to be the spirit of Jonathan Blevins. They said that he is a hateful and angry ghost. I lived down there for a year and didn't see his ghost. I was out there alone, by myself, a lot, so I was afraid to run into him. I guess I wasn't very open to seeing him.

Jonathan Blevins is buried there. Sometimes Mr. Hatfield would come down from the ridge and give John Blevins a hard time. One time John Blevins was drunk while he sat on his porch. He threatened Hatfield, saying simply, "Get out of here. I'm going to shoot you!" Mr. Hatfield turned his horse around to ride away and Blevins shot him in the back.

Some of the graves are unmarked. It was too steep for Indian settlements, but the pioneers and loggers were there. The log house where we lived was built in 1816 and was a weaver's lodge. Inside were holes for the spokes of the weaving looms. The managers still live there; the cabin has to be kept in historic condition. We go down there all the time. My son lived there from age 2 ½ until 3 ½. So he has very fond memories. Every year we return to visit. If you hike in to the Lodge via the short trail, you used to have to cross the creek over large boulders.

He ran down to the creek and exclaimed, "Charit Creek! I'm home!" He was just a little bitty kid.

Two's Company

It wasn't until after I had gathered notes on the mild-mannered ghost that used to inhabit Jane's business/home on High Street, in Lexington, when I realized her business's name, "Two's Company", might refer to an unseen companion. I've enjoyed my brief conversations at the Duke Road Postal Station with postal employees, Jackie and Jim. Jackie offered to help me scout out some local tales of the unusual. Jackie heard some mention of a ghost from Jane's employee, Rosa. Rosa had heard unexplained sounds in Two's Company when Jane was away. So, let's start at the beginning...

Jane is a cheerful and smart woman who grew up in Louisville. Her family owned a number of businesses, including a funeral home. Jane's friends visited and played at her residence at the funeral home. Jane said that she often felt the presence of the spirits of those recently deceased bodies when she went downstairs through the funeral parlor to get the laundry from their basement. She was used to having the funeral business in her home. She didn't give those feelings too much thought. As she grew up and starting hearing ghost stories in school, she realized what was happening in her own home.

Jane's business operated in Chevy Chase, Lexington, for years. She bought the building on High Street East in 1994. The Witt family originally owned this 1920's duplex and a building across the street. Jane said that she heard that two sisters lived in the duplex, one above and one downstairs. When Jane was a new resident there, she often heard the sounds of drawers being opened and closed in the kitchen. Sometimes, when she was up late at night, Jane felt a presence behind her. She identified that presence as being female.

Jane reports that the ghost was active about once a week, sometimes slamming the cabinet doors. Her cats would prick up their ears when they rested on her bed as they sensed the spirit of the woman. Jane's employees downstairs were puzzled by hearing footsteps above them, particularly when they knew Jane was away. They heard the sound of furniture being moved around on the floor. Jane's employees went cautiously upstairs, in pairs, to have a look around, only to discover that nobody was there and the furniture seemed to be undisturbed. One time they heard the sound of someone entering both locked doors and walking up the stairs to Jane's apartment. Again, their investigation led to empty rooms.

Jane actually had a few interesting experiences with the spirit world since she was a girl. She had a near-death experience when she was ten years old. She went down to a basement refrigerator and opened it up, not realizing that the basement was flooded. Jane was electrocuted and described herself as traveling a tunnel toward the light.

When Jane was living in Houston, she awoke one night about 3:00 AM to the sounds of chimes tinkling. Thinking her noisy neighbor with the loud bug zapper had now added chimes, she went outside to check it out. But there were no chimes, and five minutes later Jane got a call from Lexington to let her know that her friend Paula passed away. Jane's sensitivity to spirits from the other side must have continued with her children; she says that her two daughters have reported visits from their grandfather (Jane's father) more that once. In fact, Jane's mother relates an incident where she was driving along an ocean highway in Florida. She was returning from a bridge game with friends and suddenly noticed she had company in the back seat of her car. It was her mother, father, and her aunt, all of whom died some years earlier.

One of them said, "This is a great place to come for a vacation."

Jane's sister Judy calls on the telephone and Jane will pick the phone up before it rings. They seem to have a psychic connection to each other's thoughts and feelings. Jane has seen spirit activity at the home of friends and has heard ghost stories from other families. She knows a friend from her high school days in Louisville who tells his mother's interesting tale.... When his mother was 17, her sister traveled from Louisville to Chicago. They all thought that perhaps she went there to seek a job, but they were concerned since they hadn't heard any news from her. The woman in Louisville was awakened at night to find that her sister was sitting on her bed. Her sister asked not to be touched, and they walked together out to the porch swing to spend the night talking. She had been ill with diphtheria and told her sister that she was dying. They freely talked until daylight came and then the woman faded away. The news reached the family in Louisville that morning that she died.

Finally, Jane stated that her aunt had, many years ago, suffered a stroke while driving and wrecked her car. Her aunt was unconscious at the hospital.

One night, her aunt suddenly awoke from her coma and announced to the bedside nurse, "My mother's coming to get me to take me home."

The nurse talked with her aunt and they played cards together. When the nurse went away for a few minutes, she returned to find that Jane's aunt had died.

Historic Haunts

Ashland, Lexington

One of Henry Clay's children was brave enough to detail a ghostly encounter with no less a famous ghost than that of Daniel Boone. When I visited Ashland, volunteer Mary Ellen Carmichael gave me a copy of the article that reproduced Susan M. Clay's amazing story. Susan Clay reports that her husband looked up from his library desk to see a man dressed in the "backwoodsman's style" take shelter from pouring rain. Mrs. Clay saw him at the same time as she entered the library to visit with her husband. The apparition rested on one of their chairs, with his rifle at his side for several minutes. The frontier ghost answered a few questions by Susan's husband in monosyllables. After he left, Mrs. Clay noticed that he had brought not a single drop of water from his clothing, despite coming in from the rainstorm.

The folklore of Ashland tells that neighbors have seen figures in the upstairs window. One Lexington resident reports seeing lights in the windows when she was present on the grounds for a musical performance. The tour guides are fond of pointing out a dark figure in the recesses of a large beech tree near the tombstone of one of Ashland's less famous residents – a cat! The only tombstone found on the property of Ashland's original 600 acres was located where Lakewood is now, and carried the name "Sarah – beloved consort". Ashland opened as a museum in 1950, but the house was closed for two years in the early nineties. That was when a workman reported seeing a mysterious person walking down the mulch path, the same path where Henry Clay had walked while composing his speeches. It was there that I met one of Ashland's neighbors, Margaret Ryle, who loves to walk about those hallowed grounds and attune to nature. Margaret is a former volunteer who has walked across Richmond Road from her house to Ashland to find a peaceful retreat where she can release stress and grief.

A former employee of Ashland is reported to have often smelled the scent of spices near the 1882 reproduction oil painting of Henry Clay. Years later, when she found herself in the Civic Center, she was puzzled to smell that same scent there. She looked up in amazement to discover that same painting was now hanging in the Civic Center. The portrait now again hangs in the hallway at Ashland.

One more interesting tale came from a man I met in Lexington, who lived near Ashland. He recounted how he often walked the gardens and grounds there. One day, while walking alone, he looked up to see a man, dressed in 19th Century attire, bicycling along merrily, about six feet up in the air!

Whitehall, Madison County

Some families have all the ghosts. If you take Interstate south to exit 95 and follow the signs to White Hall, you can visit the home of kinfolk to Henry Clay. Cassius Clay and Henry Clay were first cousins, once removed. General Green Clay built a marvelous house in 1798, Clermont, and his son Cassius Clay had it greatly enlarged between 1861 and 1870. White Hall has a number of stories and its own ghost tour. Tour guide Keven McQueen compiled the old mansion's unusual tales into part of a book he is writing. Keven wrote a biography of Cassius Clay, in which he clears up many misunderstandings about that notable statesman. Folks have smelled ethereal pipe smoke and unexplained perfume. The old piano, which hardly can make a sound, has occasionally sounded a few pinging notes without the action of mortal hands. Keven notes that the spirit activity seems to have quieted down since the summer of 1989 when extensive repairs were done. But, Mr. McQueen said, the house did have a reputation of being haunted long before the state opened White Hall for tours in 1971.

The master bedroom is the site of General Green Clay's death on Halloween, where shortly before his death he said, "I've just seen death come through that door." This room has seen a mirror repeatedly come falling down for no apparent reason – it's still intact. Another room, the Blue Room, seems to often prompt some visitors to inquire if White Hall is haunted. Faint, muffled voices and the sounds of moving furniture have been heard in the Blue Room, and when the tour guides go up to investigate – you guessed it, nobody is there, and everything looks to be in its place. Keven says that it was more noticeable before air conditioning was installed. A room got cold right before some spirit phenomena happened. Anybody see the thermostat scene in the movie, "The Sixth Sense"? Son Brutus Clay's room displayed a lamp that prefers to stay on, despite a security guard repeatedly turning it off. One room has a doorknob to an empty room, which keeps turning back and forth.

In addition, the employees heard ballroom music, that once sent an employee straight back out to the parking lot, and smelled the unexplained scent of burning candle wax. Guide ropes swung without the benefit of any wind. Folks caught a glimpse of a woman in a hoop skirt pass around a corner into another room. A whole tour of visitors with their tour guide watched in amazement as a woman dressed in black came downstairs to the second floor back hallway, walk <u>through</u> a guide rope, and disappear into the back closet of one of the bedrooms. Mr. McQueen reports four other incidents that have occurred in that area of White Hall. Even the gift shop has a few bizarre tales, according to Kathleen White, the gift shop manager.

ꝶexington Ghosts

Mark, a Lexington resident, had numerous close encounters with ghosts. Mark worked at Camp Woodman, which is located out Tates Creek

Road. When returning to camp, late one night, Mark and his friend saw a light-colored object within the dim headlights of their truck. He got out to investigate, and was shocked to come directly upon a tall stranger. The man turned to face Mark; his eyes were a vacant stare. Mark turned on his heels and jumped in the truck, and urged his friends to drive away. They warned the other staff about the stranger. A search of the area later revealed neither track nor trace of the stranger. Some of his friends in the truck, and at the camp, were doubtful of the truth of Mark's experience. But it was not much later during that same summer season when a different camp counselor saw the tall stranger. His fellow counselor saw the ghost at the same fork in the road. Once again, the tall stranger looked at Mark's friend with the same vacant stare. Mark's second sighting of the ghost was when he was shown an historic picture of the cabin on the camp property. There photographed was the tall stranger who used to live at the cabin, except the photo was dated from the 1920's.

Mark and his father worked at the Holiday Inn South on Athens-Boonesboro Road near Lexington. They were cleaning up after a banquet and his dad asked Mark to go to the kitchen. As Mark came up to the basement, under the banquet room, he saw that the lights were turned off.

"These lights down here are never turned off!" he said to himself in surprise. Puzzled a bit, Mark walked through the dark basement to put a box into the kitchen. When he set the box down, and turned around to return, the lights suddenly came back on. Mark heard a thud, and the sound of footsteps coming toward him. When the sounds stopped, Mark left the kitchen, and walked back through the basement.

He told his father, "Okay, Dad, that was really funny, scaring me like that".

But his father denied any involvement with Mark's unusual experience, and asked him to carry another box to the kitchen. Mark's suspicions were again aroused as he saw the basement lights out. He carefully walked through the basement, and after arriving in the kitchen, he noticed the lights went on again. The same thud hit the floor, and this time there was the sound of heavy breathing as the footsteps approached. The steps and the forced breathing advanced right up to Mark. He stood, frozen in fear. Then the ghost simply let out a sad sigh and Mark felt himself freed to escape.

When he got back to his dad, his father simply told him, "So you've finally met the ghost in the basement."

Perhaps the ghost was from the suicide, which happened years ago. It seems that back when the hotel was a Sheraton, a man checked into Room 168 and killed himself. People reported that the bloody mattress was left for weeks on the loading dock; no one wanted to touch it. One of Mark's coworkers, the cook, also had a ghostly encounter. But this man had been at his home where he saw the ghost of his deceased wife. The cook was feeling guilty about remarrying. He fondly recalled the love that he and his first wife shared. While he was sitting on his couch, he watched in complete amazement as the spirit of his dead wife walked from the kitchen to sit in the chair across from him. They talked for some time, with his former wife offering supportive comments concerning his upcoming wedding. The next day, when the cook came to work, Mark noticed his changed attitude and lighthearted spirit. He was relieved of his burden.

Mark had one more ghostly experience, at Waveland. He lived near this historic building. One night, Mark and his friends went up there to hang out. They talked with the caretaker, who told them the story of a black slave who was supposedly forced to be a mistress to one of the white men there. It seems that the woman tried to escape, but fell into the cistern. Since she was unable to swim, the woman drowned.

Mark was by the soda machine when he heard singing.

"It sounded like a Negro spiritual, and it was a woman singing".

When the other boys showed up, Mark found that they, too, heard the singing. None of them confessed to having made a sound. But then, as they all stood there, they caught the sight of a woman in white rags running past. They tried to pinpoint her figure in the dark with their flashlights; but the light shone completely through the female figure. They all watched in utter amazement as the woman seemed to fall down into the ground. They rushed up to the spot where she had disappeared, only to find the ground intact and no one in sight.

Visitors From the Past
Pat Ellis, Lexingon

On Madison Place, in Lexington, is a house owned by Pat Ellis and her husband. Pat actually feels as if she's lived in the house before. Her strong connection to this house was augmented by sensitivity to the spirits found inside. An aunt of an old friend died sometime ago in the house. She was cared for downstairs and was diabetic. Pat believes she saw this woman after her death. Once, she caught a glimpse of the tail end of a yellow dress; the ghost moved with a sort of limp, just like the deceased woman. Another ghost, the spirit of a woman who was robbed and beaten to death, appeared as a form blocking the light from Pat's television. Pat believes that an older gentleman who passed away in the house, Mr. William Morris Lamb, was the source of many sounds and activities. Mr. Lamb had a heart attack, and died two weeks later in the house. Pat felt his spirit make a cold air on her face.

After feeling his presence for a while, she simply spoke to him and said, "it's okay with me if you want to show yourself".

The most difficult aspect of his haunting was the times that things would disappear. Her son laid down a CD on the table; then it vanished, only to later reappear. Pat claims that the ghost loved to make the twist ties disappear, the ones she needed to bag up the recyclables. Two brand-new kitchen potholders poofed and never were seen again. She often hears the noise of a shutting door. Pat also hears the sound of things falling to the floor, but she no longer pays any attention to the noise, as she knows she will find nothing.

One of the homeowners was a temperance lecturer at the Chautauqua gatherings in the late 1800's. Another former male resident was a rather mean father. He supposedly went into his son's room, stated that he was now too old for stuffed animals, and put all his teddy bears into the fireplace. To compensate, Pat keeps dozens of beautiful teddy bears in that room. Pat heard about the event, which took place in the 1950's, from the boy's sister. Pat claims a native psychic ability. She is the seventh of nine children; she was born with the veil over her eyes.

Pat led me through her home on a brief tour; there are 13 rooms and 5,100 square feet. Later, we sat out back, drinking lemonade, as Pat told of a spirit in her neighbor's home. She pointed to the adjacent house to the east, and said that at the home of Phyllis Walters, a ghostly girl would come and brush her face.

Pat told me that in December of 2002, a ghostly gentleman came to her bedroom door and opened it. He seemed taken aback, as if he didn't know the room was taken. He said nothing. Pat went to look about the house, to see if she might have mistaken him for someone there. But she found no one else was at home then. At first, Pat thought the ghost was her sister's deceased husband. She didn't recognize the ghost, although she felt it was someone who lived there. She calls this ghost, "Jimmy". He has grey hair, blue eyes, with glasses, and is in his mid to late seventies.

Hurricane Hall

Mary Lynne Mackin Salazar, Lexington

Hurricane Hall's main block was built in 1794 with additions in 1805 and 1840. It remained the same family (the Quarles-Thompson clan) from 1803 until 1962 when Stanley Petters bought it. He began extensive remodeling, which may have brought to life the inhabiting spirits. I talked with Betty Stephenson, who grew up in the house with the last family before the Petters. She said she never saw a ghost. Amazingly, she remarked that just before they moved from Hurricane Hall, her father dug a big hole and put in all the family photos, toys and mementos and covered it up. Betty also reported about her cousin who was "mysteriously" thrown down the well by other cousins. I assume he is the malevolent-acting ghost in the house. I suppose if my cousins threw me down a three hundred foot well that I'd be a little upset, too!

I had my own experiences in Hurricane Hall, which led me to question and hear many stories from the Petter children. I talked to the son. At first he was reluctant to say anything, but eventually his comment was, "You should be happy we are not alone in the house."

When I told him I was jerked around he responded, "That son-of-a-bitch has been jerking me around for years!"

He told me when he was a child, sleeping in the nursery, some invis-

Hurricane Hall, Lexington.

ible spirit frequently pulled off his covers. He also had his head jerked back and forth. But the most alarming event happened when the ghost put a pillow over his head to smother him.

I also talked to the stepdaughter who told me about a young girl with long dark hair wearing a white nightgown. She evidently died in the corner bedroom while giving birth. She was often seen when the family had babies in the house – standing over the crib. In the early 1990's, the son brought home a new wife. She was a woman who nearly matched the ghost woman's appearance. He had an interesting encounter with this young female ghost while both slept in this haunted bedroom.

His wife, also wearing a white gown, got out of bed and walked down the hallway to the bathroom. This was a straight-line path from the doorway of that corner bedroom. He watched her go into the bathroom and shut the door. Directly she returned to bed and sat down. When he reached over to touch her, he felt no body there. Then his real wife walked out of the bathroom to find her husband toting a loaded shotgun down the hall.

When he told her what just happened, she asked him, "Who are you going to shoot?" Certainly that was a logical question!

The daughter related several interesting tales about friends who came to visit. A girlfriend from New York came for Christmas. While walking up the stairs, she happened to look into the first bedroom and was surprised to find a teenage girl, dressed in period clothes, smiling at her. The girl then disappeared. I checked the graveyard for teenage girls and located just one grave. Her first name was Marie. The family plot is on the property near a barn. When I searched the family cemetery, I was amazed to find nearly all the deceased were children of various ages. I remember the slave cemetery also had a collection of youthful dead. One couple lost their baby, each year for several years. These young spirits made their presence known to me.

The daughter had a friend from Prospect, Kentucky, stay one evening. After a lot of partying, he went to bed in the first bedroom. An hour later he was awakened to hear tunes from the 1940's playing on an old radio that sat on a bookshelf in the bedroom. He got up from the bed to walk over and turn off the radio. But as soon as he set the radio down, the music resumed playing. Impatient to get back to bed, he thought he'd take care of the problem for good by pulling out the plug. But upon reaching for the plug, he realized it was not in the wall outlet but dangling free and unconnected. Astounded, he held the unplugged but playing radio in his hand. He simply set down the radio, returned to bed and pulled the covers over his head for the night. At the break of dawn he made a hasty retreat.

My experience at Hurricane Hall began in 1993 when I housesat. I was happily in residence for the first week with no warning of what was to pass. At 11:00 PM I went upstairs to the corner bedroom. My two dogs were with me: a greyhound and a deaf poodle. They slept with me in the first bedroom. I lay down, turned off the light and within minutes I heard the soft laughter of children playing. As the noise got louder, I realized they were coming up the stairs. Directly the dogs flew around the corner into my bedroom. Small rugs were flung about as the dogs leapt on my bed. They both were crying and shaking.

I told my dogs, "Yeah, I hear it, too" and I grabbed the greyhound's neck.

Right about then my head was jerked twice, as if to nod in agreement and out of my mouth, in a male voice came, "Hello Mary." Then as quickly as it started it was over. I promptly got up, got dressed and got gone!

The next day I returned to Hurricane Hall with my husband. He was not quite sure what to think about my reports to him. We came into the rear of the house through the kitchen.

As we walked into the dining room, which is directly below the first bedroom, I asked aloud, "Okay, where are you spirits?" We both immediately heard a rock, with the loud thud, hit the second floor landing.

I turned to tell my husband, "They're upstairs, come on" but he was already on his way out the back door.

I slowly walked into the hall and took three steps toward the second floor. Suddenly, it dawned on me that I really didn't want to see the ghosts waiting for me. So I backed down and left.

From that day on when I entered the house I said, "I'm coming into your house. I accept the fact that you are here but I do not want to have any contact with you." And I never did see or hear the ghosts after that, until the Petters moved.

One other thing I later discovered was actually connected with Hurricane Hall happened in my own home. It was in 1994. As I lay in bed, I suddenly heard a loud sigh. It scared me although I didn't tell the girl I worked with. But a day or two later, when I was sending a fax, I noticed a strange look on Rheta's face.

She looked around the room then looked at me and asked, "Did you hear that?"

I replied in turn, "Hear what?"

She said, "Well, I don't know, but it sounded like someone sighing. It sounded like someone who was really tired and sighing."

I jumped up from my chair and told her, "Are you serious?"

Rheta replied, "Yes, and I just heard it." Although I heard nothing at that time I could tell she was shaken.

I then revealed to her, "I can't believe you just said that because I heard the same thing a couple of days ago at home."

We reported this to our boss who said nothing that day. But a few days later as he sat between us he said he needed to talk to us about the sighing. Just then the phone rang and for whatever reason he didn't again bring up the subject. Later, I recalled that his wife often used to sigh like that.

When the Petters moved in the early 2000's, I returned to Hurricane Hall to help them pack up. On my last night in the house around 8:30 PM, I worked to finish in the hallway. Suddenly, I heard a woman start to wail. She was sobbing as if heart broken. I looked up the staircase toward the third floor but saw nothing. Then I decided it was time to leave Hurricane Hall. I often wondered since then if the ghostly lady who cried that night was Mrs. Petter. She put so much of herself into the house.

Hurricane Hall was again remodeled. The parlor wallpaper, a wedding present in 1820, was removed. I'm not sure if taking that out caused more haunting. But so much was changed that I wouldn't be surprised if the spirits are upset. Mr. Petter was a preservationist and did all he could to keep the house as it was in 1794. It seems the new owner did not have that same sense of history. I would not be surprised if they are paying for that now. When the energy of a house is disturbed, so are the spirits who inhabit that home.

Restless Door ... And More

I met a woman at the Kentucky Book Fair, who told me she had a few ghost stories. She lives in Frankfort, Kentucky, and is retired from working for the state government.

I grew up in Hardin County in a house next to a city plot with an old graveyard, where the headstones were taken up. The removed headstones were stacked under the house on the other side of the graveyard. There were three small plots of headstones, and we played around them. The house was a parsonage before my family bought it and moved in, before I was born, in the early 1940s. The house started out as a two-room log cabin and was built onto several times. It was about 100 years old. I heard voices, footsteps and other sounds in the house at night.

I was once in my bedroom when I heard, "Help me."

It sounded like a man's voice, coming from the direction of the old slave house. I felt chills going up and down my spine

One day, I noticed new black shiny rocks on the railroad tracks. I thought "obsidian". I heard my spirit guide correct my pronunciation.

"Yes, it is obsidian, like in your geology book. You didn't know how to pronounce it. Take some rocks and put them under your bed." I did so and I no longer heard noises in that house.

The second story concerns the family farm haunting. It's not the house I lived in. Things were seen or heard by at least five different people at various times. These occurrences happened as my grandparents were both dying and decided to sell the farm that was in the family since 1918. The sale was in 1977. The strangest thing was the false teeth with a gold tooth that appeared so it could be given to a grandson that wanted the gold, since he was a child. The story concerns four generations, counting the haunting of my great-grandparents.

Restless Door

These occurrences started in my grandparents' home while both were ill. Grandfather was hard of hearing, but noticed the back door banging shut at night. It wasn't long afterwards when he mentioned this to family and he was diagnosed with cancer. Family stayed to help with grandmother, who was bedridden after a broken hip. He also had several strokes during this time.

I stayed one night at the house. The next morning I was asked if I heard or seen anything strange during the night. I hadn't. Over the decades, I've learned more about the haunting of the family farm while my grandparents spent their last days.

The farm my grandparents lived on belonged to my grandfather's parents. My great-grandparents bought the farm in 1918. The house was fairly new when they moved in. In 1954 my great-grandmother passed. My grandparents moved in with great-grandfather to help him farm that same year.

When the farm was run by my great-grandparents, it was pretty much a self-sufficient operation. They fed the family from their produce during the great depression of the 1930's. Two sons had families of their own; their daughter was still at home. The farm had two fishponds, as well as several types of fowl. They had an orchard and a huge vegetable garden. Apples were stored in barrels in a barn, wrapped in catalogs, one apple per page. Potatoes were stored in a depression in the middle of a barn floor covered with hay. Mother says they never had beef, as it was too expensive to raise cattle. They did have some hogs and they had a dairy cow for milk. The land was very important to the family. They were able to live from its produce and took care of the land. I remember the Old Farmer's Almanac hanging from a hook on a wall. Over the front door was a horseshoe, with the open end up to hold in the luck.

Years later, the old frame farmhouse was torn down and a new brick one built in the same place. My great-grandfather was still alive and living with his son, but sold the farm to my grandparents. During the winter, great-grandfather lived with his daughter, my great-aunt, in Louisville. The new farmhouse was modern, having central heat, running water and a bathroom. There was also a basement. The old house had a cistern that collected rain-water. The hand pump was outside the kitchen. The back door that led to the main barn also led to the combination chicken house and outhouse. Even as a child, I thought it strange that there was a convenient concrete walkway to the barn, but no conveniences such as a bathroom in the house.

Great-grandmother kept her medicinal herbs by the cistern, where they were easily watered. She knew herbal medicine, giving tonics to her family. She nursed my grandfather through the flu of 1918, which killed many young people. He almost died. They had two other children.

By the time I was a child, Great-grandfather was going blind. At the old house, a chain hung from an overhead metal wire that ran from the back door to the outhouse. Once as a child, I played by running while pulling the chain along its overhead wire. Grandmother called me to bring the chain to Great-grandfather, who needed it to find his way to the outhouse. He stood by the back door and reached into space with his cane to find and catch the chain by the crook of his cane.

The new house, built in the same place, was laid out directionally in the same manner. Both faced the main road and had a back door to the barn in virtually the same place. The new house had a cistern under a back covered porch area, which had the back door to the barn.

The new house had a bathroom off the hallway. To the left of the hall-way was my grandparents' bedroom, on the front of the house with steps to the basement. On the right of the hallway were the two secondary bed-rooms. Great-grandfather's bedroom was the back bedroom, on the corner of the house, closest to the bathroom. Great-grandfather died in that room in 1967 in his late nineties. It was a slow, easy death. Even though he was completely blind, as he neared death, he gained the ability to see. He looked around the room. He remarked on the colors in the room, the curtains, and how nice it was to finally see his grandson's wife that had helped take care of him.

My grandmother broke a hip in the mid 1970's. She also had strokes and some cardiac problems and remained bedfast for the last few years be-fore she died. In 1976, my grandfather was diagnosed with lung cancer. He decided to die at home and not be a guinea pig for the doctors as his older son was. My uncle and grandfather had lung cancer at the same time. Grandfather died quickly, within a few months. During this time, fam-ily members stayed with my grandparents. My mother and younger sister moved into the house. Other family members rotated in and out to give relief so mother could rest. As grandfather got worse, there was one person, then two people sitting up all night to attend to his needs and those of our bedfast grandmother. These members included my grandfather's sister (whom Great-grandfather lived with during the winters) and grandparents' other children along with their spouses and children.

It was before my grandfather was diagnosed, but suspected he was ill, that he heard noises in the house. He told several closer relatives that he heard the back door banging. His sister, my great-aunt, later heard the same noise. She said the sound was that of the door slamming at the old, demolished house, not the new one they were standing in. She said it was Great-grandfather (their father) bringing in milk from the barn.

As my grandfather's condition deteriorated, other family members heard the back door slam shut. They locked the door yet it still made the slamming noise. One night Grandmother's elderly sister stayed overnight. My cousin and her mother, Grandfather's daughter, didn't want this great-great aunt disturbed by the back door noises. They locked the back door and put a chair under the doorknob to prevent the door from opening. That night after dark, the three women sat together on the couch in the living room. They were at the front of the house facing the drive into the farm. Outside, slamming car door noises started from the front drive where cars were parked. The great-great aunt got up and stared out the window into the dark. The cousin and aunt looked at each other and kept quiet. They thought to themselves, that the ghost was saying, "I'll show you."

My sister slept in the bedroom that belonged to our great-grandfather. She slept in the same bed in which he had died. Every morning, a different person would ask her the same question.

"Did you get up during the night to go the bathroom?" She would answer no, and then would again be questioned.

"Are you sure?" She answered she was sure, she would remember going. The people that sat up heard the door to her room open and close, every night. One night my cousin was about to get up to go to the bathroom, but saw a shadow move at the end of the hall, going from Great-grandfather's old bedroom toward Grandfather's room. She assumed it was my sister. She kept an eye and ear on the hall so she could have her turn in the bathroom. After waiting for a long time for my sister to exit, she got up to check on her. She found the bathroom empty and my sister in bed asleep. Again, my sister had no knowledge of what was going on.

After my grandfather died, my mother moved Grandmother into her house. The old house was just too spooky. My aunt (Mom's sister) and her daughter (called my cousin through this story) and family moved into the farmhouse a few months later and took grandmother back to her home. Grandmother died the same month, within a year of my grandfather. My aunt and her family stayed to keep it secure until the time the farm sold at auction.

Many in the family said they felt presence in the house at various times. One aunt went to the house one day with her young son. No one else was in the house at the time. She was in the basement. She heard footsteps upstairs. She went upstairs and saw no one. She felt she was being watched and quickly left. This is the aunt that Great-grandfather saw for the first time before his death.

Gold Tooth

My mother and others went through the family items to prepare for the farm auction. My mother was in the house alone one day working in the basement. While she was there, she went upstairs three times to see who was walking about the house. She heard the footsteps. There was no one there but herself.

On another day, my mother, her sister and my cousin worked in the bedroom in the basement when they found Great-grandmother's false teeth. My great-grandmother had a gold tooth placed into her upper plate. It was considered a fashionable thing at the time. One of her grandsons, as a young boy, wanted that gold tooth. Great-grandmother said she would leave it for him. The boy is my great aunt's son, my grandfather's sister's son. My great aunt told Grandfather to dispose of the teeth. Grandfather put the teeth in a small open wooden box under the bed in the basement bedroom. My mother and her sister finished up their work in the room one day and left the bed with nothing on the bedspread. Everyone left the room and didn't enter the basement until the next day, when my mother arrived and they were ready to start again. That morning, in the middle of the bed was the upper plate of Great-grandmother's false teeth with that gold tooth. The lower plate was found under the bed, still in the wooden box on top of the other contents of the box. Mother and great aunt both said they didn't want to pull that gold tooth out of the plate to give it to the grandson. Mother still has the upper plate.

The day of the auction, my aunt was very tired. She said she had little sleep the previous night when she stayed at the house. The back door kept slamming and woke her. The family always assumed it was the great-grandparents that haunted the house. Mostly they took it in stride as best they could. They let only a small number of people in the family know about it. Even now they do not want to talk about it or identify the property.

We heard through local gossip that the next people to live in the house were scared to death and didn't stay long. This repeated. The house quieted down when the inhabitants were people that knew my great-grandparents. The man had worked on the farm with my great-grandfather.

Grandfather made out the will for his estate after he knew he had cancer. He made arrangements for power of attorney for himself and Grandmother. He decided to have everything sold at auction. He told his children his wishes and told them to carry it out without any quarrelling. Otherwise, he'd come back and haunt them.

There was no quarrelling.

Help From Beyond the Grave

This last story happened after I left home. At that time, my parents were farming in Hart County. It was the time of year before the tobacco money came in, and it was a stretch to have enough cash flow to buy groceries. They tried to take some cattle to market, but it was raining too much to move the livestock. The freezer was pretty well eaten down, and there were not many more vegetables left in the garden.

My father went to the post office and there he found an envelope with enough money in it to buy some groceries. Inside were sixty dollars in twenty-dollar bills. Afterwards, the rain stopped and they got the cattle over to market. The mystery money came in a standard small white envelope, with no return address. It was mailed from that same post office. It was addressed to my father, by his familiar nickname, Jimmy.

The odd thing was that the envelope was written in my father's mother's hand. He recognized her handwriting immediately, and my mother also

Old Beech Tree, Henderson, Kentucky.

confirmed it was written by her. This happened in 1978 or 1979. She died in 1976. Despite death, my grandmother still helped our family to survive.

The Homestead, Bardstown, Kentucky

There are many lovely and historical attractions in and around Bardstown. The Homestead is located about four miles northeast of the city. The Homestead was built in the late 1700's. But when Joanne Hobbs moved to Bardstown and bought an interesting old home, no one, including the seller, knew what amazing architecture lay beneath the centuries of remodeling and additions. Joanne and her working buddies diligently endeavored to rebuild that which was fallen down, covered up, broken and taken over by raccoons. One of her workers found massive poplar logs. Slaves had hewn these logs, some 16-18 inches square, for the original building. A slave wing was added later. Today you can see that section, which is now a kitchen. Brick floors complement an open vault to the second story. On the west wall, there is a plaque with the names of the slaves that lived and died at the Homestead.

History is embedded within the home itself, and also in the land at the Homestead. It was the only stage stop from Bloomfield to Bardstown. The Union Army stopped and stayed, using one of the many springs on the property, and no doubt quartering both inside and on the grounds. As a Historic Kentucky Landmark, the Homestead carries layers of feeling, both dignified and mysterious. Joanne took me on a walkabout tour, showing me the downstairs parlors, game room, and bedrooms upstairs. I was impressed by the very large buffalo – bison head mounted above the fireplace, as well as recognizing artifacts and crafts that Joanne collected in the desert Southwest. There were Navajo rugs, Indian pottery and kachina dolls.

The bedrooms available are the Farm Room, the Log Guest Room, and the Victorian Guest Room. I slept in the Victorian Guest Room, which had antique wavy-glass windows facing Bloomfield Road, a fully dressed up dress form, and a hutch with television and video player. There was little traffic on Hwy 62, and I slept well. In the morning, Joanne fixed a hearty country breakfast, with eggs, sausage, homemade biscuits, and preserves. While I ate breakfast, I noticed that the kitchen was stuffed with genuine antiques, flower sack slave dresses, kitchen tools and pottery. Joanne told about a couple who came from England. She worried beforehand, trying to study about teas and British teatime, to be good hostess. The couple arrived, and when Joanne asked them about their preferred drink, they noted that they drank only coffee, no tea!

After breakfast, I explored the grounds, walking out the whistling path to see the stone cellar and milk house. I wandered toward the driveway, past a tree that is much older that the Homestead itself. There is a little stream and an arched wooden bridge over the spring-fed stream. Behind the house I found a family set of a dozen gravestones propped up with a metal rod behind each one. Joanne said that the headstones were removed from their original site, farther back on the property. We chatted out in the warm sunshine, as Joanne plucked hard pears off the tree, tossing them to the chickens.

Joanne befriended many local craftsmen, and her B&B is filled with carved folk art, jewelry, antiques and Christmas ornaments. Joanne hosts an annual Christmas Open House. Joanne is an artist, too – she hand-makes goose feather Christmas trees. Eventually we talked about the haunting at the Homestead, and I was an attentive listener.

Joanne:

The ghosts chase my dog, Daisy. I believe there are mostly all slave spirits here. Patti Starr told me that every place having multiple spirits has one protector spirit. She told us that she noticed that spirit in the game room, at the end of the bar, by the window.

The Homestead, circa 1800's, view from the west.

Gravestones found on the Homestead property and propped up behind the house.

The electrician who did remodeling work was not a believer in ghosts. But he kept having problems, which he fixed, and then they were unfixed by the ghosts. Then he had to fix them again.

He said, "Something's going on in here."

They had a terrible time with the telephone line. I couldn't call the phone company to report that it was a problem with ghosts. They would think I was crazy. One day I was brushing my teeth, leaning over the sink. I heard a faraway sound of a phone ringing. So I turned off the running water, but then I didn't hear the ringing. I resumed brushing my teeth, and again I heard the ringing sound. Then it sounded as if it was coming from the drain. Then five minutes later the phone really did ring downstairs, but only from downstairs. I finally took the phone out of the game room, as it kept ringing.

I've always had trouble with smoke detectors here; it's been a nightmare! I had trouble with one smoke detector on the stairway landing. One afternoon it started beeping and I put in a new battery but 30 minutes later it again started beeping. It started and quit on an off until by 10:30 I had enough and I turned off the electrical breaker switch. But even then it went to beeping again.

The electrician came over with his wife Becky. They brought a brand new smoke detector. Becky picked up Daisy, who was shaking like a leaf. We were three puzzled people with a very scared dog.

Becky said, "There's somebody blowing on my neck."

We took out the battery and put in a new battery. While we all stood there, with the electrician holding the old detector which no longer had a battery – it started beeping – without any power!

When Patti Starr came to conduct a ghost hunt, we had about a dozen visitors. Daisy kept close to my daughter.

Joanne asked, "I wonder what we're going to find tonight."

Patti said, "I'm going to try and get in touch with that 12-year-old girl I saw yesterday. I think she's in the sunroom."

So Patti went off through the game room and talked with the protector spirit. They all swept through the house and over to the sunroom. People were also standing in the dining room. Cindy was at the end of the dining room, sitting on the floor, scratching Daisy's belly. Patti asked questions and used the dowsing rods to get answers.

"Are you the little girl I saw yesterday?" Her rods seemed to indicate, by their crossed position, "yes".

"Do you think you can call Daisy over to you?" There was dead quiet, and no answer. Patti repeated her question, and then, very slowly, one rod turned to point to the dining room. Patti asked very quietly, a third time, for the ghost girl to call Daisy over. Then Daisy jumped up, wagging her tail, and went over to Patti's feet. My daughter's face showed that she was so shocked.

When the pest technician came, he always seemed a bit leery of the place. He knew there were ghosts. I have an old wagon outside, filled in season with flowers. There is also a birdhouse that was leaning against the shop wall. Once, the pest technician was working in the side yard, putting termite traps in the ground in the flowerbed.

The man came running up to me, shaking, and said, "You've got to come out here. I can't believe what's going on. You've got to come out here to see this!" When I followed him outside I saw the wagon was flipped over. Then a second later the birdhouse fell over. There was no one else around and no wind.

I sent Patti Starr via email photos taken in my house that had orbs. A guy from Louisville enlarged the photos to wall size, where people could see faces in the orbs. The picture was from the loft room. On Patti's first ghost hunt here she contacted a ghost who claimed to be 54-years-old and was not a slave. The ghost was walking away, through the farm room, loft and over by the window. The spirit whirled around back to the stairs. It seemed this ghost didn't want to communicate, though it did answer that its name was not on the slave plaque downstairs. I had found a photonegative of a black girl; it appeared to be taken in the late 1800's. Patti asked if the spirit of that girl was present and she received "yes" in reply.

In 2003 I heard the loudest voice I'd ever heard. Patti connected with a man who had not lived here who was looking for his

Child and dog at the Homestead c. 1890

daughter. He reported dying 25 years earlier and said his daughter was still alive. Patti tried to help by asking all the guests to gather in a circle and since nobody claimed to know him, they sent him on to the light. The group went back to the living room and went over the cassette recording. Patti ran back in to tell me the ghost had recorded his voice on the tape, saying in a loud voice,

"Oh yes, you do know who it is!" While Chuck, Patti's husband, held the camcorder and filmed me, we saw orbs coming to my outstretched hand. Patti suggested that I walk out to the porch and put out my hand. Some kind of white thing showed up by the window. It looked like a nurse, kneeling down.

Patti asked, "Are you the protector spirit?"

The ghost nurse said she was, that she helped care for 34 injured Civil War soldiers who were injured and quartered in that room.

Since there were only three houses between the towns of Bloomfield and Bardstown, the Union soldiers set up camp at the Homestead. Those three homes each had water springs. One of the family members from this house was a big drinker. His name was Henry Nicholls, and when he was drafted he didn't want to fight in the Civil War. The night before he was to appear before the draft board, he drank castor and mineral oil. The next day at his military physical, they noted his "consumption of the bowels" and allowed him to pay someone else $5,000 to go fight in his place.

One of Joanne's overnight guests got up to use the bathroom that is in between and shared by two rooms. She tried to open the latch to enter the bathroom but it seemed stuck.

She knocked, and heard a faint but sweet female voice say, "I'm in here."

The bathroom door never opened, and the next day the guest asked Joanne who was staying in the next room. I told her that nobody else but me was staying over night, and I slept downstairs. My grandson wasn't here either – just Daisy and me.

In the old kitchen, the electricity sometimes goes off.

When I was shopping for antique feed sack dresses in Tennessee, I saw a young girl carrying a small bouquet of wildflowers "jumping the broom".

Becky said they've come home. Standing, showing guests discovered the dresses came from Louisville and were sewn with string, not thread. Patti said one of the ghosts who are here owned those dresses.

Lights came on in kitchen. I heard the little bells on the doors ring. It sounded like sleigh bells, and got Daisy barking.

Two weeks ago I was working on an order to make goose feather Christmas trees. Some folks came up to the kitchen door and called "hello". I heard a woman's voice answer "hello" back from inside my house! But there was nobody else inside. I turn off the TV when I go to town. But when I return I sometimes hear people talking…So I know it's not the TV sound. When I come through the dining room, the talking stops.

A long time ago, when I was in the game room pricing items for a yard sale, a friend came in, white as a sheet. They said, "A man is by the bar, talking." She also saw somebody in a long, black coat coming down the stairs. Another time, my sister and her husband and I were watching TV. Her husband said,

"Well there he is!" He was watching TV but, out of the corner of his eye, saw a man. I have never in my life been in such a place that I've felt so much spirit activity. My brother-in-law, Fritz, remarked one time, "This is the reason why I keep my cap on all the time, because my hair is standing on end!"

But I'm not afraid of the ghosts. I guess because I've been here living with them for so long. Sometimes things wake me up. I hear the sound of glass breaking, but after I look around I don't find anything broken. One time I heard a very loud noise in the living room, then I saw Daisy trying so hard to get away she ran into the wall!

One day the ghosts were just driving Daisy crazy. They chased her around, making the sound of fingers snapping. Then that started making me upset. I scooped her up, saying to the ghosts,

"You all quit this right now – 'cause you are scaring Daisy to death!" And they stopped bothering her.

So many things I've intuitively known about the Homestead have come to be true. I really wanted a tin and pewter chandelier for the dining room. I tried to strip the paint off the mantle. I worked so hard to burn and scrape off the paint. Then all of a sudden, I worked down to a lower layer. It was pewter color.

Byron Crawford visited and wrote about the Homestead. He published a story in his book, "*Crawford's Journal*" and wrote an article titled, "*Unseen Visitors Occupy This Inn.*"

Haunted American Castle

Lexington has a few faux castles. There is the Lexington Art League's Loudon House with a turret and some castle-like elements. And out Versailles Road, folks can take their eyes away from traffic on U.S. 60 for a moment and, from a distance, see the "nobody has been in there", low but wide, castle to the north. But in Loveland, Ohio, there is a bona fide castle made of stone, by one man. It has a number of mysterious apparitions who make themselves known in sight, sound and by moving objects.

The Loveland Castle Museum has a fair size parking lot. I was not impressed at first, since I imagined a larger structure perched atop a big hill. In my imagination, of course, there would be colorful pennants and a surrounding moat. The ground measurement of the Castle is 65 by 96 feet. But while touring the castle and after hearing the story of its construction, I began to appreciate the castle and the efforts of its solitary builder.

Harry Delos Andrews, born in 1891, received five academic degrees from five universities. He served as a medic in World War I. After the war he worked as an architect. During 'retirement' he proofread for Standard

Publishing Company. Harry bought the hillside property overlooking the Little Miami River and mixed his first batch of mortar on June 5, 1929. He didn't live on the site until twenty-five years afterwards. Harry was an idealistic man and inspired some of the local youths, who he taught in Sunday School. He initiated a group of "knights" whose vows were the Ten Commandments. In addition to creek stone from his property, Harry made concrete and poured it into milk cartons. He molded over 33,000 concrete bricks and constructed an amazing castle before his death in 1981.

The castle features a number of architectural elements related to medieval castles. There are slot windows, turrets, crenellated battlements, a tower keep, roof holes for pouring molten lead, a dungeon, and a door with 2,530 nails driven into it. The nails protect against strikes from a pole-ax. In addition, Harry created a secret room with access from one of the arch walls in the flanking garden. The secret room was unknown until after his death, when the caretakers found a partially collapsed wall there.

Harry was a busy man. He constructed the winding road down to the castle for which the county later took over maintenance. He dug a sort of dry moat above the castle, for diversion drainage. With the stone and earth from the dungeon and the ditch, Harry made terraced hotbeds that were heated by railroad lanterns. He also wrote a guidebook for the U.S. Immigration Department to help immigrants who were seeking citizenship. One dramatic aspect to accent Harry's achievement was his constant effort to rebuild after vandals knocked down walls, stole construction equipment, and even assaulted Harry while he lived on site.

Inside the castle, you will find memorabilia of Harry's life. There are old photos of Harry in WW I and of some of the over 120 men who were knighted into the Knights of the Golden Trail. Harry's tiny office is intact; he was a notary public. He often quipped to folks who came for that service, "I let them swear but not curse".

Upstairs, there is a display case with medieval weaponry. Some of the stones inlayed with the local rocks are various stones from other states. There is petrified wood from Arizona, sandstone from Tennessee, granite from Maine and more.

Sir Nick Fantetti was behind the counter on the day I visited. Nick answered the same questions countless times in the decades since Harry died. Nick took photographs of the castle that show odd misty-white images hovering in front of the battlements. I asked Nick about ghost stories from the Loveland Castle Museum website. Nick smiled and stated that there were spirits, but that he didn't believe that Harry himself haunted the Castle. As a caretaker, Nick locked up the castle then when he opened up the next day found chairs moved and some of the wooden game pieces shifted about. Nick believes that the spirits of two young children visit the Castle at night. Unfortunately, these two children died in a nearby house fire. When they were alive, the brother and sister walked down a path through the woods to visit Harry and watched the Castle being built.

Sir Nick reports that he and others heard the dramatic sound of horses at night. When they looked out there was nothing to see. He believes that the spirits of Shawnee Indians are active in the area. Since he spent many years since his adolescence visiting Harry, Sir Nick feels that he really knows the Castle and which ghosts are haunting there. Nick said that he felt a less friendly ghost above the main room; he feels that Harry brought back that ghost from his tours of European castles after the war.

The Loveland Castle Museum website reports additional and fascinating ghost stories. Here is one story reported by Lady Donna Jean.

"I was supervising a Scout Overnighter in May of 1989 and all of the Scouts and their leaders were down by the river at the Fire Ring. As is my habit, I did a complete perimeter check of the Castle. When I finished it was between 11 and 11:30 pm. I sat down on the round cement step to relax. As I sat there, I looked over to my right and noticed a figure on the road by the Port-a-Potties coming up to the gardens. The figure was transparent, whitish in color and her clothes were flowing. She was a woman with shoulder length hair and in a long billowy gown. She walked up to the garden area where I was and disappeared. That scared me, but as I sat there, I remembered that Mr. Andrews told the story of a man and his wife that built their cabin at the front of a cave down river from the castle and made moonshine. One day there was an explosion and Mr. Andrews with his Knights and Squires ran down to the cabin to find it ruined from the blast. When it was safe they entered the half cave and half cabin and found the woman dead under a whiskey barrel. From that time on she was seen many times, not only by Mr. Andrews and the Knights, but many visitors as well."

There are other reports of mysterious knockings, unexplained doorbell ringing, swinging overhead lights, lurking shadows, and even a Viking ghost complete with sword. There is no guarantee, of course, that you will have a spectral encounter.

The Doctor Is In, But They Wish He Was Out

I met "Edna" and her husband in 2001, and told them I collected ghost stories. They invited me into their home, built in 1885, which sits in the area of Baxter and Bardstown Roads in Louisville.

Edna:

The first time our grandson Chappy came into this house – he was eight years old – he said, "Well, you got other people living in here. There's a man."

I know he's a very intuitive child. He said the man lived here before, and we all lived together somehow. His parents bought my Dad's old car after my Dad passed away. They needed a car and I needed to get rid of it. He actually stayed with me for more than two hours – people he had never stayed with alone. He felt very, very safe and secure in this house; he didn't want to leave. Even at nine years old he still kisses me and Jim goodbye. He's always gravitated toward us both.

His dad doesn't like me to encourage this intuitive connection with him, which I think is a shame. This is the child who once spoke, "Shall we talk of the four worlds?" So in our house he said, "Can you see him?"

And I asked him back, "Where is he?"

He replied, "He's right over there by that door."

And I said, "Yeah I see him. But Chappy, what does he look like?"

He answered, "Well he's average kind of height, no taller than dad."

His father is about 5'8" or 5'9". He's got a big mustache and kind of like buck teeth.

I said, "Well that's our man".

I saw him one night. He didn't scare me, per se, but he makes me feel mad. I believe this emotion is a carryover from a past life when I was living in this house with him. When a psychic visited she was trying to convince him that he wasn't here anymore as a mortal. She told him that he could no longer have anything to do with me and he needed to go on into the light. But he didn't listen to any of that. He's very jealous.

I always had an uneasy sense in this house. I feel like I'm being oppressed and I ask help from Jim's (deceased) first wife, Rachel Rebecca. Usually it calms down after that. When my first husband and I lived here, we went down to the Historical Society. The Historical Society wanted my father to put the house on the Historical Record, which we didn't do because we'd have to have every single home improvement approved. But they gave us the name of Dr. Rosenberg as the first owner of the house. Then we went to the County Courthouse and from deeds found information about his doctor's business.

There are other things I know about this house, without knowing how I know those things. When I was fourteen years old, we looked for a house, and we almost bought his second, larger home on Everett Avenue. My father nevertheless wound up buying the first house the doctor built. So there's some kind of link here. This house was for his first wife, and since Jews don't get divorces very easily, I wonder if he may have killed her, or she just got tired of being told what to do and up and ran away.

I used to have trouble in the kitchen. I would often cut myself, or things fell on my head. I always hurt myself. I banged into things that I should have plenty of time to avoid hitting. A door swung back and hit me. I mean, I'm a little klutzy, but not that klutzy. One night the pizza flew off the counter and hit me in the back. We were cutting up the pizza and I had a piece sitting there; it was nowhere near the edge of the counter. It flew and slammed me right in the back. It's interesting that we were in the process of getting a realtor at that time. The ghost was aggravated.

We went through the house and smudged sage and things got better afterwards. We smudged a lot in the kitchen. We bought some candles from a lady at the psychic fair, and the room became very peaceful. I was able to sleep soundly the last few nights. I got so tired, and I couldn't sleep in that bedroom. My Dad was sick in that room but he didn't die there. But this other spirit feels like someone standing over me. I feel apprehensive, particularly after dark, every night. I feel dread, in my stomach. He was a very strict person. I think he was extremely orthodox.

I sat right here in this chair last Christmas and sang a German love song all the way through, start to finish…and I don't speak German. Another time while sleeping in the front room, I woke up speaking German, out of a solid sleep. I didn't know what I was doing but my husband, who speaks fluent German, recognized what language I spoke. I was raised in the Episcopal faith and yet found myself singing a German hunting song. I recognized it because I was familiar with a book on Jewish folksongs. I worked for the Printing House for the Blind. We read books for the blind and I did research on them. They gave me the books in Yiddish or Hebrew, and I had a knack for speaking or singing those books. I didn't learn until several years ago that my background was actually Jewish.

We burn candles and smudge, but it's a lot of work. Sometimes they won't even stay lit, especially in the front room, which was the doctor's waiting room. They lived in the back three rooms and one closet was his pharmacy. When I lived out of state, my dad had eye cataract surgery. My cousin came to live with him for a while, as he couldn't put the eye drops in by himself.

She told me, "I swear I will never, ever stay in your house again overnight!"

She doesn't believe in ghosts, but reported that she woke up screaming, and then cried, each of the three nights. My father got better, but she said if he hadn't then, she would have made him go stay over at my uncle's home.

I lived here before, with my first husband for three years and for four years with my second husband. My dad moved here in 1978 and lived here for 21 years until he died.

My dad never said anything to me about there being ghosts here in the house, but one time he asked me, "Edna, is it possible there are monsters?"

My dad was not someone who talked about things. He had manic-depression – seriously bipolar and he never took any medication. I think he felt a spirit in the house.

At various times my four cats, sometime in my lap, sit and look up at something invisible; their head stretch like a giraffe – as far as they extend their neck – to look into the hallway. And they're very nervous sometimes. I don't have a quiet home – the TV's on, some kid is running, music – but I'll pass the cats and they jump three feet up in the air. They are usually not like that.

One night as I sat on the sofa, talking to Jim about packing to move, the candlesticks on top the CD rack flew into the other room – all three candles.

He just looked at me and asked, "Did that just happen?"

The children were all in the kitchen. And it wasn't the cats. I saw them walk between crystal and not break anything. People visit and talk about the ghosts and then footprints appear on our floor. That would be the doctor and his first wife. I can see the footprints now, and they weren't here this morning. I ask his wife to help calm him down sometimes, and she does it! I think she comes back when needed. I don't feel her here all the time. But he is, and he definitely doesn't know he's dead.

I have a friend with very fundamental Christian beliefs. She blessed the house and, oh my Lord, all hell broke loose. They tried to get rid of this guy and send him to the Light. They anointed the windows. Good Lord, he's a Jew! He really didn't like what they did. He was very upset. Orthodox Jews don't believe in an afterlife, you must live your life the way you're supposed to in this life, because you're not going to get another one. He doesn't know it is not 1895. At least that's the time period I'm guessing by the way he looked when I saw him, with his celluloid collar. He was a very tall guy with button-up shoes.

I lived here with my first husband and it was an abusive situation. The ghost took away all the scissors. They just all disappeared. I could not find them anywhere. I probably had about seven scissors in the house.

I spoke to the ghost, "Oh come on, I've just got to have the scissors!"

The next night, when we got home, we found all seven of the scissors in the bed, in a circle, with the points inward. He took them because he was afraid my husband was going to do something with them. The points inward were for protection.

He didn't mind grandpa, but he hid things belonging to my first husband. I gave him a very nice pen as a wedding present. It disappeared for some time.

I finally said, "Give him back the pen!"

Well, we woke up the next morning and there it was under the bed sheets; we rolled over on it.

One potential homebuyer came and was very aware of the paranormal activity; she left out that door in two shakes. She literally ran for the front door. I didn't have a chance to meet her. The kids can get apprehensive after it gets dark. And I find myself sometimes unable to leave the house. I get very tired, aggravated and I take exception to everything.

Waverly Hills Sanatorium

Every town has tales of terrible tragedy and triumph, too. Waverly Sanatorium in Louisville represents one generation's attempt to deal with a deadly disease known as the white death, or tuberculosis, TB. The TB epidemic greatly reduced in the United States with vaccinations developed in the 1940's and 50's. The U.S. death rate from TB of 50 per 100,000 in 1940 fell to 22 per 100,000 in 1950. However, statistics show that, worldwide, TB is still a killer. On a worldwide average, one person dies of TB every 15 seconds. Putting it another way, every day 20,000 people develop TB disease and 5,000 die. Also note Center for Disease Control figures for the United States, which show that during the period from 1993 through 1998, the native-born had 5.8 cases of TB per 100,000, while the foreign-born rate was 32.9. The danger of TB carried by immigrants to America is a rising concern. A century ago in the U.S., TB was killing nearly 150,000 people each year. We now know a sneeze may contain over 1 million particles that can bear infectious organisms. TB sanatoriums were built in order to isolate patients from other people. By 1938, over seven hundred sanatoriums had been constructed across the United States. Other public efforts included the sale of Christmas seals and widespread chest X-rays of school children. A former state senator, Major Thomas H. Hayes, donated 125 acres of land south of Louisville for a TB sanatorium.

Waverly opened a small hospital there with 8 patients in 1910. The capacity of 40 patients was reached weeks later. Eventually 130 patients were housed there, and funds were raised in the 1920's for a larger hospital. The new hospital was designed to treat 400 patients at a time. Its construction took two years and Waverly opened in August 1926. In 1932 there were 478 patients admitted with an average stay of 393 days. Waverly had a working farm, female and male nurse dorms, a steam heating plant, laundry building, children's pavilion, classrooms for children, and workrooms for crafts. The craftwork made by the patients was sold at the Kentucky State Fair to assist in defraying hospital expenses. Treatments for the TB patients included sunbaths, rest, fresh air, plenty of healthy food, occupational therapy, and also some surgical procedures then considered progressive. These surgeries included pneumothorax and thoracoplasty. On the southwest side of Waverly, the patient rooms faced a long solarium porch way. Patients were moved out to the solarium on wheeled beds to take the fresh air, even during winter. Electric blankets were used. The TB epidemic decreased during the 1950's and in 1961 Waverly closed. The structure was renovated and continued in use as a nursing home from 1963 until 1980. Waverly's ownership changed hands several times as the building was vacant and subject to several decades of vandalism. The current owner, Charles Mattingly, purchased the property in 2001. He coordinates the annual Haunted House within Waverly and opened Waverly to walk-through ghost tours.

My tour of Waverly Hills Sanatorium, courtesy of Keith Age and the Louisville Ghost Hunter Society, LGHS, was late on a windy Friday night in August. It was perfect night for fright as lightning from an approaching thunderstorm flashed all around. After meeting owner Charles Mattingly, I was taken into Waverly via the loading dock entrance on the east side. Keith Age twirled the numbers of the combination lock as I looked at my tour mates, thinking, *this is it*... Two "cabooses" accompanied us. These were two LGHS volunteers who tailed the tour group to make sure that we didn't wander off into a dangerous spot, step in a hole in the floor, or bump our heads on hanging hazards. I felt better knowing that these folks had been here many times, and one of the cabooses was Jason, a reassuringly big guy. By the way, on one tour in which Sherri was bringing up the rear, she was surprised to feel an invisible hand tug at her ponytail. All abandoned buildings have that look – dark window openings seem to invite the curious, but curiosity can have a cost. I wondered if I wanted to have a ghostly encounter. I felt nonchalant and fairly brave with my guides. We went up a floor and saw the corner solarium. We walked past the haunted house, sectioned off by plywood, painted with ghoulish murals. Keith pointed out the original marble stair steps, and our flashlights searched for evidence of life in Waverly from the previous century. Keith told us that, over the years, an estimated 6,000 people died here. It was hard to imagine a warm, light, caring place as we walked down the dark hallway and saw old operating rooms in dull flashlight.

"Doors just close by themselves" reported Keith. "They close in the direction opposite from the prevailing west wind." We were taken in one room that reportedly has a spirit who gets upset by the presence of pregnant women. I felt a kind of tentative heaviness in the air, combined with a sense of due respect for those who fought for their lives. I was relieved when we were guided to the open fifth floor area/rooftop. There were wonderful views of Louisville and New Albany. Someone noted that the roof had been a children's playground with swings set up there. We enjoyed the breeze and prepared for the second half of our tour. And things got interesting...Back down on the fourth floor Keith showed us a metal door that had been repeatedly hacked with an axe. He told us how some trespassers had the door mysteriously shut on them. Thinking it was locked they screamed and tried to open it with repeated blows. A guard heard them, came up the stairs, and opened the unlocked door with ease.

"Doors will open for some people and not for others," Keith said. Then he added, "Let's try something – turn off your lights". After a minute, our eyes started adjusting to the dark. I looked down the long hallway. Shafts of ambient, outside light came in laterally in both sides from the old windows. The shafts of light flickered as reflected lightning flashes pushed their way indoor.

"There, did you see that?' Keith told us to look for dark shapes that interrupted the light from the windows. Everyone in my group saw dark shadows, moving here and there. I felt like the guy who didn't get the Magic

Eye poster. Maybe my eyes were just too tired from the work week. Maybe I didn't have the second sight. Keith pointed a laser guided thermal sensor down the hallway while the two LGHS guides pointed EMF indicators in the same direction. The EMFs, electromagnetic field indicators, have a visual gauge and also an emitting sound to show that there's a local surge in the electromagnetic field. Since there is no electricity in Waverly, I was surprised to hear their EMF meters sounding louder and louder, as if something was approaching us. I felt like the spaceship crew in the Alien movie, waiting for the aliens to drop out of the ceiling. I took a picture with my digital camera. The moment the flash went off, the EMFs fell totally silent. I felt a little guilty, as if I scared off Casper. There are some other interesting stories including the tunnel used to take out the bodies. I think there's something about haunted places that lets us approach several taboos in our lives – death and the past. Normally, both are inaccessible in terms of temporary visits. You can't live or visit the lives of your grandparents and their generation. But at Waverly one may hear those voices, as they try to call to us. I'm sure that the proprietors can't guarantee a spirit encounter, but you never know which ones among us that the ghosts will choose to touch.

Photo of a Ghost Nurse

Ashley Campbell, Louisville

I've been to Waverly several times. It's set up so that when you enter the building you come in by the incinerator. That's where they used to throw the bodies. That area is really eerie. It's dark and dreary; the windows are further down. When you walk through you come underground and past the incinerator and then into the building. I teach construction management at ITT and I had my students with me. I had six students with me, five men and one woman. We walked through Waverly to see what kind of shape it was in. One of the areas we walked through was what used to be a waiting room. This is where the people sat and waited for the patients to come down and see them. It's in the corner of the building and faces out on what was then a huge field. It's nothing but windows. This is the area they believe the families gathered to meet the patients.

There is a child's play ball that is left in this room. It's said that there is a young boy who came to visit, contracted tuberculosis and then had to stay there.

Ghost nurse to right rear of plumber Tim Faust at Waverly Hills.

They believed he then died there. He liked to play with a ball so that is left for him.

So as we walked through Waverly and later returned to this big room we saw the ball had moved to a different part of the room. I've been to Waverly four times and each time the ball was in a different spot from where it was when I first walked in – always! It's very interesting.

The patient rooms all go out into a common exterior walkway. These look out over the south lawn. We walked through and looked at all the rooms. Right in front of the big first floor waiting room the building angles straight off to the patient rooms. In that spot on every floor my female student got goosed. She thought it was the guys in the group. But by the time we got to the fourth floor, there weren't any guys around her.

She said, "Somebody's following me and they don't like this spot."

One day the project manager who I worked for was with the plumber on the fifth floor. This is supposedly where the nurses took their lives, dove to their death because they couldn't stand the illness anymore. The plumber was standing in front of Room 502, which is a bathroom. They were the only two people in the entire building. The project manager took pictures with his cell phone while the plumber stood there. When he first looked at the digital display screen on his cell phone, he didn't see anything unusual. But when he later transferred the pictures to his computer he was shocked to see, very distinctly, a woman in a white nurse's uniform! Some have said the photo was doctored, but Kevin is not that good with computers so he couldn't have fabricated the photo.

It's said that since plumbers have to get in the walls during renovations, they often disturb the spirits more than folks who simply walk through old buildings. And he was there to figure out which walls to tear out.

The Return of Waverly
Kevin Milburn, Urban Designz, Louisville

The picture I took that has a mystery figure in the background also shows Tim Faust, who is a master plumber. For a number of years he was the director at the Division of Plumbing in Frankfort. He retired this past August. I used to work with him in Frankfort and I've known him for many years. He was there when the picture was taken along with another gentleman, a local plumbing director. I tried to bring anybody that we needed for the Waverly Hill restoration project to walk through the building and make sure we did everything correctly. Since it was to be an historical rehab, we had to follow certain guidelines.

Per the owner's request I brought these professionals in groups (so we didn't just wander the building). These included folks with the city and any others involved with the project.

We had that walk-through in late July 2008. While we were on the fifth floor we got to Room 502, which is basically a bathroom. There are two bathrooms on the top floor. As we stood there we were a group of five or six men. Standing next to me was the other plumbing director, Floyd, and the guy with the City of Louisville.

We took cell phone photos when we were at Room 502, since it had some folklore attached to it. Me and another guy took pictures of the room. It was my idea to take the photos and I had Tim's cell phone to photograph him in front of the room number. I didn't know how the picture on Tim's phone turned out until later. At the time we didn't feel or see anything out of the ordinary. That was probably the fiftieth time I had been up there.

We had an invitation-only project announcement. This sort of event brought in everyone involved with the renovation. We gave them the data and then we'd see if they would bid for it and so on. Folks who came included local councilmen, people with the state and anyone being brought in to work on the project. On that day, August 4, 2008, we had about eighty people on the roof. At that time Tim showed me the photo of himself and the ghostly-looking figure. He couldn't figure out how to get it off his cell phone. It was a state-issued cell phone and took a while to get the image off. We beat our brains trying to figure out if there was any possibility that there was someone in our group who could have gotten behind Tim while the camera took his picture.

The photo was taken in the women's restroom and the men's restroom is on the other side. There are openings off the bathroom. One doorway goes to the dayroom. Another opening behind where Tim stood goes out onto the roof. We tried to figure out if there was anyway someone got in the background but we couldn't think of anyone in our group getting back there. We later digitally enlarged the photo, but you loose the detail beyond what you can see from a regular view. So we couldn't enlarge the image to pull out any distinguishing facial characteristics that might help us to try and eliminate someone we knew being the figure in the background. Whoever it was back there was wearing all white and had gloves on their hands.

But that is not the only odd experience I had at Waverly Hills. I hired Marty who created a video titled *The Return of Waverly*. You have to understand that back then Waverly was like a miniature city. It was a progressive and a self-sufficient place. We had it in mind to bring things back to that wonderful time – not only the building but also the community. It had a lot of potential for bringing in jobs, income and so forth.

The video had a lot of the old photographs and we shot the same scenes. We ran the video during the project announcement and people watched the old scene dissolving into the current view and then showing the renovated look. It was interesting that the photographer for these scenes ended up with pictures showing large, white orbs. He took hundreds of photographs to create the images for the video. The idea was to bring Waverly out of its disrepair and return it to a place that is happy, joyful and cool. Unfortunately six weeks later the entire project fell apart.

The project plan was to take the first floor administration back to where it was originally. Where the nurses' quarters were on the first floor would have become hotel rooms. The second and third floors, which used to be hospital rooms, were also going to become hotel rooms. There were plans to renovate the fourth floor back to its original 1925 hospital status that could be used for historical, educational or paranormal tours. And the fifth floor on the roof was going to be used for different venues, open with some awnings and set up as a green roof. It was a really cool concept.

The main entry would remain the same, leading to the hotel check-in. What was originally the ambulatory entrance we planned as the valet service. We tried to reuse places similar to what their prior purpose had been. The original director's office would become the hotel manager's office. The laboratory would be returned to that same use. Leaseable spaces were available for a health club, onsite psychic and a beauty salon and spa.

Technically there are two buildings at Waverly. There is a smaller two-story structure that was called the refectory building. It was originally designed for services and dining. Here we had someone interested in taking over the 20,000 square footage for hospitality services. The first floor would be meeting rooms with the floor above that intended for a restaurant, small night club called the Sanatorium and a few other rooms to be leased out for various venues.

The original nurses' stations were going to become hotel rooms. In the corners of the floors were great rooms that we planned to remain in a similar function. They could be rented out for parties and as a gathering place before folks left on tours. We set up different traffic flows separating the hospitality guests from the paranormal tourists and from the regular hotel visitors.

We designed the original Waverly Hills Sanatorium "WHS" logo to be a boxwood maze viewable on the north side. We also designed the removal of some of the middle windows to build a conservatory. This was the only real addition to the building and led to Wellness Gardens. At one of the gathering rooms there are reports of a ghost named Mary who waves from the windows.

We found the building in phenomenal shape. Currently people who come to visit drive up by the golf course. We planned to keep that for employees and paranormal tours only. But we were going to return the use of the original entrance off Pages Lane.

We planned a subterranean parking garage out back with a great lawn on top of it. Folks could walk out of the lobby onto the grounds. And the parking lot where it is now would still be there although not visible.

I have to know the property on any project with which I get involved. And due to the unique nature of Waverly's history we had to have consultations with someone who was experienced in terms of the paranormal. I walked through the building while talking on my cell phone to a paranormal consultant. Her name is Doris. She gets what she refers to as impressions from old places but does not call herself psychic. I chose someone from out of state. I wanted to use someone who was not familiar with the building or the history.

Doris and I also worked together to do history and archival research.

We went to the libraries at the Filson Club and the University of Louisville. We came across the name of a woman mentioned in a newspaper article back in the 1950s. Her name was Kay, or Nurse Kay. The article mentioned that she lived in New Albany, Indiana. I took a shot at contacting her and did an Internet search for her name. Her name came up. She used to work on the fourth floor operating room in 1945. Kay and her son came as our special guests for the project announcement.

Three weeks later she and her son and I did a special walk through at Waverly. I took my tape recorder. I wanted to have her go back in her memory and pull out some history of what it was like when she worked there, especially in the operating room. There was only one operating room at Waverly. They did two operations per week on Wednesdays only. From our research we figured that perhaps 8,000 people died at Waverly over those years. The operating room was way down in the corner.

As we walked around she commented, "I don't believe in ghosts."

Years ago when ghost tours were being done at Waverly and someone interviewed her she kind of rebutted that notion. But she had not been back to Waverly since 1945. As Kay and her son went on the tour he took photographs (being a professional photographer). As we walked down the first floor corridor toward the area of the main door he and I were about four steps ahead of her. I was in front turning on lights as we went.

Suddenly she said, "I'm sorry."

I asked her, "For what?"

She said, "I just ran into you."

Her son turned around to mention, "Mom, we're like two feet ahead of you."

She answered, "No, I accidentally hit you again."

She described it as being a push or poke to the upper chest.

It seemed to me that she changed her tune a bit after that mysterious incident.

I felt things as I walked through Waverly. It often felt like someone was following me around. I swear that the door going up to the fifth floor didn't like me because it used to "bite" me. Each time after I unlocked the combination lock and lifted the wooden bar I'd somehow get splinters in my hands. Or it would slam in front of me. There was a lot of door slamming going on.

There were several people who I had out there who told me they felt pushed or nudged. There's energy in Waverly. The building is just full of energy. I'm far from an expert on the paranormal but after renovating three houses I feel I've connected with spirits. This last renovation where I live is where I met my ghost Hattie. She is an older African-American worker who used to be the cook there. All that is in David Domine's second book, *Phantoms of Old Louisville: Ghostly Tales from America's Most Haunted Neighborhood*.

Kerry Hall-Evans of Track Plans Inc. is a colleague and architect who did all the verification drawings for me. She walked through every nook and cranny of that building; she got into places I wouldn't even go. They originally gave us two drawings; one was from 1924 and the other was from the 1950s. Each was only one sheet and thus showed only a portion of the entire building. So we had virtually nothing to go by. Kerry told us that she didn't want to hear any ghost stories until she was done. She spent six weeks primarily by herself going through Waverly. She did a heck of a job.

The only thing she was afraid of was the raccoons. There are raccoons that come out in the afternoon and the owner feeds them. Now it turns out that she also had several doors mysteriously slammed in her face too. Without any windows there was a lot of air flow through there. But sometimes it was a still as it could be and a door would slam.

I used to play kickball with a ghost that is called Timmy. There were a few kickballs there and after I kicked a ball down the hall it seemed to come back down later. Our interior design guy Mark and I walked through right before our August event. Well there was Timmy's green ball so as usual I kicked it. I told Mark what I was doing and he said that he really didn't believe in that stuff. When we got to the complete other end of the wing, there was the green ball. It freaked him out to no end.

The Ladies Club and the Women's Club of Louisville raised all the money to build Waverly Hills. Waverly did not become a state project until the 1940s. And then it came under the jurisdiction of the local Health Department. Originally it was all privately funded. There were hundreds of acres. Now it has 30 acres. There was a Negro hospital, a children's hospital and children's quarters. Not only were there kids at Waverly with tuberculosis but also there were healthy kids who were abandoned because their parents had TB. There were doctors' houses as well. The only other building is the laundry room. A previous owner tried to tear down the building in 1998. It's reported that they tried to dig away the foundation but it is built on solid rock and would not budge. They had gorgeous gardens. Waverly has terraces all along the south side. To the inside were patient rooms and staff quarters.

There was a network of walking trails around the main and other buildings. These were considered Wellness Trails. They had two group walking trips every day. If you could walk to the bottom of the hill and back sometime during your time at Waverly then you were considered cured. Nurse Kay told me that the average stay for someone at Waverly who had tuberculosis was from two to five years.

They had some experimental but gross operations at Waverly. They would go in and slice out your ribs and squash the infected lung. Then they'd sew you back up. As you started healing they'd go back in to re-inflate the lung. The operating room was about 20 x 20 square feet. I mentioned to Nurse Kay that I saw no drains in the operating room.

I asked her, "What did you all do with the blood on the floor?"

She answered, "We got a mop bucket. Then when we were finished we took it down to the incinerator."

She added, "It looked like a stuck pig in there sometimes."

The so-called tunnel that is connected to Waverly runs from the top of the hill northwest to Dixie Highway. It was constructed to bring the employees and supplies in and out where the buses stopped there on Dixie Highway. It has steps on one side and on the other side is a ramp with a wooden winch. Where the golf course is now, back then was the Waverly farm which included enclosures for the hogs and cattle. They brought other supplies up through the tunnel or chute.

There was only a three-body morgue at Waverly. It's my opinion that the bodies were taken through the refectory building hallway, because it was out of the main hospital, and put on a gurney and then they shot the gurney down to the bottom of the hill and on a hearse. That way they kept the infection away from anybody else and it kept up the morale. There is a place at the bottom of the hill where the hearses would line up.

There were two documented deaths of staff at Waverly. One was the nurse who hung herself and the other nurse jumped off the fifth floor. I believe the hanging suicide could not have occurred in Room 502 because at the time the death happened there were no pipes on which to hang a cord or rope. What seems to me more likely is that she hung herself in the sub-grade level where there are lots of pipes.

I noticed that on the roof there appear to be pipes cut off that once might have supported a fence. I think after the woman jumped to her death from the fifth floor that a chain link fence was added. I have noticed both before, no fence on top, and after pictures, with fence, of Waverly.

The original TB hospital was downtown at the general hospital. The Women's Guild then started to raise money for a Sanatorium. They wanted it to be top of the line, state of the art. The gentleman who owned the property where Waverly was eventually built had two daughters. This was in the late 1890s. Since there weren't any schools out there he brought a lady in from Nashville, Tennessee, to be the teacher. Her name was Lizzie Harris. They built a one-room schoolhouse and it eventually grew to be one of the main schools out Dixie Highway.

The teacher was right out of college and in her early twenties. I did some genealogical research for my family. My grandmother's name was Elizabeth Harris. She used to go by the nickname Lizzie with her friends. She was from Danville where I'm from. I thought that was an odd coincidence. But it turned out that my grandmother's family was from Baxter, Tennessee, and from right outside of Nashville. I found Lizzie Harris! The information on Ancestry.com said she came from Nashville and she was a school teacher. She was my great-grandfather's first cousin. We always knew we had Native American Indian blood. It turned out that my great-grandfather was a registered Cherokee and his first wife was Creek.

This one-room schoolhouse was at the bottom of Waverly Hills. Lizzie Harris named Waverly. The name came from a book she read which was titled "Tales and Romances by the Author of Waverly." So she named the school Waverly Hills and they took the name when the Women's Guild bought it and built the Sanatorium. So my great-grandfather's first cousin was Lizzie Harris who named the place. That is bizarre. I feel there was always something that pulled me to Waverly.

Shadow People

Roberta Simpson Brown, author, Ghost Hunter, Louisville

My husband Lonnie and I have been on several tours of Waverly. We have encountered many things we could not explain logically. On our first visit, we were right behind our guide Keith Age (founder of the Louisville Ghost Hunters) when a heavy door slammed in our faces. We were startled, but Keith opened the door easily and we proceeded to explore the second floor. The kitchen used to be in the second floor area and some in our group smelled bread baking. Lonnie and I did not experience this. As we walked down the hall, camera lights and flashlights were focused on the floor. We came to a spot where rain had blown in and puddled there. Suddenly, out of that puddle came wet footprints! We just stared in amazement! Something was walking out of that puddle with bare feet, but we couldn't see who was making the tracks! We saw about five or six footprints and then they stopped! I had the eeriest feeling I had ever experienced! *Something invisible* had actually walked among us! We continued to explore the upper floors and saw *shadow people* moving back and forth across the hall. Some appeared to float rather than walk. They gave me a comforting feeling, though, because they seemed to be going to rooms to care for patients.

On an overnight tour, we were with a very large group from the American Ghost Society. The "caboose person" and I decided to make a hall sweep to be sure we hadn't left anyone before going to another floor. The rooms on this floor had two doors. One led to the balcony walkway and the other led to the inner hallway. The caboose person took the inner hall and I took the balcony.

As I walked by one room, I saw two things happen. The caboose person walked by the door in the inner hallway and a figure inside the room rose up and went out the door after her. The figure was wearing a white coat like a doctor, but the rest of the figure was in shadows. It looked so real that I thought at first glance that it was one of our group. Then I realized that I had not seen a bottom to this figure in those shadows! I hurried to the end of the hall and arrived just as the caboose person came around the corner.

"Oh, my God!" she said. "Something just followed me down the hall!"

When we compared notes, we realized we had seen the same figure!

Later that night, I took the group to Room 502, which has the reputation of being the most haunted room. This is where the nurse is said to have hanged herself. When I walked in, I felt a noticeable drop in temperature. Some EMF meters peaked out. I stepped out to let others come inside. An experienced ghost hunter stepped inside and backed out so fast that he almost tripped over me. He insisted that he could not breathe in that room. He had to go sit down for a few minutes to regain his composure.

Then he was able to go back inside the room and take pictures without any problem.

Ghost Next Door

My next-door neighbor had a number of encounters with what we feel was the ghost of the previous owner. Let me tell you a bit of history about the area. It was a large dairy farm owned by a still well known family in the city. About 55 years ago it was parceled into lots for home building.

A woman, while being the second owner, loved her home. She and her husband originally owned another home they built on the same street. After her husband died, she and her son purchased the home discussed for this story. Her son died young and tragically in an auto accident. Don't know if ANY of this has relevance....

When we moved to the neighborhood, this elderly, ill lady lived at home with aides for about 10 years. They provided 24-hour day care. One day one of her workers told us that money had run out and the lady suddenly quit eating. She wanted to will herself to die in her home, rather than go to a nursing home. She almost did it. She languished in the hospital for about 3 days and then died.

A younger, single lady purchased the home almost immediately after a new roof was installed and some clean up was done to the smoke-stained home. You see, the old lady and her aides would smoke together constantly. Not long after the new owner moved in, she sheepishly admitted several years later to odd things that happened. She frequently heard noises in the kitchen. And she smelled someone smoking but neither she nor her guests smoked. On many nights she also heard the sounds of shuffling slippers going down the wooden floors of hallway. One night something fell from kitchen counter, breaking into pieces!

With each new boyfriend or renovation she would let her presence be known. If she liked the man they would smell baking cookies at night but a decrease in evening sounds. If she did not like the male visitor then she would increase the kitchen noises. They could hear stepping downstairs to the basement. Most of the activity happened at night.

Later two cats came to live at the home. Some of the sounds were dismissed as kitty activity. The cats though, were not immune to ghostly visits. During the day the cats sometimes suddenly looked at something across the room. Then they reacted and ran away into another room.

The current owners have done extensive renovation with no more activity from Mrs. "Smith"...at this time.

Tales From the Mountains

I receive stories through many kinds of connections. I met folks with ghost stories when I was at book fairs, storytelling, or at other social occasions. Sabrina Blackburn somehow found my first book, *Shaker Ghost*

Stories. After she read the book, she sent me a letter to tell me she had a few tales of her own to share. She wrote that letter through the publisher, Author House, and after months passed away, I received the letter and wrote her back. She wrote additional letters detailing both her experiences and also about odd happenings with other family members. Sabrina called me to add more details, and I heard from her mother, Mary Bentley, as well.

My name is Sabrina Blackburn and I'm from Pikeville, Kentucky. I also have Dutch, Blackfoot and Cherokee blood in my family line. Our family comes from Wheelwright, in Floyd County, Kentucky. My mom's maiden name is Price, and my maiden name is Harris. We also came from Cowpen in Pike County, Kentucky.

Everywhere I go I hear and see spirits. I have seen visions of both men and women. I heard spirits talking. When I was young, the ghosts sometimes told me to do things, to act up. My aunt once told me that my tenth great-grandmother was burnt at the stake for witchery. I don't know where that happened.

My husband doesn't believe in ghosts, but I do very much so believe in them. I would like to learn more about the spirit world. I am 28 years old. I'm a short little girl. Ever since I was a child I heard and felt a lot of unexplained things. Some of my own family and others outside my family think I'm crazy, but these things really happened to me and my mother. Since childhood I saw visions of spirits. When I was about five years old, I walked into the bathroom and I was surprised to find a black bird lying in the bathtub. The bird was dead, but there were no windows open to let it inside. I don't know what kind of bird it was, but I called my mom and she took it outside to bury it.

My mom believes in ghosts, spirits and the afterlife.

She told me, "You see more than you should."

But she still believed what I told her. She often would take me into another room, away from my sisters, and let me tell her about what I saw. She actually listened to me." Mary cut in to add, "You can't scold somebody for seeing things when you see them yourself. I've seen the same things. I just told Sabrina not to tell folks outside of the family. I didn't want the other children making fun of her." Sabrina continued with her tale.

When I was a young child I thought I saw a ghost. This happened in my old house. My mother, Mary Bentley, told us that she felt someone touch her one night, but when she woke up there was no one there. She thought maybe she was just dreaming and went back to sleep.

When she woke up she saw a small child standing at the foot of her bed. She yelled for my sister and I – we were in another room. She told us to get back in bed, but we were already in bed on the sun porch. So we woke up to our mother yelling at us.

When I was eight years old, I was in my bedroom. I was angry at my mom and I said a bad word. Then right before me, my papaw appeared. He shook his finger at me and then disappeared. He died when I was four years old. My sisters don't believe in ghosts. They teased me and said I was re-tarded, that it was all in my imagination. My oldest sister didn't want to hear about the ghosts. She knocked me on floor then set on me like a pretzel. She told me she wouldn't get off me "until you talk some sense".

Our house in Peach Orchard Hill in Pikeville was haunted. We moved into the house in 1982, but the family before lived there in the 1960's. The man and his wife with their three-month-old baby lived there. The man beat his wife nearly every day. One night he came home in a drunken rage, killed his wife and hung his baby from the doorway. He then shot himself. When my sisters and I slept on the sun porch, we saw and heard the woman singing to her baby, and rocking it to sleep on the chair. We heard this every night. On stormy nights we saw her outside the house, crying and hold-ing her baby. Down below our house, was another little house where that woman's mom and dad lived before they died. We saw the ghost there too, rocking her baby on that porch.

We heard footsteps going down the staircase. One night, between mid-night and 12:30 am, my mom awoke and saw a little girl at the foot of her bed. She thought it was me, so she told the ghost girl to get back in bed. Three or four times that night, when my mom rolled over, she felt the girl with her in bed. Finally she rolled back over to see her, and the girl vanished.

On another night, my mom got back from a date. She heard Jughead, our German shepherd dog, cutting a fit upstairs. Something told my mom to go up and check on Brandon, who was napping. By the time my mom got up there, my dog pulled Brandon off the bed. My mom reached down to pick up Brandon, and took him downstairs. Then she heard a loud crash-ing noise. She went up to see what happened – the ceiling fell right where Brandon was sleeping. It looked as if someone cut the ceiling with a saw.

Once when we lived at Brammon's Creek in Floyd County, my husband and I were arguing about my ex-husband calling all the time. As we argued, the bathroom door, all the way across the room from us, started swinging open and shut. It was doing this by itself, with none of us nearby. We looked at that, and both decided to stop arguing to see if it would stop. And it did! My husband then told me he heard the sound of children in the hallway, playing. Many times he heard children's voices. At night, he thought the kids were up playing, but when he checked on them, he found them fast asleep.

I moved to Huntington, West Virginia. The house I now live in has the ghost of a little old woman. I hear the ghost sometimes, but my mom has seen her. About four days ago, my mom saw the ghost as she appeared in a white night gown. She looked at my mom and then vanished.

Little Boy Ghost

I lived at Mudd Creek in 1994. My hollow was called Bear Fork. I lived in a one bedroom little yellow house. It had a bath, living room and kitchen. I was fifteen years old and pregnant with my first child. My ex-hus-band locked me in the house with padlocks on the front and back door until he got home from work. I lived right beside a graveyard.

One day I heard a noise outside. I looked out my window and I saw a man dressed in an Army uniform walking in my front yard. He turned and looked right at me – it felt like someone took my legs right out from under me. I heard a small baby crying, and I went looking for the child to comfort him. He found me, in my living room, and he was about five or six years old. The boy was three feet high, with blond hair and green eyes. He had dark skin like an Indian. He was crying like someone hurt him.

I asked, "How did you get in here?"

He pointed to the floor. I believe he was buried there.

Then he hushed his crying and asked me, "Will you be my mommy?"

I told him, "Baby I can't be your mommy, because you've already got a mother." I turned away from him since I heard a sound, then when I turned back to ask the little boy where his mom was he was gone. So I thought I was seeing things, since I was in the house all by myself. I was scared with the graveyard close by. I never did like graveyards because of something that happened when I was a child when I was playing hide and seek. That night I woke up hearing the little boy crying again.

I went to him and asked him, "Honey, why are you crying?"

He said to me, "Will you be my mommy?"

I said, "No baby, I'm not your mommy."

Then I realized he was a ghost child, and I asked the boy, "What happened to you?"

He said his mommy and aunt cut out his tongue, and then killed him to keep him from telling about the bad things they did to him. For three years I saw that little boy. He followed me around everywhere. And every night he showed up at my side of the bed, cried, and then disappeared. I actually kind of got used to him. The odd thing was he looked like my own son. But since my son was born I no longer saw the ghost boy. In some sense, I think I became that little boy's mother, because my son looks just like the boy I saw.

The house where we live now is haunted. I hear noises and also a small child speaks my name. It is an old house, built in 1909, and I know there are spirits of those who used to live here. My dad didn't believe in ghosts and he thought people who talked of such things were crazy. But Papa had an experience when he was in the Army. He was a prison guard. He may have been in North Carolina. He told my mom, brothers, and sisters about how he once saw witches. He said he lay down in a big green field and went to sleep. Sometime after midnight but before one in the morning, he woke up seeing stones set up all around him. Then he saw people in black outfits dancing around; they wore sharp-pointed hats.

I asked Sabrina, "Since you see the spirits of the dead, have people come to you asking you for information, to contact the ghosts of their loved ones?" Sabrina answered with a story.

A woman friend came up to me and asked, "You see dead people, right?" She wanted me to get something about her deceased ex-boyfriend. She told me he was a nice man.

I told her, "We'll I'll see if I can do it."

I sat down there and right away got a vision of a man in a bar fight. Her boyfriend stabbed another man sixteen times. Then when he was out in the parking lot the other man came out and shot him in the back of the neck. I got scared to death seeing those things, because this man was an evil person. He was mean, not at all nice.

My friend confirmed all those details, but I told her, "Don't you ever ask me to do that again!"

My mom used playing cards once to read someone's future. We have no explanation for how and why she did that, but she told her brother how many times he would be married, when he was going to die, and how many kids he would have. She saw him marrying a second time to a woman whose name also began with the letter L. He married later to two different women named Loretta. And when his oldest girl turned ten years old, on her birthday, he died when his heart exploded. It was said that she wished him dead, because he was seeing another woman. His daughter wanted him to get back with her mom, but he was getting ready to marry the other Loretta. My mom decided she would never look at the cards that way again.

The same night she looked at the cards, my mom saw us girls in a sort of haze. She went to our room, but some force kept her from getting through the doorway. She saw a smoky black shadow like the devil and it was fighting with a white shadow over the top of us. She felt it was good and evil fighting and the devil came to take us to hell. She hollered, and finally fought her way into the room. We never woke up or heard her yell. She said that happened before she became a Christian. Since the Bible speaks against fortune telling that was the last time she read the cards.

My mom and her daddy saw my mamaw walking up from her grave to the sky. The sky was like a blue paved highway, like a staircase to heaven. Two angels were at the foot of the staircase, and both the angels and my mamaw disappeared along with the beam of light. The old man neighbor saw her, too, before then. He said she walked down toward the gate of our family plot in Cowpen, Kentucky.

Our family has a sense to know when one of our loved ones is ill, or died. I was in a mental facility in 1987 when I saw my sister, looking out at me from a mirror.

Then I told the staff, "Do you know that she can see everything I do?" The staff didn't see her, but I did. At the same time I saw my sister I also saw my mother in the bathroom. She waved her hand for me to come to her. I understood that she was sick and I felt that.

One night, when mom was sleeping – this was in February of 1995 – my sister came to her to tell her something was wrong with the baby. That night my mom went to the hospital. The doctors told her that my sister was very upset, and when they left her to write charts, and then later checked on her, she was peaceful and sleeping. The doctors confirmed the time my sister was sleeping peacefully was when my mom saw her vision.

Mary Bentley's Stories:

My Last Halloween

In 1969, at Matheny, West Virginia, my brother, sisters and I went trick or treating. I was eleven years old. My mother didn't want me to go out that night. She had a bad feeling that something was very wrong. But I cried so much that she let me go after all. A good friend of my parents lived in a house next to the graveyard. When we got there, they had a Halloween party for some people who lived near there.

A woman came in the house after me and my brother. She was dressed all in black. They asked us if she was with us, and we said "no". She went inside and sat down in the middle of the room. She would not touch the Bible. When my brothers and sisters and I left, we walked about ten steps down to the car wash when we heard footsteps behind us.

We heard a voice saying, "I'm coming to get you!"

When we looked behind us we saw nobody yet the voice came again, "I'm coming to get you!"

We ran into the car wash to hide, still hearing the footsteps along the street. We took off running, down by the graveyard, just in time to see the little old lady turn off into the graveyard. Once she got in the graveyard, she just disappeared.

Even though I'm now 48 years old, that night still haunts me every Halloween night of my life.

Ghost in Clear Fork, West Virginia

When I was six years old, my family planned to go fishing the next day. In the morning, about 5:30 AM, I woke up to a big crash. I got up out of bed and found the cook stove on. But the stove wasn't hooked up. It had no power to cook. And it came on two more times. I was so scared I couldn't get back to sleep. Later that day we went fishing. My brother said he felt like some-one was trying to push him off a big rock into the lake. But nobody was near him. He didn't tell our parents until we got back home.

Our mama said, "Jimmy, why didn't you come to us right when it happened?"

Historical and Hysterical: The Culbertson Mansion

The Culbertson Mansion has both 19th Century charm and 21st Century haunting. The Culbertson Mansion overlooks the Ohio River and is located on Main Street in New Albany, Indiana. It is across the Sherman Minton Bridge from west Louisville. I went to the Culbertson to tour both

Culbertson Mansion, New Albany, Indiana.

the state historic home and to investigate their "Literally, A Haunted House" which happens behind the big home in the old Carriage House.

The Culbertson staff provides a fascinating tour, with 25 rooms, three floors and 20,000 square feet. We walked through 11-foot tall doorframes and marveled at rebuilt walls, reconstructed plaster and recently painted designs. There are hand-painted panels, marble fireplaces, an impressive rosewood staircase, gold leaf ceilings, a tin roof imported from Scotland, and lots of woodwork done by local ship builders. The ongoing and meticulous artwork carefully replicates period designs; one ceiling renovation in just one room cost nearly $40,000. Besides the paid staff of five employees, the Culbertson operation relies on a pool of over 100 volunteers.

William S. Culbertson spent $120,000 to have his stately home built in 1867, as a wedding gift for second wife Cornelia. He was an entrepreneur, creating a dry goods business, owning his own utility, and investing in railroad stock. He was active with local charities and civic projects. Two of his three wives died and he married a third time at the late age of 70. When he died in 1892, Mr. Culbertson was worth millions.

Some 20,000 visitors per year tour the Culbertson Mansion, with about 5,000 of those arriving for the haunted tour in the Carriage House. The curator suggested that people come early; during prime time the wait to get in can run two hours. We walked outside and to the Carriage House, where I previewed the scary exhibits in the calm daylight hours. I can't reveal details, but I will say there is more than enough gruesome visual, sound, sensory and movement to entertain anyone's Halloween freaky fantasies!

In addition to the Carriage House tour, the Culbertson offers "A Ghostly Undertaking". This overnight stay involves limited reservations but maximal fun. The Ghostly Undertaking involves willing adults who pay to stay overnight at the Culbertson, from 6:00 PM to 6:00 AM. They receive a catered candlelit dinner, scavenger hunt with non-kid prizes, ghost tour, and storytelling in the upper level. A period wood casket is set up in one parlor. One might wonder if misbehaving grownups might be asked to sit in the "punishment room".

Besides the Carriage House excitement, and the overnight adult sleepover, the Culbertson also offers weeknight Ghostly Happening Tours. They are given, two per night. Visitors see the Mansion and hear about weird, unexplained things that have happening in the last 25 years. Finally, the Culbertson hosts "Scary Storytelling" on the third floor in late October.

Author and storyteller Roberta Simpson Brown reported on folklore from the Culbertson. She noted that a woman has been seen on the third floor, and opinions vary as to whether she is the first or second wife of William Culbertson. Additional reports of unexplained activities include mysteriously moved furniture, odd sounds, a spinning wheel that moves on its own, helium balloons that traveled about the home, pipe smoke scent, voices and that "heebie-jeebies" feeling! The curator noted that, "This place feels very differently at night!"

Ghost Tour Guide in Off Hours

I met Robert Parker, Mr. Ghost Walker, in Louisville one September when I volunteered to work at Corn Island Storytelling Festival. Robert gives ghost tours in downtown Louisville, and published the matching stories in *Haunted Louisville*. Although fascinated with ghostly legend, Robert maintains a healthy skepticism, awaiting the evidence of photo or material manifestation before commenting. In this instance, Robert found both!

Robert:

My sister and I went across the River to the Culbertson Mansion for their haunted house tour. Eileen was our guide, and she and I know one another and share the same passion about ghosts. We were in the master bedroom, and Eileen was detailing the ghostly activity as well as the historical significance of the master bedroom. Eileen reported that a handprint appears into the bedspread of the bed, usually on the right side of the bed. Eileen walked on the three sides of the bed providing information. We were almost ready to leave, when someone in the crowd pointed out that they saw a hand impression in the bedspread. The group went insane. Sure enough, on the left side of the bed near the middle of the edge was the imprint of a left hand.

In the photo, Eileen was pointing the flashlight toward the imprint. In the image, you can see the four fingers and a slight area of a thumb. Now here is the creepy part. Since Eileen is acquainted with me, she allowed me to come around the velvet rope and get close enough to take a better picture of the bed. I crouched down low at the foot of the bed for this shot. As I crouched down and steadied myself, I felt two, large hands on my shoulders.

As I took the picture, I thought it odd that someone would place hands on my shoulders, since I wasn't in some precarious position or in any danger of falling. I could feel the hands with pressure on my shoulders, but I didn't feel like they were going to push me down. I snapped the picture and sprang up, looked around, and saw nobody near me, since I was on the inside of the velvet rope. My body felt funny, tingling, as if I wanted to just collapse for lack of energy. The tour continued to the third floor. Eileen had us seated upstairs and she told some more history of the house. When

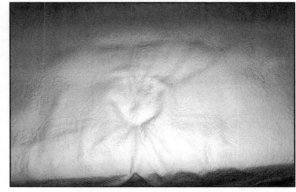

Hand impression in bed, Ghost Tour, Culbertson Mansion.

she was alone, I asked her, "Eileen, tell me who put their hands on my shoulders, when I stooped down to take the picture?"

She told me that nobody was near me, and she was standing to my right side. I corrected her and said that I felt, two big, strong, firm hands on my shoulders when I stooped to the foot of the bed. She just responded that it had to have been a ghost. I also added that the strangest sensation swept over my body – near exhaustion once I stood back up.

Of course, word spread in the group that I'd been 'touched' by the ghost. In the crowd were two Indiana University Southeast students doing research for an article. They interviewed me afterwards for their publication. Anyway, once we reached the end of the tour and were in the gift shop, Eileen told

Robert Parker at the Brennan House.

the other employees, and they ushered me to the back room so they could hear first hand of my account of being touched by the ghostly hands in the master bedroom.

Now, I don't put a lot of stock into this, but as we were leaving the master bedroom, one of the women on the tour shouted out that the velvet rope was swinging back and forth. I saw it moving, but it could have been knocked by someone.

First Sighting of a Ghost

Danny Downs, New Albany, Indiana

My wife believes in ghosts more than me. I never saw ghosts before. After this experience, then I wasn't really too sure about it. I mean, I believed. We lived in an apartment on Eighth Street in New Albany. Real early one morning I awoke and looked in the doorway of our apartment, our bedroom door. I saw a man standing there with dark hair and a T-shirt. He was about fifteen feet away from me. He was looking at me. I got kind of like goose bumps and a cold chill.

I jumped, it scared me and I said, "What are you doing in my house?" and when I looked down there was no lower half.

The man had dark hair, dark eyes and was apparently a young fellow. I would say he was in his 20s or early 30s. As I looked at him, he looked at me like he was as startled that I was looking at him. We had direct eyeball-to-eyeball contact. And as I started to wake Pam he began to disappear. It was like little crystals that started to glow and faded away.

I woke up my wife Pam because I thought I was possibly dreaming. I shook her to wake her up. Then the ghost just kind of disintegrated into little clusters and slowly disappeared.

And she said, "Oh, that's just nothing. It's just a ghost, go back to bed."

So I had goose bumps for probably an hour before I could finally fall back to sleep. And that was my first experience seeing a ghost. It was eye opening. I've never seen him again. It was a great experience because now I'm a true believer in seeing ghosts.

There are times I've gotten up for work at 4:00 or 5:00 in the morning I hear voices and I'm the only one up.

Odd Happenings

Pam:

I had a little crystal tray that I kept my jewelry in. It was a divided tray. It was actually for hors d'oeuvres at a party or something but I used it for my jewelry and I had that sitting on the edge of the box. When I would come home – I cannot tell you how often – I would find the tray upside down on the floor. My jewelry was all over the floor and no longer in the tray. I would find it on the floor all the time upside down but it was never broken. And the floor was tile.

My sister came over for Christmas one time and she heard people walking upstairs. She heard the footsteps walking back and forth.

She said, "I hear somebody upstairs and we're all right here." But it wasn't two minutes later and she was gone.

"I got to go now."

Our rocking chair would rock on its own. We came in before and we said well maybe the cat jumped on it. We had one cat then, and the cat would be curled up on the couch asleep. We walked in many a time in the middle of the night and this rocking chair would be in slow motion just rocking away.

What was so neat about the rocking chair is that it had the old sawdust stuffing and the old springs. So when it would rock we heard the springs squeaking. That really made it sound and feel eerie. It would just squeak away and I thought *as long as it was rocking I am not going in the front room.* But we still would sit on the rocker.

When we lived on the house at 1836 East Spring Street, we constantly thought we saw someone go down the hall. It was a large house, built in 1913. It's a frame Craftsman style house. I think the husband died there and maybe his wife passed away there too. They had the house built and they lived there until their deaths. It was in probate for 2 years when we bought it.

We lived in several old houses. We also lived in apartment on Eighth Street by St Mary's in an old, old house.

We haven't had nearly any activity here, other than an obnoxious female spirit who yells at us to get up.

She says, "Can you help me?" That's usually the first thing we hear.

Then it's usually "get up" or "Mom." "Hey," is the other one. And it's always when we're asleep. You don't go to bed imagining somebody's going to say "hey" or "Mom".

Now there were times we heard voices on Spring Street. Both my children had imaginary friends. Janna's friend was Setta. I think the imaginary friend for our younger daughter was also named Setta, It makes me really wonder who Setta was. She would appear upstairs in Emily's bedroom, in what had previously been our attic, after we had finished it into rooms.

For Janna she lived in the pantry. Our daughter Janna would go in there and shut the door and we would hear her in there talking. This happened when both were three to four years old. After they got to be older their imaginary friend was gone.

Janna:

She just wanted to talk to me. We had hairbrushes that were always missing – and shoes too. We had shoes thrown out the door. Once, one shoe was in the house and one was outside hanging in the cherry tree. We later found the hairbrushes on a bookshelf or somewhere else. This was constant and they would never be where they were left.

After Her Death She Came To Talk
Bonnie Casto

My sister-in-law Francis and I were always close. She lived in Louisville and I lived about forty-five minutes drive from her in New Castle, Kentucky. When she died I had surgery the week before and I couldn't get down there to go to the funeral. It really bothered me. I last saw Francis on February 11, which was a Sunday. I had surgery on the 13th and she died the following Monday. The doctor told me not to drive to Louisville.

Danny is my only brother and I had nightmares from my guilt of not being there. But Francis came one night to talk to me. I work an odd shift for UPS and sometimes get just a few hours sleep. It was nighttime when I went to bed about 10 PM. I know it was before 2 AM when I heard Francis' voice. Immediately I felt calm and it was a big relief to hear her. I sat up in bed and she sat on my bed and we had a conversation.

Frances McDole

She assured me that I would have gone to see her if I could have gone and she told me "everything will be alright". We had a long conversation and she reminisced about the things she enjoyed doing.

She said, "I want you to watch over your brother."

She didn't talk about heaven it was more like just us girls chatting.

Danny and I were always close more laid back than our siblings. We are hard workers who didn't get into trouble with more in common that the others.

Since that night when Francis came to visit I no longer had nightmares. Even though my husband did not believe in ghosts I always believed. Now he believes too.

Our House Ghost

We bought a house in New Castle, which was built on the same foundation as a house that burned down. It wasn't until after we moved in when we found out that the previous owner died in that same fire.

We noticed little things happening around our house. We moved in twelve years ago and one of the first times I heard the ghost was when I was home by myself with the doors locked. I heard the door open and close and someone walking along the hallway.

Once my (then) ten-year-old son come to say that someone cleaned up his room, saying, "Mom all my tapes and CDs are put away!"

When he got home from school he didn't clean his room and neither did me nor my husband. It could only have been the ghost.

We often lie in bed at night and heard the ghost move about the house. I heard his breathing which at first I thought was the furnace making noises. The ghost was very active when my brother-in-law stayed with us for a month.

He was bothered by the ghost and I told him, "It's just that he doesn't like you!"

For the first five or six years the ghost acted up when we had visitors. Folks told us that he was a good person. They said the man loaded up the wood stove for the night but he didn't shut the stove door. When the fire engulfed the home they couldn't get him out. I believed in ghosts all my life and I wasn't ever scared by our house ghost.

A Big Wind

Last year (2008) a tornado tore through our area. They say that when you turn fifty years old your life changes. I felt like my life flipped upside down.

The windstorm hit on February 6 at 1 o'clock in the morning. Earlier that evening, about 11:30, I checked and there was no news of bad weather. Before I went to bed I asked Travis to keep on his radio so we'd have warning for tornado or straightline winds.

We woke up just as it hit and the wind blasted through our patio door, into the dining room, through the living room, hitting some of the kitchen and out into our front yard.

Travis called me to say, "Our house just got hit!"

We had no windows in the living room but our patio door and small wall were taken out. There were seven telephone poles down between our home and New Castle. The wind pulled the electrical lines out of our house.

It was like the Wizard of Oz tossing things around. But it could have been worse since we have siding on the house. We had good insurance coverage. But I believe he watches over us.

Power Tools in Heaven

When I was taking graduate Art Therapy classes, I stayed after class once and talked with one of my classmates, Jean. Jean is bright, friendly, and often looked out for the welfare of others. Somehow we must have talked about either life, or death or ghosts, because Jean told me her experience with a friend of a friend. That friend of a friend was a ghost, as it turned out. Oftentimes, the ghost of our deceased family or friend will appear not directly to us, but to someone else who can handle seeing us. This indirect approach spares us from a complicated grief, allowing us to receive a message by proxy, without causing us more trauma and hurt. A few years after sharing that story, after Jean and I graduated and we were both busy working in the field of counseling, Jean came to my home and again told me her story, from the beginning....

Jean's father grew up in a small Italian-Irish American family, with a half dozen brothers and sisters, in Chicago. Jean's sister reported that her great grandmother came into her bedroom and tucked her in, singing her to sleep. This was after her great grandmother passed away. So their family believed that ghosts could be friendly and peaceful, or also scary sometimes. Jean's dad and uncle slept in the attic when they were younger. Her dad thought he woke up in the middle of the night to see the aunt checking on them. She told him to take care of his brother. The following morning, they found out the aunt had died the night before.

Jean's dad and grandfather told the family that when Jean's (paternal) grandfather and grandmother were married, they lived across from a cemetery. When Jean's grandmother was pregnant with her first child, her grandfather woke up to see a man standing on her stomach. And, in what he thought as the time was a dream, he tried to fight off this stranger. In the morning, both discovered bruises on her stomach.

Jean went away to a church camp in southern Alabama; she was in 7th grade. At that time, her family lived in Tennessee. She said, over the Fourth of July weekend, they went somewhere to see fireworks. She said, every time she called home, it seemed like her mom, dad or sister weren't home, so she talked to her great-grandmother, who lived with the family. This was Jean's Mom's paternal grandmother. By her choice, as a way to help serve the family, her great-grandmother did a lot of the family laundry. She wanted to feel that she could contribute to the family's welfare. She also helped clean house, despite being 94 years old.

She was an immigrant from Ireland; she arrived by boat through Ellis Island. Jean and her family called her "Gaga." When Jean called home from summer camp, she tried to talk to Gaga. She said she seemed like she was doing great, feeling great.

"She asked how I was doing in camp, and told me she'd see me in a couple of days. She died on the 5th of July, and my parents had to call and tell the camp management to tell me. So I was driven back early, instead of going home at the end of camp. Although I was at first upset, I later had a feeling of calm. I actually found out she had been quite sick when I talked with her. I couldn't tell it on the phone.

Old Sandstone Gravestones.

"When we got back, we found out she had put the dress that she wanted to be buried in, into the washer and dryer. She picked out the dress 15 years before, and put it in the closet until then. It seemed she knew that she was going to die. My mom went looking for this white dress, and found it in the dryer. But I still had that peaceful feeling about her passing on. Oftentimes, since then, when I returned home, I stayed in her room. I woke up in the middle of the night, and felt peacefulness, knowing it was her room."

Jean went to college at Western Kentucky University in Bowling Green, Kentucky. The dorms are old, with a lot of history. She heard the typical campus ghost stories, how one student was killed and how another committed suicide. Many of her classes were in the historic buildings, Potter Hall, Van Meter, and were 70 or more years old.

"At Western, the campus sits atop a hill. It's an old fort. They still have part of the walls of the old fort. There's a mound in the middle, and it's the highest point amongst the surrounding five counties. In the middle are the old buildings, once dorms, and later converted to classrooms for theatre, dance, and journalism. That's why the mascot is called the Hilltopper. Potter Hall, which is the Administration Building, is very creepy. During our orientation, they talk about the ghost stories and which buildings are the most haunted.

"One of the dorms, still a dormitory, was then called Schneider Hall. I had a friend who lived there who swore up and down that she saw a glowing orb moving down the hallway. She heard footsteps, too. Schneider was one of the few dorms that stayed open during the holidays, because most of the international students lived there. The third floor was reserved for visiting lecturers. The building was horribly old. You could see the original plaster and gaslight sconces. Although, as a residence hall, it wasn't up to date; it had character, with big columns and entry foyer. The hallways had big marble staircases. When I was in there, I had a creepy feeling.

"When I was at Western, one of the students died. He was driving back from a basketball game. He was from rural Kentucky, and his last name was "Turner". While driving home with a friend, their car hit a deer. It was on the side of Interstate 64, just outside of Louisville. They stopped to check the damage to their car, and another car hit him. I didn't know him; I never met him. At that time, when he passed away, I didn't really know anyone close to him. I was living in The Tower at PFT. I lived on the 17th floor and I had a friend who lived on the 9th floor. I went down to see him; someone else on his floor was a really good friend – "Daryl". Eventually Daryl and I became really good friends. Daryl and Turner were fraternity brothers. Daryl had a dramatic personality; he draped his dorm room door entirely in black fabric. He put up a little memorial, fake flower wreath, on the door, to commemorate Turner's death.

"Daryl and I would go out and do things. We became fast friends. I knew that he was friends with this guy, Turner, but I didn't know more about it. He seemed to have some continuing grief issues. I guess they had some fights before Turner died.

"I started having dreams with this man who was wearing glasses. I saw him in my dreams, and I didn't know who it was. But it was okay. You know how you have a dream of someone, and maybe they were a composite of people from your daytime activity. He was fairly good looking. Sometimes he would be sitting there, smoking. A lot of the dreams happened when I was in the Schneider dorm.

"It was a nice friendship; we watched movies and fell asleep. But I kept having dreams when I was in Daryl's room. In my dream, this guy sat at the edge of the bed, just smoking a cigarette.

"Daryl was going through a lot of emotional stuff at the time. He was having a hard time with depression issues. He was into a different lifestyle than the fraternity supported. A lot of his turmoil started before I met him. So I was a friend for his rough time.

"I would wake up and feel kind of awkward. I remember wondering about this person in my dreams. Who was he? And then we started talking. He never really said who he was. We'd talk about being worried about Daryl. 'He's struggling, and he's not going to classes anymore.'

Then one day, Jean got a message from the man with the glasses. She awoke from her dream, remembering that he had been at the end of the bed, smoking, and said,

"Tell Daryl that there are power tools in Heaven."

"When I woke up, I thought about it for a second, and then that thought was replaced with 'I'm late for class!'"

Jean set the dreamy message aside, but later she thought, "Is this something that someone's trying to tell me?" She wondered if there was a message behind the phrase, 'power tools in heaven'. Jean didn't normally have recurring dreams, but she kept dreaming of the man with the glasses and they talked. After that, Jean noticed more than just dreams.

"I went to Daryl's room to nap; Daryl wasn't there. And even though he smoked, I awoke from these dreams and the room smelled like someone was smoking. Also, Daryl had an ashtray at the end of the bed. A couple of times I was awakened by hearing elevator noises or some loud students returning from partying. Then once awake, I'd notice the cigarette smoke smell again. Even though Daryl religiously cleaned out the ashtray before bed, when I woke up, there were cigarette buts in the ashtray. I thought some more about this dream man's message. Why would I have a dream about 'power tools in heaven'?"

Then one night, Jean and Daryl returned to campus from a shopping trip to Wal-Mart. It was a typical college student outing, at 3:00 AM.

"The only people around were the maintenance workers, cleaning the floors. It was the middle of the week. I remember feeling a pressure. It felt like *something needs to be done*. We walked across the street, going back toward the dorm. But I still had that anxious feeling, as if *something's off*. I felt like there was someone following us. You know that unsafe feeling, when you always look over your shoulder. Something didn't feel right, so I told Daryl how I felt."

Jean suggested that they take a walk around campus. Even though it was night, the campus was well lit. They circled around the dorms, walking past his old fraternity house. That's when Jean made a connection in her mind. She realized that the man with the glasses in her dream was Turner. Even though she never met him, he came to talk to her. The realization and the implications flooded her mind and emotions, and Jean quickly started talking to Daryl about her dreams, the man in the glasses, the cigarette smoke, and their conversations about concern for Daryl.

Daryl listened politely. Other people had already offered condolences for his loss – people that knew Turner. He brushed off her babbling, thinking, *How could you be talking in your sleep to my best friend?* Daryl looked at Jean with doubt and amazement, thinking, *Maybe she's crazy; she's just trying to get attention.* But Jean persisted, and continued to talk to Daryl as they walked together up the hill to the old fort walls.

"We sat on the steps of Cherry Hall. It's another old building with its own story. It has a statue in front. We looked down the street, where you can see all the way down the hill. And then it blurted out of me, and I said to Daryl, 'There are power tools in heaven!' He looked at me with the biggest look of shock. Then he started crying. But I still didn't get it, until we started talking again and he told me the rest of the story."

Jean recounted how Daryl and Turner, when they lived together, had become blood brothers. The formed a bond beyond their fraternity attachment, cutting and putting their hands together to ritualize their friendship.

They reassured each other that there would always be a special bond between them. Turner knew that Daryl had a lifestyle that was different than his fraternity brothers, and he was okay with that. But they had a strong connection. Daryl continued, sobbing uncontrollably. When he stopped crying and calmed down a bit, he resumed talking about their unique friendship.

"When they were living together in the fraternity house, as roommates, they had some serious discussions about death. They agreed, should something ever happen to one of the pair, one would watch over the other from the spirit world. They talked about heaven. Turner, it turned out, was really into power tools. For Christmas he'd ask Santa for a power drill set. So he told Daryl, 'Heaven won't be heaven unless there are power tools there!'"

Jean noticed that after that night, her dreams about the man with the glasses stopped. She felt that Turner was present that night, urging her to talk about the dreams, saying, "You have to do this now!" Jean felt that she was a carrier for the message from Turner to Daryl that it was going to be okay.

"It was not something we talked about after that night. Maybe because of my family ghost folklore, I was open to that experience. Maybe that's why Daryl and I became fast friends, because we really didn't have a whole lot in common, although we spent a lot of time together. It was about eight months later, Daryl and I returned from a trip to Lexington. It was late spring, and we were shopping there. But instead of taking the Bluegrass Parkway, we went via Interstate 64 to a small town to visit the cemetery where Turner was buried. Daryl drove us to the cemetery, off the beaten path. On the way there, we stopped at the BBQ place where Turner worked. There were not many fences, just a rural graveyard with stone markers and the caretaker's house.

"I think it was a little past closing time, but we drove in anyway and parked. I asked Daryl, 'Do you want me to walk to Turner's grave with you?' He said, 'No.' It was still very painful for him. He was there only once before. This was a couple of years after his friend's death." Jean continued telling her story.

"I sat in his pick up truck, while Daryl was visiting the grave. He was away for about 30 minutes. I moved from the passenger to the driver seat so I could work the clutch, and start the car to listen to the radio. From where I sat, I couldn't see Daryl and Turner's gravesite. It was dark outside, the truck cab dome light was on, and I was messing with the radio. The doors were locked. I looked up in the rearview mirror, and I saw Turner's face, with his glasses. He made a clicking sound, like when you want to get a horse going. I immediately turned around, but no one was there. It was a little bit scary, but just then Daryl came back to the truck. I could tell he was crying. His face was puffy and red. I didn't tell Daryl what I saw."

House Built Over Indian Battleground

I met Bob in college, at St. Mary's University. He was funny and friendly, and we both hit it off as friends. Bob was a year behind my graduating class, and it was hard to say who offered whom the better wisdom. I admired his generosity, and he had a knack for knowing people. Bob and I shared a dorm room for my junior year, and then we rented a half-house together during my senior year and for part of my first year in graduate school. We played guitar and quoted Monty Python movies. We were silly, and I miss that fun time we had.

I shared my interest in true ghost stories with Bob. So he told me about his house in suburban St. Louis, and this is what I recall...He grew up in Creve Coeur; it's a well-to-do area west of the I-270 loop. Bob told me that when he and his younger brother first played in their backyard before they put down sod, they found bits of bones and old bullets. Years later, their father finished half of the basement. Being an architect, his father paid extra money to have the cement basement anchored to the Missouri bed-rock. Concrete pilings went down to secure the basement from cracking. It was guaranteed not to ever crack, Bob reported. But over the years, a long crack slowly appeared in their basement foundation. It ran the entire length of the basement.

The finished side of the basement, on the west, bordering the back-yard, had wood paneling in the style of the time, the 1970's. Bob's father directed the work crew to leave a crawl space between the wood paneling and the concrete foundation wall. This allowed the exterminator to access the south, west and north finished sections to spray for insects. The man came several times a year for many years. But on one visit, he admitted that he only sprayed the shorter, south and north sections.

He said, "I can't go back on the west side. It doesn't feel right."

On the other side of the basement, the unfinished half, there were storage shelves and washer & dryer. Bob's younger brother tied up his ka-rate punching bag from the wooden supports under the first floor. His brother would walk down the steps a few times each week, to work out, punching and kicking the four and half foot bag. Besides the sound of his grunting and kicks, the bag made a conspic-uous squeaking sound when it moved. Then he hugged the bag, to fully stop it from further swinging, and walked back up the stairs to the kitch-en. His brother reported that each time he returned, when he was halfway up the stairs, he heard the chains holding the bag squeak again.

College friend.

Indian Mound, Cahokia, Illinois.

Bob reported some sightings in his house too. But the most dramatic event came when Bob and his parents went out for the evening. His younger brother was home with their dog. When they returned, there was no one in the house. The framed pictures on the wall were all askew. They found the pair next door; the dog had its tail between its legs, and Bob's brother looked very scared. His brother said that all at once, he heard a pounding. He said it sounded like someone was hitting the air ducts, and that was when he and the dog ran outside and to the neighbors.

Double Trouble

Beth Wilder, Jeffersontown, Kentucky

This story appeared in a Nashville newspaper around the mid-late 1980's, possibly early 1990's. My great aunt sent me a copy of the article. It is true, although of course, I may be remembering some parts like the storm a little incorrectly but in the way I imagined it as I read the news clipping. I have arbitrarily made up names for the characters, since I do not remember them.

It is a tradition among some Southerners to sit overnight at the funeral home with the recently deceased. Crystal offered to sit with her deceased father on this particular night. Mr. Tompkins, the funeral home director, told her he would be leaving soon and that he was going to lock all the doors behind him. Consequently, she would be locked in the building until he came back the next morning. Crystal said that was fine. So after a final check of all the rooms, Mr. Tompkins left, locking the door behind him.

About that time, rain started, eventually building up to a thunderstorm. Crystal sat calmly by her father's side for a few minutes, until out of boredom, she decided to move around a bit.

She walked into the adjoining parlor and saw a casket sitting in the room. Curious to see who was in it, Crystal walked across the room to gaze upon the person who passed on about the same time as her father. Her heart melted when she saw the handsome face and beautiful brown curls of a young man who could not have been more than eighteen. She lingered a few moments, thinking about this life that had been prematurely cut short then Crystal returned to her vigil at her father's side.

As the storm picked up, Crystal quietly sat next to her father, listening to the rain and thunder, watching lightning flash periodically. Suddenly, she noticed a figure standing in the doorway – *but the funeral home was supposed to be empty!!!* Her eyes grew wide with fright as she realized she was looking at the young man who had been in the casket across the hall.

"What are you doing in here?" she gasped.

The young man merely looked quizzically at her, slightly cocking his head to one side.

"Who are you?!!" she cried.

The young man remained silent and slowly began to approach her. Crystal backed away from him as she felt her heart rate increase to an almost painful tempo. As if the event unfolding was not frightening enough, Crystal heard one of the funeral home doors creak open – *what else was she going to have to try to escape?*

Crystal was in a panic when she saw a familiar face appear behind the boy who was moving ever more near to her. It was Mr. Tompkins! Thank Heaven!

Mr. Tompkins took the young man's arm and patted his hand. Noting the horrified look on Crystal's face, he quickly explained.

"I am so sorry. I just realized that I never saw Jamie leave this evening. You see, Jamie's twin brother is laid out in the parlor across the hall and Jamie was here for his visitation. Jamie is deaf and he must have been in the restroom when I was locking up the place. I hope he didn't frighten you too badly."

Scared By the Dead

This ghost story happened in a cemetery somewhere in downtown Louisville. A friend of my ex-boyfriend was crippled, and he told Dennis that he never told anyone the true story of why his shins got shoved up into his thigh area, because he thought no one would ever believe him. He said he'd been smoking pot and walking around a cemetery where the ghost of an old woman was sometimes seen rocking in her chair on the front porch. He saw the ghost, but at first thought it was a **real** old woman. He figured maybe he should leave, since she was watching him.

All of a sudden, the old crone shot up out of her chair and flew towards him, chasing him. She was not there from the waist down, just a blur. While running, he turned to keep an eye on her and accidentally fell off a drop at the foot of the cemetery. It may have been like a retaining wall or something. That's when he damaged his legs. Having smoked pot, he never told anyone what happened, as he knew they would not believe him. But according to Dennis, he said he was high, but he wasn't **that** high. He really saw the old woman chasing him.

Living With Ghosts

Andrea Yussman generously invited me over to a dinner with her family and friends. On another occasion, Andrea and I met at the local Borders Café, where she told her ghost stories in detail, which I recorded on cassette and later transcribed. Here are her stories.

Andrea:

Growing up, I always had premonitions of things that later happened. I saw them in a dream – and I never knew how to explain it. It's almost like, "Do I go out today? Do I not go out today?" One of the first signs of this was when I was 18. I had a premonition that I was going to be involved in an automobile accident. And I saw exactly the way that it was going to happen. I got up and I kind of discredited it. I went ahead and got on with the day. Shortly later on that day, guess what happened? – an automobile accident. It happened in exactly the same place, to a t, dream-wise. It happened on Eastern Parkway, I went down to the University of Louisville. I was an art student down there at the time.

My brother and I were always very close growing up. It was like we had telepathy. We were in different rooms and we read each other's mind. I thought *maybe we will do this or that*, and then he came in the room and suggested we do the same thing. My brother recently moved back from living in Las Vegas, even to this age those things happen. My brother and I went to Bass Pro in Clarksville, Indiana. My husband and brother looked for a Father's Day gift for Dad. I didn't know that, before looking for a gift, my brother was upstairs in the snack bar sitting at a table. He was sitting, with his feet propped up on the chair next to him. After sitting there a while my brother left to look for us. He found us in the fishing area, and my husband and brother left to hunt for a perfect gift for Dad – which turned out to be a pair of camouflage gloves. Meanwhile, I went upstairs to sit at a table in the snack bar. Well I ended up at the same table, same chair, and propped my feet up on the same adjacent chair. When my brother arrived, he exclaimed,

"I cannot believe this!" We do things like that and don't realize it; there's just that bond. We look at each other and say, "Okay, I know what you're thinking." It's kind of weird when you think about it. By the way, before the men went looking for a gift, I picked out what I thought would be a good gift…camouflage gloves.

Speaking of ghosts, I had a lot of what are called out of body experiences. I really don't know what else to call it. People looked at me and said, "you're a little on the far-fetched side here". My grandparents died, my grandmother died three weeks before my wedding. It was very devastating. We didn't know if we wanted to go ahead with the wedding. But we did. Shortly after my grandmother died, we were at the funeral. The whole room filled up with the Shalimar scent, but nobody was wearing it. She wore Shalimar perfume. It was like her spirit was there. About three years later I expected a child, and we were deciding what to name the child. My husband wanted to name the child after his side of the family and of course I wanted to name the child after my grandparents who died. One evening, I can't remember if it was a dream, but I sat up. I saw, at the end of my bed, my grandparents, and their bodies were levitating. I tried to wake up my husband.

I pushed him, saying, "Get up – get up! Oh my gosh!"

But he seemed to be in a trance. I could not wake him. Then I looked at them and said, "If that's really you, let the telephone ring." It was three in the morning – I had my clock by the bed – and the phone rang. I immediately picked up the phone, and there was nobody on the phone. I sat there with the phone in my hand and looked up at the end of the bed at both of my grandparents. I put the covers over my head, and then took them back down. Then they just slowly started to fade away. I put the phone down.

All of a sudden, my husband got up, and I said, "My grandparents were just in this room! So we're naming the baby after one of them."

Prior to my grandfather dying, I saw that in a dream. It was another premonition. I actually saw him having a heart attack. The phone rang the next morning, in the dream, that was my father telling me. I could see my grandfather calling for help in the dream. The next morning, the phone rang, and I said to my husband, "Don't answer that. I know what it is." We were supposed to go bowling. We belonged to a bowling league.

And my husband said, "Well I'm answering the phone." He answered the phone, and he said, "It's your father."

And before I could tell him, what the conversation was, I could tell by the look in his face, I said, "You don't have to tell me – I already know."

I was living in Virginia at the time, and my grandfather was here in Louisville. At the time I dreamt about his heart attack, it was the time he was actually dying.

Some people have told me, well you're psychic. Tell me what am I going to do, what's going to happen to me?

And I told them, "I can't do it that way, it just kind of hits." I moved back to Louisville and we bought this house from two little old ladies, cutest little old ladies. We slept in their master bedroom. I kept having this dream. I was running. And as I was running I tripped, every time, and where I fell there was a tombstone. On the tombstone, there was no name, but a date, it was August 1981. I had this dream for three consecutive nights. I woke up in a sweat, and I just couldn't sleep – I wouldn't want to sleep – because it scared me. On the actual day, in August, I was afraid to go out of the house. I thought maybe that was the day I was supposed to die. I actually started physically believing that.

I said to my husband, "I can't go out and do anything today."

About noon, I got a knock on the door – it was my next-door neighbor. I looked at her, her name was Elaine, and I said, "Hi Elaine, what can I do for you?"

She said, "I just wanted to come over and tell you that, the people you bought the house from, the mother, Mrs. Ledbetter, died this morning." I thought *Oh my Gosh*. That explained the tombstone, and we were in their master bedroom. They moved to Georgia upon the sale of the house and corresponded with Elaine my next-door neighbor. Elaine was the woman who told me about Mrs. Ledbetter's death, and after that I never had that dream again. So somehow I got a connection with her. After that happened I never had that dream again. It was gone forever. But it was scary to think *this is the day I'm going to die.*

My house has some ghostly activity in it. We believe we have numerous ghosts in the house. I collect a lot of antiques, and it sounds crazy but sometimes spirits are attached to some things that you bring into the house. Last summer (2006) my male rabbit Oreo died on July 19. He was a Dutch black and white rabbit that I had for about six years. That was the same date as my Aunt Anna's birthday. Anna was an animal lover and grew up in Taylorsville, Kentucky, with lots of brothers and sisters. She especially loved dogs and since she never had any children of her own the dogs were like her children.

I came home from the veterinarian empty handed, because they said there was no hope – it was an older rabbit. I was very devastated. I felt very much attached to the rabbit, which I had for ten years. It just happened so quickly. I came into the house and felt very upset, because they asked me if I wanted to take the rabbit home to bury it on the property.

And I told them, "No, I don't want to do that."

I was in the kitchen, and I heard a door shut. I thought my daughter was coming in the house, but it wasn't her. All of a sudden, a woman walks across my dining room. I thought *somebody is in the house*. I looked into the dining room, and suddenly, it was gone. It didn't dawn on me until a few days later, that it was probably my aunt. She actually died on June 26. Since I was upset, maybe she knew to come and comfort me – "The rabbit's okay, it's safe with me." That was sort of a strange event, that particular day. The ghost I saw was a female, an older woman, she had her hair back, away from her face. The color of hair was like white, but really was no color at all, and it just sort of faded away. I thought, *my gosh, am I seeing things? Am I losing my mind?!* I didn't want to say anything about that. It was a short figure with curly hair. It looked like the dress I buried her in, to be honest. It looked like the pink, flowing dress in which she was buried. I really couldn't tell the color. She always dressed to the nines.

Keys are another thing. We always place them in a basket on the dining room table. The keys went missing for two and a half weeks. We finally had another set made, so I was using my husband's set. After I had those copies made, two months later, I came in the house, and there are my keys, sitting on the dining room table. That happens all the time. My husband had a wallet – he put his credit cards, everything in it. They like to take things and hide them around the house. His wallet disappeared. He had to cancel the credit cards and get a new driver's license. One year later, I went up to our bedroom, and in the middle of our bed sat the wallet with all of the stuff in it.

My husband said, "Where did you find that?",

I told him, "It was in the middle of our bed." It's just unbelievable.

We have toilets that flush by themselves. Lights will go off and on. I finally just got used to living with it.

I would tell them, "Stop! Just quit it!"

My daughter, when she was younger, slept in what is now the guest bedroom. We had to move her out of there, because she was so frightened. She said there was a little girl in that room who wore a bonnet. I'm not sure of the time period for how she looked, maybe the 1800's. She would always appear at the end of my daughter's bed and wanted to play. I never saw her. We don't know of any murders in our house. The land was the McMahon farmland and might have been where the slaves lived. I have a

Genna Yussman and friends – look for odd image in this photo.

Picture detail with unexplained figures.

photograph, taken when my daughter was young, with her friends. The picture was taken in front of our house, near sunset, and back behind the children in the window is an image of a black family. You can see a man, a woman and a baby. We're not sure if the baby was the ghost my daughter saw, or maybe somebody else. We are in the house, and all of a sudden, we see something white. It's a glimpse of something and it goes by really fast. When I'm sleeping, it sometimes feels like someone is standing over me. It's a really hot feeling, like someone is right on top of me, almost like touching.

I say aloud, "Stop it!"

And my husband says, "It's not me, it's not me!"

We learned to live with it, actually. We hear footsteps coming up the stairs – there's nobody there. I have my jacket hanging up, and it starts swinging back and forth. You know that they're there. They don't do anything mean, they just get irritating, like when things are missing. What happened recently is they turn statues around.

My husband likes everything in its place, and he asked, "Are you moving the statues?" We had friends over the other night; we were all in the kitchen. We heard a grinding noise.

They said, "What is that?" I answered,

"I don't know."

I went in the living room and discovered that the two oriental figurines on the mantle had been turned around to face the wall. Nobody was in the living room. We were all in the kitchen. There is another figure in the dining room; for some reason they want to turn those around. That's the latest happening. We just thought that was a little strange. I flip them back, and they turn them around.

There is a black man, a black woman and a baby. There was the woman who walked across my dining room who I believe to be my aunt. And there's a little girl with a bonnet. My friends want me to have ghost busters come out to our house. But the thing about it is the activity is not all of the time, it just happens sporadically. I don't pay attention to it anymore. We were in the living room and the lights went off and on and back off again. I think *okay we're having a power outage.* But it's not an outage, since it's off and on, off and on, off and on.

And finally I'll just say, "Stop, I know you're there!"

And it will stop. I wonder about myself being sensitive to spirits. My daughter has that ability and so does my mother, to see or feel or know things will happen before they happen. Our first dog, Sparky, used to back up, just looking into space. He was afraid to go into the back room of the basement. He stood there, seeming to bark at nothing. We had pictures of ghostly figures but they were all lost when the basement flooded in 1997. We snapped a series of pictures and later we pieced together those photos which each had glimpses of something, and saw one whole figure. We ruled out camera effects such as flash or double exposure.

When my daughter saw the ghost girl with the bonnet, she drew a picture of the girl.

She said, "This is the person who keeps coming to play."

At first I thought she had an imaginary friend, but when started drawing her, she was so hysterical, I knew something was going on. I went to the Edgar Cayce foundation in Virginia when I lived there. A person told me I have a lot of psychic ability, but I "didn't know how to channel it". They held up cards with symbols for me to guess, and I was pretty much on the money. My daughter was supposed to go out of town – this was about two years ago – in 2005. She planned to go to Alabama for a concert on her birthday. I had a premonition that she was involved in an accident; there was water. I saw her body lying on the concrete.

My husband said, "If you call up and tell her that you have this pre-monition, she's going to think you don't want her to go. She's 27 years old – you can't stop her!"

I said, "No, I can't have her go, because there's going to be a terrible accident."

He said, "Don't call her up and tell her that."

So I was biting my tongue on this one. I worked at the time, so I got up at 6:30 to go to work. I thought, *I can't stand it – she's not going.*

I called her and said, "I have to tell you what my dream was."

She said, "You don't have to tell me – I'm going to get killed in an automobile accident. There's water."

And I said, "That's exactly what I saw in my dream."

She said, "I'm not going. If you had the dream and so did I, then I'm not going." Now here's the odd thing. My mother-in-law died a couple of years before she planned to go to the concert. She was from Alabama. That's where she was born and raised. My daughter said she saw herself lying on the concrete and then she saw my mother-in-law, floating through the am-bulance to pick my daughter up off the ground. She said that's when the dream ended.

I said, "You know what – you're not going."

She said, "No I'm not."

So she did not go because of that. We never really know if that ac-cident might have happened, but there were too many signs there. She gets a lot of the same things I get, and we see things before they happen. She bought the house next to us.

She comes over and says, "You know, I felt a spirit or a presence."

And I say, "Yes, you don't have to tell me, I know."

She deals with vintage clothing and antiques, so I told her that the stuff she brings into the house has spirits attached to them. These would be people she doesn't know. She had a woman in her house – this was kind of strange – the woman just kept looking at the clothing. Maybe she owned those clothes in a previous life – I have no idea.

My uncle had a lot of spirits in his house in Okolona. He sold his house and moved. That particular spirit would turn everything in the house upside down. They locked the house, went away for a while, and when they came back and the doors were open. The checkbook was lying out on the concrete. They called the police who were baffled. Why didn't they take anything? There were times when he saw that same little girl, with the bon-net, in his house. In fact, he thought it was one of his little daughters when they were younger.

He said, "Gosh, why are you wearing that stupid hat?"

He got up, late at night, and saw the ghost at the end of the hallway. In his house, the girl could actually mimic some of the voices, to sound like his children. And both he and his wife saw this girl ghost.

He sold the house, and he thought *please, whatever you are, wherever you are, don't come with us – we don't want you!* So the people who bought the house, he never disclosed that there was some activity. They heard running in the wall, scratching sounds. He thought at first it might be squirrels. He could never figure out why they did some of the things, turned everything upside down. Once again, it's not mean things but annoying things. What happened in his case, he moved away, bought a new house.

The man called who bought his house and asked, "Did you turn in all your keys to the house?"

My uncle said, "What do you mean?"

He said, "Well, we came home and all our doors were open. They had the locks changed. But last we heard they were still having problems with the doors being found open. They even brought in a psychic. His name is Albert. They couldn't figure out why the doors kept opening.

We had a relative that was killed July 1st, 1975. It was a horrendous automobile accident. She was five years old. Jenni and Debbie, her mom, were coming back to Louisville. Debbie died first and Jenni was flung out of the car and she didn't survive. Jenni wore a little bonnet.

When my daughter drew the picture of the girl ghost, some of the family members said, "Well that looks like Jenni!"

But my daughter was not born yet to see that, and Jenni was not in our house. So I don't know why Jenni's ghost would come back to our house. Genna and Jenni were cousins. Jenni, if she was haunting my uncle's home, was a cousin to his two daughters as well. I haven't had any sightings of Jenni in a long time.

I had one out of body experience. I know I was very sick. This was about ten years ago. I was running a very high fever. It was so vivid in my mind. I was on a bridge. It was very cold and icy. I was trying to walk up to this bridge. All I could see were these two white lights; they looked like headlights on a car. It was so windy that I thought I was going to get blown over this bridge. I touched the railing, putting one hand over the other to hold on. I never got to the other end of the bridge, but as I neared the middle, I saw my grandfather. He was waving 'go back', like 'it's not your time'. I remember in the dream saying "Grandpa, grandpa!"

I woke the up the next morning and I found marks on my hand. They looked like railing marks from the cold metal railing. You know, how things get iced over and you put your hands on the icy metal and you almost tear your skin. That's what I had on both of my hands. I went to the doctor later that day. I didn't want to say, "I've had an out of body experience".

I felt sick – I had the flu with a high fever. I asked, "What is up with my hands?!" He looked at my hands, and asked, "Did you touch something?"

Well, in my mind, I knew what I'd touched. I thought *yeah, but nothing you're going to believe.* So I told him, I just woke up with my hands that way. He told me he had no explanation. I was very, very close to my maternal grandparents.

When my mother-in-law passed away, I was the last one in the house. I had a premonition to go over there. It felt like something was wrong. The anniversary of her death is July 1st, same as little Jenni. She died in 2002.

I went over to her house, and she said, "I've been trying to call you."

I said, "I know. I'm here."

And she said, "Take me to the hospital. I don't want to go in an ambulance."

So I literally carried her out – she was very tiny – and put her out in my car. We went to the hospital, and they admitted her. Then she said, "Oh, my house is a mess."

I said, "I'll go back and fix everything and you'll be back in no time." She later passed away. My husband's father died, so I think she grieved herself to death. They died about ten months apart. I felt really bad, because I told her she was coming home. It kind of haunted me. I thought *I made her a promise, she's coming home, and she didn't*. It was six months after her death. I felt like there was no unresolved business. I didn't feel anything. We visited the gravesite and put flowers down. Then one night, she came to me in my dream. This is going to sound really weird. She didn't talk, and this really bothered me. She led me down the hallway of her condo, and everything was empty. It wasn't a normal color. Everything took on this super, bright light. She went back and opened up the closet, and it was empty too. There was another voice speaking for her. It said that she wanted to come back and tell me that it was okay she didn't get to come home. I asked,

"How's Dad?" This other voice answered,

"He's fine. Everything's okay – Dad is just Dad." She looked at me and the other voice, speaking for her, said she was at peace, and she would not be coming back. The only time she did come back was in my daughter's dream. Then the conversation was over and it was like her body fell back, and out of her mouth came this little vial.

I asked, "What is that?"

This voice answered, "That allowed her to come back to earth one last time." That's all I got – it was so bizarre. I wondered what that vial contained.

I hate it when I hear a bird hit the window. I heard from my grandmother, Josephine Frank Weiser, that if a bird hits the window and dies, somebody is going to die. Once when a bird died hitting the window of my sunroom, a few days later my cousin who suffered from cancer passed away. In the mid-1990's I took a group of kids in my van to drive them to an enrichment program. We went to the ice cream factory to see where they made ice cream cones. We also went out to lunch, and to other different places in the city.

A bird hit the grill of my van, and one young man said, "Oh, you just killed a bird."

I said, "I'm sure I did and I feel terrible about it."

But he was the one that made mention of it, nobody else did. Shortly after that he was killed in an automobile accident. He was sixteen years old. I thought back to that day because he was the only one that said something.

My husband is missing some paperwork right now, and who knows? We have no idea what happened to that folder. It's a nice size folder but it just disappeared in thin air. We searched the house but we have no idea where it is, but it will turn up. It will eventually come back but no telling when.

Anna went to the hospital. She was comatose. They only gave her three days to live, but she was in the hospital for 17 days. I brought in balloons. I talked to her like she was awake.

One intern said, "Why do you talk to her? She can't hear you."

And I thought how people have said that the hearing is the last thing to go.

So I told him, "I'm going to talk to her until I can no longer talk to her. He kept trying to call her my mother, but I corrected him saying,

"She's my aunt." She was comatose, living on borrowed time, but I told her, "I really would love to hear your voice. I wish you could wake up and talk to me today. I set some balloons by her bed, kissed her and as I walked out of the room, I thought I heard her call my name. I thought *she's comatose, what am I thinking?*

So then I heard my name again, "Andrea! Andrea!"

I thought *I have to go back* and I turned around. *I have to go and find out. I have to see if that's really her calling my name.* I went back in her room – she was sitting up in the bed. *Oh, my, I thought, this woman is supposed to be comatose.*

She sat up and said, "You look so pretty today. I like your orange top you have on…she talked about how she liked the balloons, and general conversation. I told her how the weather was outside.

Then she said, "I'm so thirsty. I'd like a drink of water."

I hit the button to call the nurse in and said, "I just want to validate with someone that she woke up."

They gave her water, just a little sip, and she said, "You know, I'm tired now, but I just want to tell you that I love you."

Tears were rolling down my face, and I said, "I love you too."

I kissed her on the forehead, I walked out of the room, and she went back into the coma. The next day, I didn't get to make it up there at the same time because we closed out everything in her apartment. The movers came to take the last bit of furniture. I stood in the room and looked around and thought *I'll never be in this place again.* And at the exact time I was closing the door – she died.

I got a call from my mom, who said, "We need you to come over here" – they wanted me to be over there so they could tell me that she passed. I was so upset because I wasn't there. I felt guilty that she died alone, that none of the family was there at the time of her death.

Later at home, I shuffled some papers around, and thought *I'll need to write an obituary.* A book fell off my cabinet, opened to a page with a picture of an angel, all dressed in pink. That's the color she always wore. And the book passage talked about how you're never alone. I still have that little book. So when we went for the funeral, I took that passage. I don't know where that was quoted from, but it made me feel better to know that no one is ever really alone. I used that for a prayer card at her funeral – it made a really nice saying for the back of the card. That was strange, for something like that to happen. And it was even stranger for her to wake up. I felt like it was a gift, personally, to me, because after that she never spoke again. She died the next day.

I worked as a teacher in Jefferson County schools. My vice principal and his wife lost a child.

Suddenly, the other staff said, "Don't talk about it – it's a sore subject."

It was very detrimental to him. He just didn't want to discuss it. It was during the same school year, about three months later, I had a premonition that his wife was pregnant, that they were going to have a baby boy, and that everything was going to be fine. So I asked myself – *do I go in his office and tell him?* I couldn't stand the urge.

I knocked on his door and said, "Can I talk to you for a moment? I know you don't like to talk about the loss of your child, but I want to tell you that your wife is going to be pregnant, you're going to have a baby boy, and everything's going to be just fine." He turned white as a ghost, just looked at me.

I asked, "What's wrong?"

He said, "My wife just called. She found out she's pregnant and nobody knows." So there was someone, not family, that found out ahead of time.

Suddenly everyone asked me, "Can you tell me what's going to happen with me?" I said, "No, I can't. It just kind of comes and goes."

There were a lot of strange happenings in the house across the street from us. An older couple bought the house and turned it into a nursing home. Then of course, over the years a lot of people passed away from old age. The finale happened when the owner of the house got cancer and did not want to leave the house. They had hospice come out. He died in his own home. The house had lots of different rooms. He actually died in what was then a bedroom. That area was a garage which was converted into a bedroom. After he died, the house was foreclosed on and sat vacant for two years. The new owner bought the house, said he was going to get rid of that bedroom and put the garage back. So while he tore it down, he came over to my house – me of all people to pick. He looked as white as a ghost.

I said, "Can I help you?"

He asked, "Did anybody die in this house across the street?"

And I answered, "Well actually, yes, several people did. Why do you ask?"

He said, "Well, every time I put my tools down and go to do something in this room, my tools seem to float across the room."

I said, "I know who that is, that's C.R. He doesn't want you to tear down that room. He died in that room and doesn't want it messed with. He probably thinks that's the way it's supposed to be and you're ruining it."

He just looked at me like 'what?!' But they went ahead and tore it down, and new people moved in, and to my knowledge, the new owners never said anything about a ghost. But they're moving now and so the house is going to be vacant again.

You have to be a believer in it. Because most people would say that it's just not happening. Why he came over to me, I have no idea. There were neighbors closer but he came to my house.

We once went to Danville to the Playhouse and to shop. We went to the cemetery to look around. I saw a dog running around the cemetery.

I asked my friend, "Do you see the dog?"

And they said 'no'. I tried to follow this little dog because to me it looked real. My friends kept saying, 'I don't see it'.

Lost Camper

There is a plethora of folklore and scary stories about ghost children and other creatures which, every summer, camp counselors tell to young listeners. In rural locations across America, by flickering fire and during the nighttime made creepy with muffled odd noises from the woods and stream, stories are told of dead campers, revengeful counselors, and strange things that rise up in the dark. Kentucky has many camps, from Hickman to Hindman, across the state, and as with many businesses over time, there is property now used for suburban homes where once campers played. On Lake Herrington, in Mercer County, outside Harrodsburg, there were and still are numerous camps lining the lake. One family discovered that a camp may have left one of their charges behind, and their home, built over the site, is active when they try to sleep.

Eruma (pronounced "Erma") Taylor and her husband live on Paradise Camp Road. When I was in Harrodsburg to tell stories at Old Fort Harrod State Park, I had a break after a book signing and before the evening telling. I went to Olde Towne Park on Main Street to eat the tacos I brought for dinner. This lovely park is an open-air tiny park between tall brick walls. At the back of the park is a low platform and behind the platform is a replicated section of the Kentucky River Palisades. A fountain of water flows over the tile wall, decorated with flora and fauna of the Palisades.

A man walked near me to sit and enjoy the shade. We watched swallows dip and glide in the blue sky. He was smoking and I didn't want to breathe the secondhand smoke. Despite that impediment to socialization, we started a conversation. He was intrigued when I mentioned I collect ghost stories. He called his wife to join us, and she began to tell about their haunted house.

Eruma is from the county seat of McLean County, Calhoun, which is located on the Green River and Kentucky 81. It seems that ghosts have visited her family many years ago. Her mother lived on the Green River in Jewel City. Her parents ran a ferry and lived on a hill above the river. Eruma was the seventh of eight children, seven of whom were girls. Eruma's mother reported that she saw a ball of fire come out the fireplace chimney, roll around on the floor, and whoosh back up the chimney. She wondered if their home was situated on a Native American burial mound, since there was unusual activity there. Eruma's mother said when she slept in her bed she was sometimes awakened by a popping sound from the corner of the room. She fixed her eyes on the spot for up to an hour with no further sound…until she looked away, when it happened again. Eruma noted that house is no longer there. It was torn down years ago. After living in Jewel City, her family moved to Lewisport and then to Calhoun.

Eruma and husband moved to their home on Paradise Camp Road about 2001. She said her husband was the first person to notice some strange sounds, asking her if she also heard the mystery footsteps across the upper level wooden floor. Many times her husband was downstairs in the laundry or dart room when he heard the footsteps cross above him.

"I just blew him off" Eruma said. "Until I was doing laundry one day, then I thought I heard him upstairs. I looked up there but he wasn't home. I thought that was strange."

Another most bizarre incident involved a ghost girl who may be a lost camper. Eruma related how her stepdaughter came to visit in 2006. She visited their lake house before, but this one night was different. She awoke to see a girl hovering right over her. She said she felt like she was gasping for air, and that the girl was trying to "suck the air out of her mouth". Eruma reported that she was scared so bad, she still won't return to spend the night at their home. Her stepdaughter described the girl as appearing to be about nine or ten years old, with a "Buster Brown" haircut. She thought she had brown hair with straight-across cut bangs. Something odd later happened, which could be connected to that disturbing apparition.

Eruma:

"In 2005 we remodeled the bathroom. We tore out the cabinets including a medicine cabinet. We put it away in a downstairs room. Since a friend was also remodeling, we offered for him to take away that medicine cabinet." He picked up the cabinet, but before he removed the cabinet, he showed Eruma and her husband a photo he found inside. He asked who the little girl was in the picture. Eruma and her husband had never seen the picture before, and it bore no resemblance to any family members. There was no identifying writing on the photo. But it looked very much like the girl described by her stepdaughter. The strange sequel to that story was the photo, which Eruma said she must have placed on a counter top or in a drawer, simply vanished.

The mystery of their ghostly cohabitants only deepened after they invited some investigators from Kentucky Paranormal to check out their home. Eruma said they took photographs which did not produce any anomalies, but their recordings produced a few EVPs, Electronic Voice Phenomena. They heard unexplained voices not noticed during their walk-through. In the kitchen, and outside of the kitchen over the garage, they detected activity and also recorded an unexplained female voice say, "Marilyn is a bitch".

This voice, which sounded more disgusted than angry, repeated the statement. In addition, they recorded a male voice downstairs in the garage, after they asked if there were any spirits present. The answer, only heard on playing back the tape recording, said, "We've come home."

Eruma reported that the voice sounded frightening.

Eruma is not aware of details of the history of the house and property. She said the camp used to have lots of children who swam in the pool. The pool was cemented over. Their neighbors have not offered any comments about the land or house. But things continue to happen at their home. While I talked with Eruma in the Olde Towne Park, she told me that just the night before, her daughter's friend, visiting from Virginia, received a comforting pat on the back. She overdid it at the lake with lots of sunny, outdoor time and ate lots of junk food. She had trouble getting to sleep, and when she finally gave up tossing and turning, ready to get to sleep, someone patted her back, almost as if to say "everything's gonna be okay". She turned to see her friend, Eruma's daughter, facing away from her, curled up, with no hands extended to pet her on the back!

Eruma mentioned that three months ago, a couple from Lexington came to spend the night. In the morning, the woman asked if Eruma was moving boxes around. She reported that all night long she heard the sound of boxes moving. She said it wasn't the sound of hangars scraping on the metal bar.

Eruma told her, "I don't have any boxes in that closet." One time when her husband was out deer hunting, Eruma watched a television movie, only to consistently hear footsteps on the outdoor deck.

"I heard deer and other animals on our deck. It did not sound like that it was big footsteps, like a person. I turned down the television to make sure I heard those footsteps. It would not stop interrupting my movie, so I called out, 'You need to stop that you're messing up my movie' and it stopped! I thought *that worked well.* But they seem to be friendly ghosts. They're not causing havoc."

Yet the ghosts are restless there. Did a young camper drown, to come back and try to draw life's breath from another? Who was Marilyn and why did she displease the female ghost? Perhaps Eruma will call on another set of ghost hunters to help the spirits cross over. But life goes on, for both the Taylor family…and the spirits.

Meeting House Bed and Breakfast

There are times when one wants to have a functional, quick stay in a chain motel, and there are the occasional times when one wants to stay in a Bed and Breakfast, to slow down and enjoy getting to know the people and place. Frankfort, Kentucky, has two B&B's. Gary and Rose Burke own and operate the Meeting House. The Meeting House, in Frankfort's historical district, is just blocks away from the Old Capitol Building and a short walk from the Kentucky History Center. The Meeting House is a Bed and Breakfast, Café, and gift shop.

The Meeting House is a three story brick building, brightly painted

The Meeting House Bed and Breakfast, Frankfort, Kentucky.

and pleasantly landscaped with flowers. I entered through the side, café gate, and walked along a brick outdoor patio that had round tables with umbrellas. I met Rose Burke, who was busy hanging party lights along the awning. Rose is bright, cheerful, small in stature but mighty in energy. She took me in through the long, narrow café and bar, past the gift shop, for a brief tour of the dinning rooms, bedrooms and library. The library was originally the children's room for S.I.M. Major's two daughters. Alfred Z. Boyer built the house in 1837. He was a four-term mayor of Frankfort, and hosted many learned men for regular meetings of the Lycerian Society. Talented and bright teachers came to visit, read at his extensive library and discussed topical matters. S.I.M. Major called somebody to a duel, and when his opponent didn't show, Major was put under house arrest for breaking the law by attempting to arrange a duel. After Major's wife died, he made a series of unwise business deals and lost all of his wealth. Major's son survived and married into the prominent Brown family at Liberty Hall.

Rose and Gary came from Massachusetts via northern Kentucky to live the dream of owning a B&B. Rose had a café and shop in New York but she bought and refinished antiques for their dream B&B. After buying, refurbishing and painting, 260 gallons just on the interior painting, the Burkes opened The Meeting House in March 2004 and the café one year later. There are four adjacent tenant homes built in1890.

I stayed in the second floor Commodore William S. Harris room. The full size bed was plumped with pillows and I found a pewter plate with chocolates. Two chocolates were made to look like little mice with thin almond shavings for ears. The U.S. Naval Commodore was the original landowner. Back downstairs, Rose and Gary outlined some of the Friday night possibilities with wine tasting or a short walk to the Old Capital grounds for live music. Gary joined me and we walked three blocks to hear blues and country music. The area was filled with happy families, open shops and food vendors.

Rose:

The first unusual thing we experienced in our new home, after we moved, was when we went to bed one evening in August. Gary was already asleep when all of a sudden we heard a HUGE noise. At the same time we felt a chill in the bedroom and there was a sound of a big rushing wind. It sounded like a Nor'easter!

I sat up in bed, and asked Gary, "What the heck was that?!" It sounded like a storm howling through one of the old houses back East.

I said, "There must be quit a storm brewing outside." So I walked over to pull the curtain aside and look out the window. There was not a leaf moving. This wind lasted for four of five minutes and then it was gone.

We host many special events in our house, and we're often up late, putting things away or doing the dishes. There are many times when we feel the other person walking into the room, and we turn around to talk with them – but there is no one there. I never feel alone in this house.

We have a Pomeranian named Napoleon. And before Napoleon we had another Pomeranian for 14 years. His name was Cam. And Cam loved to get away, run upstairs to the library. He liked to lie down there, and, since it was the children's nursery, we wonder if their spirits are still present. Our newer dog does something different. He will sit up, and follow something we can't see. He turns to watch something at the ceiling as it apparently goes around the room.

The previous house owner, Jewitt Sheetinger, adopted two young teenage boys. They were adopted out from the Boys Home of Kentucky. Jewitt reported that one of the boys, Lee, was apparently fond of seeing his bodily fluid cascade – not into the commode as with most folks – but sail out the third floor attic window. It was sometime later when Jewitt found a secret room in the attic which had a lamp, silver, and a great big picture which now hangs in the library. When Lee saw the picture of the original house owner S.I.M. Junior, he reported that it was the same man he saw in the attic. He confessed to Jewitt that one time, when he was up there urinating, he saw a man behind him who wore a military uniform. That was likely S.I.M. Major Junior who was the ghost in uniform. Both boys said it was a very spooky house in which to grow up.

Another man who was a guest at the old house when Jewitt owned the home came by to visit me.

When I opened the door, he asked me, "Have you seen them yet?"

I asked him back, "Have I seen who?"

And the man continued, "The girls – well I saw them and I'm not kidding you. I stayed in the Harris Room and once, when I slept, I woke up to the sound of children laughing. I opened my eyes to see two little girls at the foot of the bed – two girls who were not there. It scared the you-know-what out of me! I'm not lying!"

He swears he saw the little girls' ghosts. The history of the house says the girls died in what is now the library. Since it was the 1860's the girls could have died of anything back then.

A couple of guests stayed at our

Kentucky Country Scene.

place. They were very into the paranormal and they told us there was some presence in the house. Another woman, who is a tarot reader, said she felt the presence of some very kind young spirits. She felt they are not bothersome, very happy. Finally, she reported that there was a time of turbulence in the house. Interestingly, just six months ago I found out through a local historian that S.I.M. Major committed suicide in the house. The newspaper article euphemistically noted that "he lay himself down to die". He was likely over-whelmed by his wife's death, and the poor business decisions in which he lost his money and the house. But the house does not have a scary feeling to it.

Once when we were renovating, I was up on a ladder in the S.I.M. Major Sr. Room, and I nearly fell. I was on top a twelve-foot ladder. It was late at night and Gary was sleeping. I leaned way over to reach the wall and I lost my balance. I should have fallen and I have no idea how I regained my footing…I think somebody helped me to stay on the ladder. My husband Gary is not a believer, yet he feels there is a presence here.

It was not long after we moved in, when I went outside to take a bunch of photos. I went across the street and pointed the camera at the front door and the wing on the right side. It was afternoon and there were no lights on in the house. But when we got the pictures back, we found little circles of light in the photo. I sent copies to my cousin – he likes to study ghostly things – and he told us that ghosts can appear as orbs in pictures.

Another thing happened with picture taking and the previous owner, Jewitt. He did all kinds of renovating too, and when he finished redoing the nursery, he took a photo of the wall to show the new color. When the photos came back, there was an image of a lady on the wall. But no picture was really there of someone on the wall!

House Ghosts

Becky, Louisville

I had experiences when I felt my mother's presence. I felt her put her hand on my back, after her death, and I was always comforted by that gesture. My sister Martha told a story that happened after MaryAnn died last April. We had her funeral on Monday and Martha was supposed to leave on Wednesday for Ireland with a group of students. She stood in the room, where MaryAnn's body was, talking to a cousin. When she turned her back to the body, she then felt hands hugging her from behind. She decided then that she was sort of inviting MaryAnn to come travel with her in spirit to Ireland. When she was alive they always talked about how they had so much fun on a trip to Germany. If she could "take" her there, then she could see all the European relatives named MaryAnn. Martha knows where our family came from, and everybody looks like us.

Weeks later, while sitting in a pub in Ireland with several colleagues, Martha was by herself on one side of the table.

Suddenly Martha sat up straight and said to the two other women, "Did someone just walk by me and grab my shoulder?!"

They answered, "No".

She replied, "Then MaryAnn is here with me and I'm so glad."

She continued throughout the rest of the trip to feel that MaryAnn traveled with her.

My husband and I lived in Lexington, on North Limestone and Seventh Street, past Whitehall and past Sayre. It was on the north side of the street. I think the house was painted red. Pater and Pierce lived there first, and they had experiences in that house, and afterwards Pierce's girlfriend Anna and I also saw the ghost lady. When you walked into the house it was ground level and then there was a stairway that went up. On the second level was a hallway with a railing. We often heard footsteps racing across the wooden floors upstairs.

You could see the white, turn of the century clothing and she was looking at us as if to say,

"What are you doing in my living room!?"

That's where his bedroom was. And we could hear a scampering down the hallway. We had two other roommates.

My friend Cathy came with a Ouija board and announced, "We have got to figure out what this is all about". We got a name on the board spelled "K...A...T...I...E", and "Bagley" as in Bagley drugstore. We also got the word "Siths" and the word "Help".

Then the Ouija board just went wild and we said, "We've got to put this away!" We turned on the lights and figured we'd get out of there and head out to a bar. From that point on, whenever we heard the ghost we called her Katie. We thought we had a name for this apparition, whenever something would happen. Pierce also lived with us and he saw the ghost. She acted as if she didn't understand why we were there. It was her house and why were these people there?

Sometimes our shoes were moved so we asked, "Katie, where'd you put the shoes?" We really had conversations with her.

The homeowner, Fred, lived below us. I went downstairs and asked him what he knew about the house. I was amazed to hear the history of the family that lived there. It was given to a young couple and the woman died of an ovarian cyst.

Since Bagley's was the local apothecary, it was almost as if she said through the Ouija board, "Give me the medicine. I'm looking for the medicine."

When we saw her for the first time, the two of us were totally shocked. We had that unreal chill that happens when the entity is going right through your own physical matter, and it happened to us both. It happened one other time and made a believer of my husband Pater.

The other time that happened was over in the area where the Licking River feeds into the Ohio River. There is a place in Covington where the Underground Railroad comes up. We were just walking and talking and all of a sudden a gust of cold wind blasted through us. What a feeling!

And in our own home here in Louisville, Mr. Pierre Vinglini walks into the kitchen daily about 4:45 PM. He goes over to that corner cabinet and pops it open. It stays shut otherwise. We're certain this was his cocktail hour when he was alive. This is really amazing, because when I first moved in here, Pater did all the research on the house. We have no photographs of their family. I'm not sure what kind of job he had. His brother built this house and was the president of the German National Bank. He was a bachelor. The house was finished in 1913.

A neighbor down the street, a woman in her 70's, was born in that house. She was a little girl when the Vinglini's lived here, so she was able to tell us about their family. We have the most beautiful signature of his name down in our nasty basement. It's carved into the cellar door, and there's another of his signatures in the concrete.

We're a little confused, because it seems they had a son who died, probably of mental illness, but actually alcoholism. He never married and never left this house. My son Hans is scared all the time. But the weird thing about this house is that you can't hear people talk to you from other parts of the house. You can't yell for someone, since these walls are so solid. You have to go find them if you want them. And that's been our family rule – don't start yelling because by the time I hear you, you'll be mad at me. So please look for us.

But everyone one of us heard someone calling,

"Mom...Mom" (stretched out). I came out in the hall, upset and looked to see who called.

"What?" I said.

But then my husband replied, "I didn't call for you."

It happened to Pater, and it happened upstairs in our bathroom. We were so sure they called us, that something was wrong. But once we got out in the hall...nothing.

My husband came out to ask, "Becky, what do you want?"

And I told him, "I wasn't talking".

So there is this strange sound. It could be the ghost of their son.

The other thing is the room that appears to be a delightful children's playroom – Hans cannot be in there. The way our neighbor described the room back for the Vinglini's was that it was his bachelor pad, with a mattress on the floor. You know, don't go in there kind of thing. I don't necessarily mind it, but I can understand how it can still have his vibe.

In Jackson, Kentucky in 1989, Pater was living there and working for the Appalachian Research Fund. I took my summer break during graduate school to visit him. I went to photograph and document the Hinsley settlement, which is situated near Cumberland Gap. There was a family that lived way up on a mountain in a beautiful, park-like setting. I wanted to draw and paint their tombstones. Previously I took photographs from the East Coast area of what seemed to be orb-like configurations around the sun. They were so bright. These pictures were taken in an area where there were stories of pirate ships.

Pater lived in a little house on First Street in Jackson. It was a shack with steps going up the hill to it. I took over one of these rooms, and had an experience in that room. One day I was sitting and going through pictures, when I saw the rocking chair moving. I saw it out of the corner of my eye, and I totally froze cold.

I said to the rocking chair, "Who are you?"

And I introduced myself. Ever since I was a child, this is the way I've coped with this kind of thing – just because it makes me feel like I'm speaking to someone who is there.

So next I said, "If you're going to sit here, then I'm going to draw you!"

I did a whole series of this moving rocking chair, in the style in which I was drawing for graduate school. They were big pictures. I drew it in an abstract form where part of it was with the chair. I illustrate the feelings I get by having these experiences. That's what motivates me as an artist.

When I was a child, growing up, we said the "Now I lay me down to sleep" prayer. And we asked Jesus to let us have a peaceful night's sleep.

But I often woke up yelling for my mother, saying, "The old lady's here!"

My mother replied, "No Becky, you're dreaming".

But the old lady checked up on me. I slept in a bed next to a closed door, pushed up against an interior door. I still have the memory of her in my mind's eye; she wore a night robe. Not only was the house big enough for the family, but my aunt Mame took in two boarders to help pay the rent.

An older man, Bernie Connors, smoked cigarettes out on the porch. I think aunt Mame had a 'thing' for Bernie. She was out there with him, drinking her Southern Comfort. Now Bernie had a hard time going up and down the steps. After he died, he would still be on those stairs.

And my sister Katie walked down the stairs, feeling his ghost, and say, "I hate that!"

That house had dead people who checked on us…all the time. It was really interesting. I never felt alone.

Fred Reaves, Henderson, Kentucky

I had an experience one day in my studio across the river in Henderson. Ever since I've been there I hear things such as people walking upstairs. I didn't pay a lot of attention to it even if it was ghosts – if it is, it is. The brick building used to be a cigar factory and is over 100 years old. Henderson was a big tobacco town at one time. It's between First and Second on Main Street. At the Henderson Historical Association they all know it as a ladies dress shop called "Bones".

That day I was coming out of my studio and getting ready to go upstairs. I saw something and I question myself ever since I saw it. *Did I really, truly see that?* But I did although I have no explanation for it. On that day a form appeared, full figure, not plain and transparent, fluttering and then it was gone. The whole thing lasted four or five seconds. It was just long enough that I saw it, stopped and looked. I kept thinking *something is going to* appear. But it didn't. It was mid afternoon in the summer last year (2007). I've seen so many effects in the movie like that. It's almost cliché. But that's the only way I can describe it. It looked like a hologram. I never saw it again.

Haunted Quaker Church

There is a story related to me by my Father David Reaves, who is 84 years old.

My Dad was born in Calloway County, Kentucky. I had told him about an experience I had and I was kind of reluctant to tell him because so many times I had told people about my experiences which they pooh-poohed.

After I told him a story about seeing a ghost in my studio, he said, "Aw that's nothing."

I asked, "What do you mean?"

He said, "Let me tell you a story." And he's never been a storyteller. Up until a few years ago I never heard a war story out of him. He was in the Army's 75th Infantry in World War II fighting the Germans. They were in the Battle of the Bulge in Belgium.

He related to me a story about being in an old Quaker church.

He was double dating with a friend. So there were two guys and two gals. This was pre-my Mom. They went to an old Quaker church in Boydsville. It was always open. They went in and sat down. This town is in Graves County not far from Murray, Kentucky. This happened in the early 1940's. He said the night was really bright. The light from the full moon came into the windows. You could pretty much see everything it was so bright in there. They sat on the bench towards the back of the room. The girl that he was with was on his left. The other guy was on his right with his girlfriend right of him.

The girl that he was with elbowed him and said, "There's somebody sitting next to me!"

He leaned over and looked around. He saw an old man with a black beard. He was dressed in a black suit with a black flat-rimmed hat sitting about two spaces down the seat from her. The man looked straight ahead and made no sound. Now when they came in and sat down there was no one there. They all got up and ran out of the church. My father was the last one out. As he turned around and looked before he went out, he saw the Quaker ghost still sitting there. The ghost never made a sound.

Murder Victim in Courthouse

This story relates to my experiences in the old Vandenburg County Courthouse in downtown Evansville. It's a neat old building. A few years ago I opened up one of my businesses as a division of another company. It was called Phoenix Media. We rented, because the rent was really cheap, a huge area in the old courthouse on the main floor. You could almost call it the basement because from street level you walk down about four steps and walk inside. It was ground level. We had construction work to do. We had to build walls, tables to hold computers, work surfaces and a darkroom.

The very first experience I had happened before we moved in. A friend, me and an employee worked one day putting shelves together. We were both sitting on the floor with the screwdrivers, pliers and so forth. I was putting screws in the shelf when suddenly something blew in my face. It was a very strong wind. I even remember that it moved my hair back. It was like someone walking up to blow in your face. That was exactly the experience. It was almost something that I did not even want to mention to anyone. It was really strange.

The other guy sat across from me. A little bit later he said, "Fred."

I answered, "Yeah."

He said, "Look."

I said, "What?"

He said, "Look over there on the floor!"

The extension cord on the drill was moving, just one little section of it, across the floor. It moved about a foot and it stopped. We both sat there wondering how that happened.

Then I mentioned, "Five minutes ago something blew in my face." We started a conversation and it came out that our office had at one time been a temporary classroom for Locklear Business College across the street. They ran out of office space and rented space in the old Courthouse for classrooms. Our particular space was a mathematics classroom. The mathematics instructor who taught in there was murdered right outside our door one evening as she left class. It happened in 1974 and is the oldest unsolved murder in Evansville.

Recently they got a break in the case. A man in Texas told an acquaintance that he murdered Ann Kline. The man didn't know if it was true or not but he called the authorities to find out if it was in fact a real crime.

Some strange occurrences happened in the three-year time span that we were in that building. We got to the point that we

Vandenburg County Courthouse, Evansville, Indiana. Copyright 2008 Fred Reaves/Image One.

would talk to this spirit. One morning we came in and of our computers were unplugged and set on the floor. There was no sign of forced entry. Someone had to get them down from the tables. We were putting a support wall in with 2x4's and 4x4's to span the space. We used lag screws and lock washers and latchet wrenches to lock it down. One afternoon we got them all tightened down into the wood. We got them so tight we pulled the washers into the wood. We came in the next morning every one of the five screws was loosened. They were backed off enough that they were off the washers.

We were always getting a whiff of very sweet perfume when in the room. The scent would just come into the room.

A had a manual slide mounter to which we dropped slides in then it would close. After a period of time it would open and drop the slide into a little chute. Sometimes the slide mounter would start firing on its own. Another time it was late night into early morning. We had a deadline to meet. My partner was leaving and I said, "I've got to finish up cleaning the darkroom and put everything away. Then I'm out of here."

It was 1:30 AM. Being in the old Courthouse at that time of night was

117

pretty creepy because no one else was in there and it was a big old echoing building. I started cleaning up. There was a big stereo in the darkroom. It had already been turned off. As I just got ready to leave, the stereo kicked on full blast. There were little things that happened. Doors would always open and slam. We were on a long hallway and if anyone ran away down the hallway we would hear it because of the echo. But that was one time that really scared me.

I've been tempted to go back and ask if other tenants in the Courthouse had similar experiences. The Henderson Paranormal Society is scheduled to do an investigation at the Courthouse. I wonder if they arrest the man responsible for the murder if Ann Klein's spirit will move on. They will also investigate the below ground arched passageways. That is reputed to be haunted.

I had always been kind of a skeptic but it made a believer out of me. I have an Aunt who is psychic – she truly is. Her name is Londa Ritchey and she lives in a little town north of Phoenix, Arizona. Her son, my cousin, who is my age, had a lot of that psychic ability as well. My Aunt and Uncle lived in a house in Phoenix where she saw a woman in white walking. My Uncle was in the hospital one evening when she was in bed. She watched as the covers came back and it was like someone lay down beside her.

She came to Evansville one time and I told her about the spirit of Ann Klein.

I told her, "I'd really like for you to come down to my office in the Courthouse." But I could not talk her into it for anything. She wasn't going to go.

All three men in the room at the courthouse experienced the events at the same time. We also had individual experiences. We never saw her figure. But there were times when we felt we were not alone. But that could have been our imagination so I don't see that as real evidence. But the blowing in the face was real and I saw with my own eyes when the electrical cord moved. When we were last there at the Courthouse the former chief of police came in. The CBS TV affiliate in Evansville was doing an update on the case. So we were there when they came in.

They asked, "Do you mind if we walk around and do some film shooting?"

We said, "Go ahead."

Before they left I told them about these experiences we had. I mentioned that her ghost was here.

They said, "Shh-right!" After that I thought *why should I tell anybody else, because they won't believe me*. I almost went back one day. I got as far as the door and saw there's some kind of office there now. I changed my mind and left, thinking *they're just going to look at me like I'm crazy*. So I never went in. But one of the guys from the Paranormal Society told me that it's empty again…

I never really felt threatened. It was always a very benign presence… except for turning the radio on. That scared the crap out of me.

Disappearing Old Woman

Anonymous, Louisville, Kentucky

My husband at the time and I were driving along the roads in Whispering Hills in Louisville. It was on a Saturday sometime between noon and 1PM in the fall. As we turned a corner we saw an old lady walking toward us along the edge of the road. There wasn't a sidewalk. Since it was a narrow road I hollered for him to watch it, to make sure he didn't hit her. There was a small ditch off the road and not really anywhere else she could have run to.

As we approached her, he swerved the car a little to make sure he was clear away from her. I turned around to look back to make sure she was okay. But she wasn't there. I thought *maybe she fell down.* So we stopped the car, got out and looked for her. There were no woods for her to run off to. Also she was older, at least in her mid-seventies. She was thin with her grey hair pulled back into a bun. Although we both specifically saw her standing her we could not find her at all then. She just disappeared.

We looked at each other and said, "Oh, my gosh!"

There was no other explanation – no hill she could have fallen down – than she was a ghost! There was only a couple of trees and a little bit of brush but nothing that could have hid her from us.

Not too long after that, the reason we were up there was because my then husband worked on subdivisions in that area. He was a planner and there was a lot of construction going on. He was in constant contact with the construction crews in the area. There was a small gravesite there, nothing major. Apparently not too long after we saw the older woman some of the construction workers reported some sightings they couldn't explain. My ex-husband saw the little cemetery. It may still be there. This was off Dixie Highway to Southside Drive. It was on the street that runs by Doss High School.

That was the first time that I had something that could be considered an experience with a ghost. We just looked at each other…It was the weirdest thing we both encountered.

Invisible Lady

My oldest daughter was born three months early. Her birth weight was only two pounds and they kept her in the hospital for a hundred days. We lived in a ninety year old home on 4716 South Third Street near the intersection of Woodlawn. I spent a lot of time with her. This happened when she was about a year old.

Often as she sat by herself in the house, in the living room, I saw her waving her hand upward as if to someone who was taller, saying, "Hi!"

I would say to her, "Honey, who are you waving to? There's nobody there."

She answered, "That lady standing there."

So I said "Hi" to the invisible lady and I thought *I don't know who you are…if you're nice, we'll be nice.* But she would often greet that woman. She was too young to give a very good description although she said she had "hair like you" (long hair). Her physical abilities were delayed being so long in the hospital from birth. She was on ventilators for a long time to help her breathe and she also had feeding tubes. But her vocabulary was very good for her age. She started out in the incubator and then was moved to intensive care for a hundred days. This happened about thirteen years ago and she really doesn't remember too much about it now. They say when people have very close encounters with death they may be closer to spirits or angels. Her lungs weren't quite developed and she had surgery two days after she was born. A lung collapsed. She was on and off the ventilator. She often turned blue. She had a lot of close calls!

A girl next door liked to come over and play with my daughter. Jackie was about ten years older than my daughter. Jackie just wanted to play with a baby and sometimes she babysat for me.

When she was there and Tori started waving at the invisible lady, Jackie would say, "Stop it, just stop it! You're freaking me out!"

She'd then ask me, "Make her stop!"

Once as I drove down the Watterson Expressway with Tori in the back in her car seat. She started to look out the window and put her hands on the window.

I asked her, "Honey, what are you doing?"

She answered, "There's an angel at the window." And she started waving at her angel.

She added, "Mommy, see the angel, see the angel!" So even though I couldn't see an angel I said, "Hi!"

It's interesting when we first moved into the house on Third Street it had an old, unfinished basement, just concrete. When we started to bring in furniture I kept hearing a music box play. It was driving me crazy because I didn't know where the sound came from.

There was an old built-up chimney which was closed up with brick that went up from the basement. The tune sounded like Mary had a little lamb. So I kept thinking *what do I have in a box that might play music?* We looked into the boxes and I couldn't find anything that would play that music. *I don't know where this music is coming from.*

My Dad was downstairs so I asked him, "Am I crazy or are you also hearing this music?" He listened for a minute, saying it was faint but he heard it too. It seemed to us both that it was coming from the chimney.

My Dad said, "How in the heck could a music box get in this concrete chimney?" It drove me nuts but we only heard it the first day we moved in to our new home. The people who lived there before moved just across the street and they didn't report anything more than some odd sounds now and then.

Call to Heaven

I have aunts who live in Cleveland. My cousins and uncle still live there; my aunt passed away in this house. She died last year (2007). My cousins told me ever since they were children they saw things they couldn't explain other than to call them ghosts. My cousin had a husband named Mike who died when he was only in his forties because of a heart attack. He died two years before my aunt passed away. They were all real close. Mike was close to my Aunt. It was a shock when he passed on.

We didn't know my aunt was fighting cancer for years and years. Otherwise she was one of the healthiest persons you ever met. She didn't want to let anyone know what was going on until the last year when it was obvious something was wrong. They were doing treatments, which weren't working. They got to the point where it was inevitable that she was not going to make it. My cousins were on shifts to help out watching her to let my uncle get some rest here and there. One of my cousins is a nurse and she stopped by the house to watch my aunt from 1:00 to 5:00 AM before she went to work. That would let my uncle go to sleep.

My Uncle had set up baby monitors around the house, one in the kitchen and one of course in my aunt's room. This was in case she hollered for him if he was away in another room. This night my cousin and uncle were standing at the foot of my aunt's bed. All of a sudden they heard a voice come over the baby monitor. They couldn't understand what it said but it was a male voice. After they heard the man speak then my aunt sat up in bed and said something in response. They couldn't make out what she said either, wondering if it was the medication that made her words a bit garbled. Then she lay back down.

So my uncle determined that somebody was in the house. He looked through the whole house for someone. He went to the kitchen and everywhere and didn't find anyone. By the time he returned to my aunt's bed she was going downhill. They took her to Hospice and she died a couple of hours later.

They believe that the male voice might have been the spirit of my cousin's deceased husband Mike calling my Aunt to say, "It's okay, let go, it will be fine." So his spirit talked to her through the baby monitor.

Destiny Calls

Me and my mother were both born on April 7. When I was pregnant for just two months approaching April we of course had no intentions of having my daughter come out that early. But I was in the hospital and what I didn't know is that my cousin who was very, very sick had been admitted into the hospital. He was very anxious for my daughter to be born. He didn't have children and it would be the first baby in the immediate family for him. He had been picking out names and he was very excited for her birth.

My family didn't want to tell me that he was in the hospital because they thought it would upset me even more. They wanted to keep me calm. On her birthday, April 7, all of a sudden, about 5:00 PM the labor pains started. She was so little, only two pounds.

I asked the nurses to come in telling them, "I think I'm having labor pains."

But the nurses replied, "No, it's just gas." But gas doesn't come every five minutes!

I asked them, "Can you check it?" Well she was so far down and so small, she didn't show up very well on the monitor. Finally the doctor came in and directed the nurses, "Get her immediately to the labor room!" But they told my family to go home, that I probably wouldn't deliver to the next day. They told us I wasn't dilated enough. They thought it would be a longer process. But my Mom always delivered quickly and so it must run in the family.

Before my family got home they called from the hospital to say, "Hey, you'd better come back. She's in full labor now!"

We waited in the labor room for the intensive care doctor because my baby would be so young. Finally the doctor got there and my daughter came out very easily because she weighed only two pounds. She was born two minutes before midnight on April 7!

What I didn't find out until a day or two afterwards was that my cousin Roger who was in the hospital that week had died. He passed away at 5PM on my birthday, at the same time I went into labor.

Spirits

It may be that spirits are ghosts, and that there is no difference between the two as they define those beings that exist within the finer substance of the universe. Perhaps using the word spirit brings more of an archaic, proper or religious tone to the discussion, whereas referring to ghosts delineates souls that are sad, earthbound, lost and somehow lower on the spiritual spectrum. I tend to perceive spirits as those beings that either did not have life as a mortal on our earth, or who have fully transcended the wheel of reincarnation. So conceivably there could be animal spirits, or the spirit of the wind, or a spirit of place. And while I feel that there is a small percentage of ghosts who are dangerous or of malintent, the majority of ghost stories seem to reflect very human characteristics, from – to simply the list – fearful to loving.

In contrast, the world of spirits may involve beings never human and intentions and actions ranging from near-Angelic to sickeningly evil. And ghosts, while possessing amazing powers to know the unknown, move about objects and stay around for centuries, may not compare to the forces of spirits. One gets the impressions, with ghosts, that there is a limited time to haunt the earth, and while some ghosts win the prize for delaying it, they must eventually 'give up the ghost' and go onward to a more stable location of energetic reality.

Spirits, on the other hand, <u>come</u> from that unseen world and seem to move to the opposite direction, toward interaction with our mortal, physical sphere. Or they may simply affect us in this world as they operate in a parallel and sometimes intersecting manner. The stories that I placed under this heading of spirits all appear to indicate beings who are on a mission, whether it is positive and protective, or mischievous and destructive. Where ghosts seem to play out the unintentional drama of human emotions, spirits may be able to more directly change destiny. They are functioning under orders from some higher power. Spirits are halfway between ghosts, and the very angels of the Lord – or fallen angels of Lucifer.

Mysterious Wavy Light

I met Pat Sisson at the Paris library and also visited with her and friends in Scott County. Pat is a friendly and talented psychic. She is listed in Hans Holzer's "Directory of Psychics" and "The Yellow Pages of Psychics". Pat was born in Bourbon County, Kentucky, but lived since the early sixties in Knoxville, Tennessee.

Pat:

This is a story that my mother and father told me. In February of 1937, when I was nine months old, Mother and Daddy went to bed, but later awoke with a strange feeling. My crib was in a corner of their bedroom. They saw, over my crib, a rectangle of shimmering light. It was about four feet long by two feet wide. Daddy threw on his clothes, put me in bed with

Mother, got his gun and went out to see if someone was outside causing this light. It was a dark night when he went to investigate with his flashlight and gun. Later he laughed and said he had no idea why he took the gun. He went around the house, finding nothing. He came back in and dressed me while Mom also dressed. The light was still over the crib but started to move toward mom and me.

Next, they high-tailed up to the Levy, in Bourbon County where my grandparents owned a country grocery. This was about 9 o'clock at night. Everyone made fun of them, but especially Uncle Ray. He just laughed and asked if maybe a posse would get rid of that ole light.

It made daddy mad so he said, "I'll go back and take care of that thing myself!"

So we left. But when he got back home, the light was gone.

For a couple of weeks after that night, everyone, and especially Uncle Ray, teased daddy. Several weeks later, daddy was at the store and Uncle Ray came in with his face as white as a sheet. He just saw the wavy light in his bedroom. Again it happened about 9:00 PM. Uncle Ray said that when he and Aunt Vesta awoke to an eerie feeling, they saw the block of wavering light floating at the foot of their bed. As he stared at it, at first he thought some of the men at the store were playing a trick on him. Then he felt himself floating over the pond in the field beyond the barn in the back field. He shook himself back to reality when Aunt Vesta grabbed him. They put their clothes on, went to the store, brought several of the men back but the light disappeared. He later told daddy he was sorry and would never doubt anyone again. I don't think that particular light was seen again. I'm not sure how the light ever got to be there.

At that time we lived in a hundred-year-old house made mostly of logs. It was also the place where my dad and I each lived when we were six years old, many years apart, and we each saw a light. My dad was born and raised in the house and we lived there for several years after I was born.

When I was six years old I had scarlet fever, my bed was in the same position as my crib when the block of wavy light hovered over me and I saw the signature sign of the flower, which my guide often gives me. I did not know until years later, *that* was my guide's communication. My dad also saw the same thing when he was five years old. His bed was in the same place when he had pneumonia.

Family Spirits

It seems that some folks have a ghost connection with their family. One Lexington resident grew up with a ghost in her home. Bridget Larmour and her family moved into a haunted house when she was just four years old. The Larmours found a lovely 100-year-old house on McDowell Road in Ashland Park. An elderly unmarried woman who was named Ms. Mutrine was the mother of the previous owner. Bridget's bedroom was the room in which Ms. Mutrine died. All the family noticed that this room was always ten to fifteen degrees cooler than the rest of the house. They even hired men to run new heating ducts to that room, but there was no change in the lower temperature. When Bridget was 15, she finally saw Ms. Mutrine.

"I was just coming in from the outside porch when I looked up the stairs and saw, as plain as day, Ms. Mutrine descending the stairs. She didn't look into my eyes; she walked on right past me as if she was going for a cup of tea."

One of Bridget's girlfriends who came over to the Larmour home stated that she really didn't believe in ghosts. She demanded proof, a sign that there really was a ghost in the house. That night in the Larmour bathroom Bridget's friend was drying her hair near the sink, when she let out a loud scream. Bridget rushed in and asked what was happening. Her friend exclaimed that the water had suddenly come on by itself at both the sink and the shower.

Ms. Mutrine seemed subdued when any work or remodeling was done in the house. She did seem to always take charge of the lights in the downstairs bathroom, which is reported to still happen. One of Bridget's friends, Jennifer, who lives at Miss Mutrine's mansion, spoke out loud to the ghost and told her that she already believed and she didn't need any proof. However, Ms. Mutrine evidently decided to slide around the coat hangers in her bedroom anyway. Jennifer reports that she prefers not to stay alone at the house.

Perhaps Ms. Mutrine is simply looking for some attention and respect from her own family who is no longer living there. The Larmours were relaxing downstairs on one Mother's Day when they heard the sound of loud footsteps and the angry slamming of doors upstairs. Mr. Larmour wondered out loud who was upstairs.

Mrs. Larmour replied, "Think about it. Our one daughter is at work and the other daughter is out riding a horse. Who do you think it is?"

Mr. Larmour went upstairs and found that all the bedroom and bathroom doors were slammed shut.

He wished out loud a "Happy Mother's Day" to the restless spirit, but later the noises continued.

Ms. Mutrine was right on cue one day when one of the Bridget's family members remarked that they hadn't heard from Ms. Mutrine lately. Bridget said that there was a deep freezer nearby which had empty Tupperware and other items set on top of it. The plastic containers suddenly took flight across the room, scattering every which way. But Ms. Mutrine's ghostly activity did actually save the day one time. One evening, Bridget turned off all the downstairs lights only to discover that they were all on again. She went downstairs several times to turn them off. Ms. Mutrine had the last switch of the electricity, however. And when the Larmours discovered the next day that many of their neighbors had suffered burglary, then they were pleased that Ms. Mutrine looked out for their welfare!

Bridget's beloved and devoted father passed on into the spirit realm a few years ago. He also proved to be a helpful spirit in that same house. Bridget said that she was overwhelmed with the newfound responsibility of tracking the business transactions for the rental properties, but one night she found herself in her father's office. She had sleepwalked downstairs to his desk, where she discovered all the pertinent papers laid out, clearly showing which bill needed to be paid to which person. In fact, one time Bridget was working in a vacant house. She looked up and saw her dad in his normal work clothes standing at the doorway.

She remarked, as she had often done when he was alive and they worked together, "How's it look, Daddy?"

He replied, "Looks good, hon'."

Then he was gone, and the smell of his cigarette smoke was still in the air.

Another time Bridget woke up in her bed, realizing that she had been talking in her sleep to her father. The odd thing was that his spot where he was sitting on the bed was still warm.

Some families get all the ghosts! Bridget's mother, Eileen Larmour, once owned Georgetown's old bank building. It was an antique store called "The Vault". At one time the upstairs had served as an embalmer's business, when that service was done to return the body for a home wake. Folks sometimes drove by at night and saw a few lights on. When Mrs. Larmour arrived in the morning however, she found the lights were turned off. One possible source of a restless ghost in the old bank building could be the spirit of the bank president. George shot himself in 1930. When Eileen purchased the building, she had to sign a document assuring the sellers that she would leave the wall with George's bullet intact. The room upstairs held antique children's toys and people heard sounds coming from that room. Also, voices are often heard. Maybe those voices and some of the ghosts came with the wardrobe, which Mrs. Larmour owned, formerly owned by Shirley Mason. Ms. Mason was the subject of a book and movie, titled *Sybil*.

Four Stories of Spiritual Battle

I met Don and his wife Cora Alyce Seaman when I found a friendly B&B online for a writer's travel trip to Evansville, New Harmony and, where their Bed and Breakfast was located, Booneville, Indiana. I felt a bit tentative, not knowing the Seaman's and staying in an unfamiliar town. But we all quickly hit it off, spending many hours that night, St. Patrick's Day, 2006, sharing stories and talking about book publishing. Don and Cora Alyce many times offered their home to me, when I traveled back to Evansville, and Cora's home cooking is delightful. Don's knowledge of the Bible is helpful in understanding scriptural discussion, and his experiences of the power of prayer are revealed in these tales.

Don Seaman:

Angel of the Lord Visits

This is an event that occurred around 1974 or thereabouts. My children were all still at home, and my son, who was a young adult at the time, lived with us in our small, three-bedroom home. When he got up at 4:00 AM to go to work, he always turned the lights on in the little hallway, in the bathroom and in the den. He was faithful in turning them off, but that was just his style. One morning I awoke with a start, which is unusual for me, and glanced at the clock on my nightstand. It was 3:20 in the morning. The strange thing about this happening was the hallway was filled with light.

I noticed since it was 3:20 in the morning, that it was much too early for my son to be up. But I just lay there. Suddenly I recognized within myself that I was not in control of the situation – I was virtually immobilized. I was unable to move and this quickly came upon me. My wife was sleeping soundly in the bed besides me, but meanwhile I sensed the presence of the Lord near me, and this great, massive light moved into the bedroom. The light moved toward the foot of the bed. I found myself quietly weeping. There was no exchange of verbal communication but I knew I was in the presence of the Lord, whom I believe to be the Lord Jesus. And I felt that this was a manifestation of the Holy Spirit confirming to me not only my faith but a newfound experience that I recently had in coming to grips with the ministry of the Holy Spirit.

Then slowly but surely, the light, as a mass, moved back into the hallway, just glimmered, and was gone. I felt myself released. In fact I can remember sighing. I was able to turn my head and glance at the clock, which read 3:35. A fifteen-minute time period occurred. I just lay there basking in the afterglow of what happened to me. It was so satisfying, so confirming, and then I drifted back to sleep.

When I awakened in the morning, I found myself almost embarrassed to share this with my wife, because it was still rather staggering to my own imagination. So it was two or three days before I finally shared it with her.

She said, "Well Don, why didn't you wake me up?"

I remember clearly saying to her, "I couldn't. I wasn't in charge." I rejoice in it even to this day, which is 30 years later.

The confirmation for me was the reality of the presence of the Holy Spirit in earthly ministry in spiritual form, not in tangible body form but very personable and very, very present and ready to listen. I felt such warmth and I felt a reception. That was a great experience. It made me realize, and I still think about this, if this is what the crossing over from life to death into eternal life is all about then I welcome it. I have no fear of death. I'll do battle with the process of dying, we all do, but no apprehension about death, none whatsoever.

In John, Chapter 5, Jesus said, "He that hears my word and believes on Him that sent me has everlasting life and shall not come into condemnation, but is" – in the Greek text it says – "already passed from death into life."

So for me it was a confirmation that, it's not just that you got it, but it's got you. And I kind of like that.

Preach or Die

He is a very well known preacher. He is still living. He is older than I am. I was at a Bible conference in Kansas City where he was one of the keynote speakers. You never knew whether he was going to preach or not.

He was sometimes invited and went places and said the Spirit would not release him to preach. Now that's always disappointing. It didn't happen there but it did happen several times. What I remember him clearly saying, when he got up to preach on his chosen text, was that he was sitting in his room. This man always expected and required anybody who asked him to come speak at a conference that he didn't want to stay in anybody's home. He didn't want to have to satisfy any one family's needs. He wanted to be separate, apart, live independently. So he always required that they put him up in a hotel or motel.

He was in nice hotel in downtown Kansas City. He said he was sitting in his room, fasting and praying. He had his Bible open to a New Testament passage that he was reading. He said, in his heart of hearts, that he didn't want to deal with that passage because he knew it was so controversial. He suddenly was aware of an angelic presence over in the corner of the room.

I remember him saying, "I did glance up and saw a form. I just glanced – I wasn't willing to look very much.

But as I read this passage again, I said, "Lord, I can't preach on this because if I do, the Devil's going to kill me!"

And he said the angel of the Lord said to him, "I will kill you if you don't."

So he said, "That's why I'm speaking on this passage of Scripture tonight." Within theological circles, we might say, he preached the lights out.

Witness to Amazing Powers

When I was a small lad – I must have been six years old – right before we came to Indiana, we went to Meadville, Pennsylvania. My mother was raised in that town. We went to visit a lady who had been a schoolmate and later life-long friend of Cora. Her name was Liddy. Actually, I know now her name was Lydia from the Biblical character in the Book of Acts. I remember that her elderly mother still lived with her. I remember my mother referring to Grandma, Liddy's mother, and what had happened to her before I met her.

Liddy was diagnosed with cancer of the throat and had extreme difficulty in swallowing. She had an obstructive mass in her throat. It was diagnosed as malignant. Since they had not been able to get appropriate care to deal with that in Meadville, they went to one of the larger cities. Liddy was an evangelical Christian and my mother told me they belonged to a Lutheran church. Some of the old men at their church gathered around Liddy's mother to pray for her, laying their hands on her throat. While they were praying she started to gag and cough and literally spit up the mass. It was so large she couldn't eject it and they had to reach in and pull it from her mouth. This story impressed me because here we were in Meadville visiting Liddy and Grandma was sitting right there as living evidence that we can be healed with the power of prayer.

To be a child of God means you are a committed believer to the Lord Jesus and you are under what we call the Covenant of His Blood. God provides spiritual gifts for believers, such as perception or for various types of healings. The anointing for healing can be different amongst the believers. One person prays well for hands and for arthritis, or for hearing. I have impaired hearing and I prayed successfully with many people for those who have hearing impairments. You then <u>sense</u> in your spirit where your anointments are once you've done this healing prayer. Sometimes you just end up praying for people. Other times you are invoking the power of God because you have the freedom to do that.

It can be very disturbing to me when I walk into a room, or even get an email or talk to someone on the phone, because I sense whether or not there is the presence of the spirit of death. I'm not happy about that, but I do sense it. So it has an effect on the way I pray for people. If I sense they are in the process of dying, then I pray more for comfort, vision and reconciliation in their lives as opposed to healing.

You have the right to ask, "How do you know that?" I can't give you a logical answer. There is sometimes often an aura of death around them. One of the most regrettable things that happens is to go into a hospital room where there are three or four or five family members sitting around with someone who is seriously ill. I felt a constraint, almost spiritually handcuffed, in praying because I dealt with a bunch of folk who are there almost like vultures. They inhibit, even prohibit, the power of the spirit in praying. I prayed with them, but it's almost a courtesy prayer and I left. There is no freedom. It's regrettable. I'm almost embarrassed to say that.

Casting Out Spirits of Disease and Death

I was living in Memphis at the time. Our living room was arranged in such a way that we could counsel someone in the living room and not disturb my family sitting in the den. About 7:30 one evening my phone rang.

A voice on the phone asked, "Are you Don Seaman?"

I answered, "Yes I am".

Then he said, "What I want to know is do you feel like doing any healing tonight?"

I responded to him saying, "If you are expecting me to deal with your problems and offer healing, or proffer healing to you, then you have a real problem. But if you are asking me to intercede on your behalf and call on the Lord to exercise healing in your life then I'm willing to do that." Well, that was the end of the conversation.

He just said, "I'll see you in a little while," and he hung up.

So I called my son who lived about two miles away. He was often a silent prayer partner with me – but in agreement. I found that if one is going to get into dealing with demonic spirits it is not good to do battle alone. You don't know what kind of reaction or manifestation you're going to be getting from the person that you're praying for, but that's another story…

He arrived and my son sat on the couch beside him. I pulled away the coffee table and sat a little to his side – I'm glad I did. We began to pray for him. I learned when I pray for people for healing or deliverance, I do not close my eyes and bow my head in the traditional form. That's crazy to do that, because you don't know what kind of manifestation you're going to get. As I was praying for him he began to gag. That's not too unusual. But what was unusual was that the demonic spirits, which were not odorless by the way, started to manifest. It looked almost like a haze. But they had formed as a glob of smoke or steam ascending over the man. Some of this haze moved over to the side of the living room and went through the wall. I followed it in my sight. Meanwhile the man continued to gag and started to retch, regurgitating on my living room rug, thank you. But we stayed with him, my son and me, continuing to pray for him. I think there was some deliverance that he received that night, but not fully.

He shared with us about some things that would border on criminal activity. I wouldn't want to share that information with anyone else. And this was a man, in his thirties, who came from an extremely well-known family in the area. We left under good conditions and I cleaned up the mess. I asked my son if he had seen a physical manifestation.

He said, "Dad, I wasn't going to say anything, but yes I did."

I replied, "I can't speak for you, but this is the first time I saw a visual physical manifestation."

He added, "Yeah, me too!"

The other story involved a lady. She must currently be in her sixties and is still a functioning successful business lady in the city of Memphis. She was a member of our very large class at church. We stayed after class many times to pray with those classmates. She stayed Sunday and asked me if I would pray with her. We walked outside of the classroom and sat down on a plush bench in the hallway of the church. My wife was there. She sat down beside her while I stood over her. She told us that on Friday she was not doing well. Her first trip to a doctor led to a referral to an oncologist. The oncologist diagnosed her with cancer of the liver. He told her he couldn't see it well, since it was on the backside of the liver, but he saw a mass. He reported that it was malignant and was uncertain whether or not it would spread. He told her it didn't look good.

She said, "Don, I just want you and your wife to pray for me."

We told her, "We'd love to pray for you."

My wife began to pray for her while I was standing, extending my hand to lay on top her head very gently. I began to pray against the principality of death and destruction, against the spirit of infirmity, and against the malignant cancer itself. As I began to call it by name, rebuking those spirits and rejecting and calling it out of her, I began to smell and experience the worst stench that I could imagine smelling. I remember being in Germany in the military, on a hot day, in the early fifties just five or six years after World War II, smelling the stench of dead flesh – that was as close as I came to that smell. But this was a living woman who sat there on the bench as I prayed for her.

We finished praying. She got up, hugged and thanked me. That happened fifteen years ago and she is a full-blossomed successful businesswoman today. As far as I know, she never had any cancer treatment or therapy beyond our praying for her that day.

My wife and I left and I said to her, "Did you smell anything?"

She said, "Did I?! That was really a bad smell. I knew that couldn't be a normal body odor."

I said, "It was indeed right out of the pit of hell. It was as bad a smell as I've ever smelled."

White Horse, Foggy Night

Two stories by Lahna Harris, Clarksville, Indiana

"Billy" and I met the summer following my graduation from Clarksville High School. The girls from Clarksville seemed to have a fascination with boys from New Albany High School, a neighboring city. My three best friends and I cruised the Ranch House drive-in restaurant in Clarksville for a couple of weeks at the beginning of that summer. Then we decided to cruise Jerry's in New Albany. We liked it, as it was more exciting. There were a lot more people there, and a *lot* more flirting going on, seemingly non-stop.

After cruising round and round for a while, we pulled in and ordered our sodas and fries. Sometimes we got brave enough to let one or two boys from another car get in our car and talk – well, flirt.

One magical night, the four of us were parked next to a car full of boys from New Albany. We saw a few of them before, and felt comfortable as we talked back and forth from car to car, joking, laughing. We never saw one of the boys before and it was Billy. He and I didn't seem to see or hear anyone else that night. He got out of the car, walked over by my window, and we connected. At age eighteen, it was easy to have an instant crush on him. When my friends and I left Jerry's that night, all I could do was talk about Billy. Pammy, Jan and Holly made fun of me and told me I fell for boys too fast. I hoped I would see him again.

A few nights went by, and we didn't see Billy with any of the New Albany boys at Jerry's. Then one night, he showed up, this time apparently driving his own car. He and I spotted each other in the circle of cars that were cruising. He stopped the flow of the merry-go-round movement by getting out of his car, walking over to my car, and asking me out. As demure as I had been with advances in the past, I immediately accepted. My friends didn't think I should go out with someone who I had only met once before. But I turned my car over to Jan and went riding around with him.

By late summer, Billy and I were parking and necking. He had a knack of finding remote places to park. One night, he drove for much longer than usual. We were on several dark country roads. I liked driving along dark country roads, and asked him if he was treating me to one of my favorite things. He explained that there was a spot to park that was completely isolated, where we wouldn't be bothered, except for one thing that I might not like. He explained that one of his friends had found a place, nestled alongside the back side of a crop field, and had a frightening experience. I asked about it, and began to feel uneasy. He said he didn't know the details, only that his friend said he would never go anywhere near there again.

Billy finally found the spot and pulled in. We were surrounded by what appeared to be hundreds of cornstalks that stretched for miles. It was difficult to see out the car window by this time, as it was beginning to get foggy. And it was *soooo* dark. I told Billy I was afraid, and he tried to ease my mind. I wanted to go somewhere else. He coaxed me to stay despite my feeling of foreboding.

My mind wandered away from fear for a few moments as Billy began to kiss me. I returned his affection, and after a few moments we were necking. During one long kiss, our passion was suddenly interrupted and turned to sheer terror. The car was shaken, and there was a thumping noise near both back windows and the rear of the car. I don't how Billy got into the driver's seat and started the car as fast as he did, but it didn't take long at all for the car's wheels to be spinning in reverse and back out on the country road. It was a blur, both because of the speed in which Billy got us out of there, and because of the fog. I saw what appeared to be three figures, though. Neither Billy nor I heard any voices.

I thanked God out loud that we got away from there. Then we began the long, slow, tedious drive through the fog, back to the city. We were both still scared, wondering if whoever was back there would catch up with us. We wouldn't be able to easily see them because the fog was so dense. At one point, we felt confident that we had escaped, but then we struggled to stay on the road, to see anything at all in front of us. I helped to navigate by telling Billy if and when I saw either side of the road.

I wondered out loud if Billy had planned the scene in the cornfield as a big practical joke on me. He looked at me in astonishment and asked if I thought he could have faked that kind of fear. That made sense to me. We talked openly about how scared we both still were, as we crept along in

the oppressive fog. We didn't know if we could make it any farther; it was becoming impossible to see anything at all.

We decided that we would be very lucky if we made it back home that night. My heart was racing with anxiety, and I began to pray silently. Then, the most incredible thing happened. Billy stepped on the brakes as we both saw a large, stunningly beautiful white horse appear just yards from the front of the car, and in the middle of the road that we could now see.

Billy was so shocked, he uttered some expletives, and I just said, "Do you see what I see?" The horse was standing sideways on the road, turned and looked directly at us, then disappeared as suddenly as it appeared. We looked at each other in complete disbelief. We confirmed with each other about what we saw, and we sighed what seemed to be a hundred sighs of relief. Billy drove on, with both us then able to see the road all the way back to town.

Deceased Resident Still Calls "Yoo-Hoo"

One of our residents, Helen, passed away a couple months ago. During her last six months with us when she was physically declining, she began a new habit of saying "Yoo-hoo!" each time any staff member walked past her door. She always sat at her doorway between meals and activities to smile and greet others as they walked. But then she became too weak to tolerate much activity and stopped sitting at her door. The staff found her "Yoo-hoo's" to be as endearing as all the other characteristics we had grown to know and love about Helen.

One day recently, I was late for work. Normally I am very punctual, so I was intent on getting to my job as quickly as possible. When I arrived, I hurriedly entered the health care facility. As I was rushing down the halls, nodding with acknowledgment toward many people on the path toward the office, I suddenly heard Helen saying, "Yoo-hoo!"

It stopped me in my tracks, and then I realized I had just walked past her room. I turned around and went to her door. No one was in the room at all. I know that the "energy of Helen's voice" could have still been in that space. I choose to believe that she was visiting that day. Helen and I had a close bond that began when I stayed very late on New Year's Eve a few days after she arrived to live in our facility. She had no family and needed help settling in. When it became evident she was uncomfortable with her room, a nurse and I literally moved her things to another room, which she made her home. She really liked it there. Who knows, maybe she is still staying with us.

Visions and Spirits

"Donna" grew up in Evansville, Indiana. She dealt with some significant family issues by drawing and painting, and finding a refuge at school. She is now happily married with two children. I met Donna at the Barnes and Noble in Evansville, where I had a book signing and Donna was exhibiting her work with other artists. When the group of artists heard about my book of ghost stories, it turned out that a number of them had ghost stories of their own to share.

Donna:

I have many dreams that are premonitions of things to happen. When I have them as dreams they were almost always bad. As a child, I dreamt my grandpa had a heart attack. I saw him in a strange hospital room, hooked up to weird beeping machines. The room wasn't really a room, but just white curtains hanging that the nurses would pull back. The next evening we traveled to Kentucky, to a hospital emergency room, the exact same strange room and machines I saw my grandpa hooked up to the night before in my dream. He had a heart attack. I remember telling my aunts in the waiting room that I saw this exact event and place in my dream the night before, and they believed me, which I thought was pretty cool.

My first marriage was not a happy one at all because we were way too young. But I dreamt about the woman with which my husband had an affair. He denied the affair until I described the photos that I had seen in my dream. I described the woman and what he and she were doing in the photos, apparently exactly as they really happened. He and his buddy's faces turned ghostly white and they looked at me like I was a freak. They told me they had thrown those pictures away days before I arrived to collect my belongings. My husband then told me about the woman he was having a relationship with and her other friend in the pictures that I knew about from my dream.

Two years ago I had a dream with no visual part at all, only my own voice saying, "Daddy's dying....he's dead."

I knew that he was going to die soon, even though this dream was different from my usual premonitions, which are usually just like watching a video or seeing still life pictures. A few days later I got a call from my father saying he had cancer. I knew the exact day he would die, but I didn't mention it. I don't know how or why I knew, I just did. He passed away a couple months later on that exact date.

I had difficulties with my mother and father. I grew up in a very abusive household and suffer from Post Traumatic Stress Disorder. While going through counseling, I needed to take a break from my mother, just to try and heal myself. I dreamt that my mother came to my house in a yellow cab and caused a huge scene. The morning after the dream I told my neighbor and friend about the dream as we walked our kids to the bus stop.

I played it off saying to her, "If you see a cab pull up today, run!"

She knows my family history well, and telling her the dream helped relieve some stress. Later that afternoon, shortly after the kids got home from school, I received a call from my next-door neighbor. She told me to close my front door because a cab just pulled up to her house, mistaking it for mine. Sure enough, it was my mother, and a scene ensued.

My premonitions when awake are much fewer. I get a very strange feeling of panic come over me, like the feeling one gets when they almost fall off a ladder, but catch themselves, and then I get a flash of information very shortly after it happens. This type is rare, and dreams like those above are much more common. I never have any control over when my premonitions happen, although I wish I did.

I know this story sounds creepy and crazy, but I swear it's true. As a teenager I had a friend who dabbled in Satanism. He was convinced that his soul was lost and there was no hope. After an evening of talking to him and telling him God was unconditional love and he could always take that love back into his life, I felt like he had heard me, and we both went home.

As I lay in bed half asleep, I felt hot breath on my ear and heard a voice that I can only describe as pure hatred and anger, say into my ear only one word, "Donna".

I jumped up and turned on the lights and started praying, I've never heard that voice again, but it made an impression on me. I truly do not understand the evil and hatred I experienced in that voice. I don't understand why someone or something could choose to embrace that type of energy. But I know that both love and evil really exist. I'm not a religious person, but I am very spiritual. My experiences have been so consistent and real to me that I know God exists, however people choose to define him or her.

I remember always having a sense that I wasn't always alone. I've still never seen a spirit, but I've heard them. The first time was at the house in which my second husband and I first lived. The floor plan was laid out so that one could walk around the entire house in a square path. Our bedroom had two doors on opposite walls, one that opened into the kitchen and the other into the hallway. We usually slept with the doors closed and one evening we were awakened by footsteps. It is so cliché, but it really happened. I was so glad to have my husband there, too, so he wouldn't think I was crazy. The footsteps paced around the house from one of our bedroom doors to the other, but never inside. I remember being startled at first, thinking someone was in the house, but there was no one there. We heard it again on several occasions, and just grew used to it. My husband even checked under the house to make sure there were no animals hiding there that could have made some noise. But he found nothing, and the sounds were definitely footsteps. We just grasped for a logical answer. He claims he never heard anything before I moved in with him.

We moved to a new house shortly after our first son was born, and we had experiences there too. One night I awoke to music, like a lullaby, coming from our son's room. I woke up my husband and asked him if he heard it, too.

He answered, "Yes, what's the big deal?"

He seemed annoyed that I woke him. I told him that there was nothing in the baby's room that played music, and I jumped out of bed and started into the hallway towards the baby's room, but hesitated as I heard the music coming from his room even louder now that our bedroom door was open. I walked ten feet or so down the hall to his room and as soon as I entered, the music stopped.

My son was safe and sound, asleep in his crib. I felt incredibly angry that whatever made the sound was in my son's room. I know it's stupid, that a ghost or angel or whatever it was, played soothing music. And it hardly seems threatening, but I couldn't help feeling incredibly protective of my son, and yelled out loud for them to leave him alone. Occasionally, in that same house I would hear the sound of bells ringing, from inside the house. I don't recall ever feeling threatened by the sound, it was actually pretty, different from chimes, but cheerful nonetheless. We had the house blessed just to be safe, but nothing troubling ever happened, and there were no footsteps.

We moved again to our present house, and we both experienced things here. The two most striking things happened were when my husband heard his deceased father call out his name from a few feet behind him. The other is when I was sitting by the piano late at night tapping out some tunes, quietly as I could. I felt a person sit down on the bench right next to me. It startled me as I wasn't expecting it. I wished for it to leave and it did. I got the distinct feeling that it was a woman, and was surprised that I noticed her.

Bright Light Figures

I met the Cassedy family, parents and six of their seven children, in fall of 1999. I traveled to their rural home where they have an organic farm and a bakery. The Cassedy's named their driveway Catwalk Road – an appropriate designation with fourteen cats. Their land of rolling hills was once the property of Squire Boone. Carol's husband Linn works as an industrial water treatment specialist, and both parents were busy for many years home schooling their children. I enjoyed interviewing Carol and finding out more about her organic business, Whitestone Bakery. Later, when I mentioned that I collected ghost stories, Carol confided in her one unusual experience. Some stories of spirits can be more powerful that other stories simply due to their mystery.

In October of 1996, Carol Cassedy was attending to her mulched crop of tomatoes and eggplants, setting up the drip irrigation. It was dark outside and she saw something very strange.

Carol:

I saw two vertical and bright – brilliant – lights walking across the field toward the pond. The lights were not from road traffic; it was the wrong angle to be that kind of light. We have a nearby pond on the ridge and from where I was I could look down on that area. It was totally dark out otherwise. I just felt there was something there and looked to see two tall figures. They were two columns of bright white light. The light was so luminescent it was startling. They just walked across the land, and I thought *what in the world is that?* I just couldn't move – paralyzed. I was too far from the house to run back or call someone, and at that time we didn't have a dog. In a matter of seconds they were gone.

I had no clue, absolutely no idea what I saw that night. There was no sound, no rustling noise of feet on the leaves. They looked to be about eight feet tall. I just froze on the spot, thinking *what in the world are those things?* I can guarantee you they were not fireflies or swamp gas! I'm outside all the time, and since that event I have not seen that kind of thing again. One of our neighbors told us that there is an Indian burial mound out there, but I have no way of confirming that information.

Gary Renard wrote, in *Disappearance of the Universe*, of seeing his wife in a similar fashion, as a vertical column of light. Perhaps what Carol glimpsed was something approaching true vision, and what we see of mundane, denser reality is really the illusion.

My Haunted Cabin
Judy Mullins

People are intrigued with the idea of staying in a primitive log cabin. A few folks who stay at the 1850's Mullins Log Cabin might have an interesting encounter with the spirit of the Cabin.

Judy explained how she came to acquire the old log cabin.

Judy:

I was at the country store in Cordova in 1991 and overheard the storekeeper asking a gentleman what he had been doing.

He said, "I've been trying to get that old log cabin torn down. If someone doesn't come and get it then I'm going to burn it."

His daughter wanted to put a trailer in the spot where the cabin sat.

So, when he said that, I spoke up, and said, "Bill, please don't burn the cabin, I'll be right over."

It sounded as if I could just pick it up, and carry it back to my farm. The process actually took all summer of 1991. My youngest son, who was 14 at the time, and Bill's son, worked on the cabin in the late evenings when the sun wasn't so hot. 1991 was a very hot summer. Bill told me to sit down and sketch out the cabin before it was dismantled.

I told him, "I can't draw!"

He said, "Well you can draw a straight line, can't you?"

So I sketched the number of logs and where the windows and doors were. Then I took pictures of each side. We numbered each log and made that notation on the drawing. My son and Bill's son climbed on top of the structure, and used crowbars to raise the logs up, one by one and dropped them over on the ground. Jarrod then loaded them on a wagon and hauled the logs to the current location. It took several loads before the job was complete. We also got the rocks from the chimney.

I then advertised in the paper to have someone put the cabin back up. I received a reply, and the guy started in November of 1991. It was completed in 1992, with several other people helping with the roofing and other work. I put the chinking between the logs myself, just to save money, using clay

that I dug up with a mix-
ture of cement. My niece
drove nails in the logs in
order to have something
for the chinking to adhere
to. When the log man got
up past eye level, he was in
trouble. He didn't know
how to get logs up higher,
and had to then admit
that he had only put new
cabins together. My hus-
band had a friend who
had a wrecker. He came
with the wrecker boom,
and lifted the logs on up
before the roof could be
put on.

The Mullins Cabin, Grant County, Kentucky.

When I first acquired
the logs, my thoughts were
to use the cabin as a work-
shop for my basket weaving and chair caning hobbies and workshops. Then,
someone suggested that it would be a good place for city folks to come out
and spend the night. I placed an ad in a Northern Kentucky paper, a couple
of newspapers ran stories as well, and as they say, the rest is history.

Thomas:

The Mullins Cabin is a pretty one-room historic home and moved
just a few miles from its previous owner. There is a loft with a cozy bed for
two and more sleeping room on the floor level with a sofa bed for two. The
original stones for the fireplace were moved and rebuilt. The logs were in
good shape since they had been covered by sideboard for many decades.

The Mullins Cabin has a front porch and is located off a pretty little
creek. Hills rise behind the cabin to the south and other farmhouses are not
far away. But the feeling is very expansive, rural and peaceful. I stayed a few
nights at the Mullins Cabin. During the day I hiked the hills, walked along
the historic rock fences and gazed at incredible starry night views. The cabin
is electricity-free and if the weather is cold you can light the wood in the
fireplace. They have a back up kerosene heater too.

I enjoyed the rustic ambiance with wood fire, candles and oil lamps.
I read poetry and imagined life full-time without television, phones and
computers. Hawks screeched nearby and the downtime was indulgent and
pleasant. The Mullins Cabin sits on six acres and walnut and other trees
shade the creek.

Judy visited me when I stayed at the cabin and told me some ghost
stories from that same cabin.

Judy:

This cabin is approximately 18 miles west of Cynthiana where three Civil War battles were fought. My mother was a schoolteacher and she taught in a one-room schoolhouse near here. This was before she was married. She boarded with this old lady who could remember the Civil War. This cabin was originally located in the same community where this old lady lived. The cabin was moved here from about a mile or so up the road.

The older woman remembered the soldiers stopping by asking for food and probably to get horses, too. I don't have any of this actually documented, but I know those soldiers didn't stop at just one house in this area.

A lot of things happened in and around the cabin over the years since I had it. I acquired the cabin in 1991 and the first overnight guest stayed in July of 1992. One odd thing that has repeatedly happened is that people have been pinched. Four people that I know of have been pinched. I'm sure there are a lot of others this happened to but they don't tell me about it.

I was one of the persons who was pinched. I stood across the creek from the cabin. This was where there were weeds growing up by the hammock. There were two stones that looked like they could be a rough pair of headstone and footstone for a grave. As I looked at the stones on the hillside on the south side of the creek I wondered *maybe some of these could be pioneer graves*. I thought *I wonder if people really are buried here.* All of a sudden something **pinched me** under the arm.

It was so hard that I exclaimed "Ow!"

I actually thought someone had come up behind me to play a joke. But I quickly turned around to find there was no one there.

I won't mention the names of the others who were pinched. Both are relatives of mine. We were sitting in the cabin one night. I had a table over by the downstairs west wall.

As we sat talking one person suddenly said, "Oh, quit **pinching** me!"

The other person answered with a question, "How could I be pinching you? My hands are here resting on the table. I did not pinch you!"

So I assume the spirit in this cabin had pinched her on the leg.

We had another lady who spent the night two or three different times. She was once outside on the west side of the cabin and something pinched her.

I believe it was September (2008) when the Commonwealth Paranormal group came here to investigate. The two men brought a lot of instruments to measure paranormal activity. They got some visual images on their infrared digital video camera. One man sat toward the center of the room with the other near the front door.

Suddenly one of them said aloud, "Something just pinched me on the arm!"

The investigators felt like there was more than one ghost present in the cabin. One man named Chris noted electromagnetic activity which seemed telling since the cabin has no electricity. He said his EMF meter gave the highest reading about midway up the steps. They took photos with some unique equipment and they will return this spring (2009) with additional investigators from their group.

They got some EVPs voice recordings where some man said, "Remember Derek – remember Derek." And then the voice said something about "wound." So I wondered if a Civil War soldier was here in the cabin and had a wound. To me all that is proof enough but they look for collaborating evidence.

I once came down to the cabin with a friend and we heard something that seemed to come from the cabin rafters.

We heard a high-pitched female voice who sounded like she was just running through the notes of a scale, "Oooo". We both heard the same sound. We called it the angelic voice. We had no radio and there was nobody else around.

One time four ladies came from Frankfort to stay overnight. One of the ladies passed away this summer (2008). There were two sisters and two first cousins. Since they were raised in a log cabin, this was like coming home to them. They usually came in the spring and fall. They cooked complete meals using the fireplace and heater.

As two of the ladies were sitting on the front porch, they gazed inside the cabin, and saw a strange thing happen to the paper bag, which was lying on the hearth.

They were shocked to see the paper bag begin to dance all about the hearth. Since they had snacks in the bag they figured a mouse got into it. They were pretty scared until one of them got up the nerve to have a look. She found no mouse in the bag. But it had been dancing all over the hearth!

I don't know if the previous owner had ghostly activity happen in the cabin. He has passed away. As it turns out this man who owned the property where the cabin used to sit, his wife, who died before I was born, was a third cousin to me. But I didn't know that when I first got the cabin. A couple of weeks ago a woman called to say that she was born in this cabin. She told me that her grandfather bought the cabin. She said when she was growing up it had three rooms and she didn't know it was a log cabin as there were exterior boards which covered the logs.

This land was previously in my family for several generations. In 1973 my husband and I bought it back. I believe it was my great-great grandfather's land. My grandfather was William Gill and his father was J.C. Gill. His father was also named John. I've been told that the type of stone fence which is in front, and runs along the road, was built in the 1850s. It runs along to the town of Berry.

Spirits Visited Me

There are four times when I've seen spirits. These were not connected with the cabin.

This happened in the house I was born in about a mile or so from here. It was built in the 1930s. My daughter was about eleven years old. She was a cheerleader from middle school to high school. She was often in the middle of the floor doing her cheers. As I sat on the couch and she stood by the door, I noticed a reflection from another room shining on the front porch.

"Janessa, there is a lady coming up to the door." I saw someone coming up sideways to the house and I thought *why isn't she coming up the steps?*

She was sort of **gliding up** diagonally.

I said, "Janessa open up the door. Somebody's at the door."

She opened up the door and found nobody there. I walked out the door and walked **all the way around** the house. Nobody was there. She had looked like an older lady wearing a black sweater and a white scarf. I don't know what the purpose was of her visit. All I know is this lady could not have run away that fast. It had to be a spirit.

For several nights after that I was scared to sit up at night by myself. That was my very first experience with something like that. It was a couple of years later when the next odd thing happened.

In the very same house, I was talking on the phone around midnight. All of a sudden a little girl appeared in the kitchen. She had her hair done in ringlets and was maybe five or six years old. Her hair was brown and she had piercing blue eyes. She was wearing a pinafore and a long dress. So the clothing style looked like the late 1800s or up to the turn of the century. She just slowly turned around, looked at me and she was gone!

I have an area on this farm I call the enchanted forest because it just has an enchanted feeling about it. There are some old rock fences down that way, too. As we walked through the woods my friend and I looked up toward the hill.

I said, "Do you see what I see?"

He repeated my question back to me as he saw something, too. We both saw a Native American chief with a long headdress on a white horse. We saw him on top the hill as we looked up from our little valley. We looked at him for maybe a minute until the Indian just faded away.

My nephew used to live in a house in Corinth, Kentucky, which everyone called "The haunted house." There was always something going on in that place. I came to visit him one night. The house had a bay window and he sat with his back to the window.

As I stood on the floor telling him, "Well, I've got to go" I saw a young man's face looking in from the window. My nephew had a distant relative staying with him. I thought it was his face.

I said, "Okay Leroy, quit playing games!"

My nephew said, "Judy what are you talking about?"

I answered, "Leroy's out there peeping in the window."

He said, "Think about it. How could Leroy be out there peeping in the window when that window is fifteen feet to the ground?"

Well, I don't what I was thinking but when I left and we walked through the kitchen there was Leroy. We saw no ladder out there and Leroy wouldn't have had time to run around the house and come back in to the kitchen. My nephew more than once saw a lady spirit in that house. She was wearing a white gown.

I often wondered about the name of the road on which our cabin is located, Scaffold Lick Road. Was the name from the old days when the Indians burned their dead on a wooden scaffold or did it refer to a hanging scaffold? I have no idea how the name came to be. Of course a lot of local roads are named after the families who lived here. But I don't think anyone was named Scaffold.

Across the creek there were what looked to be Indian mounds. So I asked a professor, Dr. Clay, from the University of Kentucky to come out and look at them. He doubted if they were burial mounds because he told me the Indians usually put vertical rocks around the edge of the graves. I have found arrowheads made of flint by the creek. I have always heard that a spirit has to have energy from some source so they can make themselves known. I am a water dowser, and there are underground streams under the cabin. One stream comes from the corner of the cabin underneath. My dad was a dowser as well. He could tell folks how deep a stream was. Unfortunately, I never acquired that skill.

Protective Family Spirit
Claudia Thurman, Sonora, Kentucky

The history of the Thurman-Phillips Guest Home in Sonora, Kentucky, dates back to William Phillips who had eight sons and relocated from The Hermitage, near Nashville, Tennessee, to Hardin County in 1820. The Phillips established and prospered local farming and businesses. William Phillip's grandson – Josiah Phillips, Jr. – built the two-story Victorian home

1897 Thurman-Phillips Historic Guest Home, Sonora, Kentucky.

in 1897 with some 200,000 handmade bricks. The home stood vacant after 1968. Over three decades later, undamaged by storms and not vandalized, Charlie and Claudia Thurman hired renovator Tony Vance to restore the family home. The 11-month long restoration commenced in 2003 and in December 2003 the Thurman's welcomed guests to both the historic home and later to the Tea Room next door.

The Thurman-Phillips Historic Home is listed on the National Historic Register. Renovators found a unique foundation with a 1/8-inch thick sheet of glass by 16 inches wide. The glass foundation deters both insects and moisture migration. The home amazingly has 90% of its original furnishings, family Bible, sales ledgers, the original parlor furniture (now a downstairs bedroom) and an iron and brass bed that has been in the family for a century and a half. The ceilings soar to ten feet high and the original dining room was converted into a very comfy den. The den has shelves with the ancestors' 150-year-old books. The home even has original paintings by the daughters of Josiah Phillips, Jr. The interior brick walls are three-bricks thick.

There is a wonderful old-time feeling in the Thurman-Phillips home. I spent a night there in early 2008 and got to know owners Charlie and Claudia. Perhaps the best one can hope for in the world of ghosts and spirits is to have the spirit of an ancestor still around as a protective presence. In this story the spirit of Josiah spoke and played with Claudia's grandson, ninety years after he passed away.

I experience spirits usually not through seeing but rather feeling them around. I felt warmth or a density, which comes into a room. When we were getting this home ready to give it its personality, I worked until very late at night. At four o'clock in the morning I knew, I just <u>knew,</u> I had helpers. Tony the restorer said that too. They drilled little holes in the wood. The tools they laid beside the hole would be gone; they were moved. We think that the spirits here thought the workers were being destructive. That was Tony's experience. I didn't have any reason to question him.

Then my seven-year old grandson visited us here. He knew absolutely nothing about my husband Charlie's family. He told his Dad that in the night an old man woke him up. The man had white hair. Our grandson asked the old man his name.

He said he didn't tell him his name but instead he said, "I like your hair."

The only thing we could figure is that there were no red-haired people in Charlie's family. And Garrett has beautiful, thick deep red hair. That's the only logic we can put behind the old fellow's comment to Garrett.

When Charlie asked Garrett to describe the man, he told him he had a short-sleeve shirt, wore a vest, a mustache and had white hair. The fellows in that period wore short-sleeve shirts and a vest. It was not uncommon. But for this little fellow to know that was validating. So we have a picture of Josiah and this family sitting on the front porch in 1915. We got the picture and put it in front of Garrett.

We asked him, "Is the fellow you saw in this picture?"

Josiah Phillips, Jr. (far left) with family in 1915, Sonora, Kentucky.

He pointed right to Josiah Phillips.

And in the following few days, he said, "I just saw that old fellow. I saw him going up the stairs and I tried to follow him. But he ran away."

Garrett said he'd play tag with him. Garrett was never for a second frightened. Josiah was a protective spirit for as long as this house was vacant. There was no vandalism. Nothing was stolen.

His father, Steven, my son, has since divorced, but when his parents were still married they lived across the street from a cemetery.

Steven commented, "That all makes sense! He used to come in our room and say, 'I can't sleep in my room because the dead people want to talk to me.'"

Steven thought it was just his way of saying, "I want to stay up." Many a night he slept on the couch. He didn't particularly want to sleep in Steven and his wife's bed. He just didn't want to be awakened. And Steven couldn't figure that out.

Cross Image in the Mirror

The bedroom in the front of the historic home was the Phillips' parlor. So it has a more ornate fireplace. The first time we noticed the cross in the mirror is when we came home and took pictures before the restoration began. The cross shows up as two intersecting bands of light.

When we got the pictures back I said, "Look Charlie, there's a cross in there!"

Mirror with Mystery Lines.

A month later we came back and the mirror wasn't above the fireplace but leaning against the wall on the floor of the library. From that photo a triangle shows up in the mirror. We thought maybe that represented the Trinity. Then when a lady did a news article on our home, she took a picture – I don't know if she even knew it or we made her aware of it – in the picture in the newspaper the cross showed up again. So now people will stand at different angles to take the picture to see if the cross will really show up for them.

Healer's Story

I'm a Reiki Teacher and Master. Toni, one of our patients, came to our New Orleans Health Center. After her initial visit with our doctor, her friend Denise came to me and said, "The doctor said that you were a spiritual guru and you could help my friend with her Crohn's disease."

I thought, *Oh my Lord, I love titles, but that's pretty gigantic.*

I said, "Well, I'll have a session with you. The only thing we can do is be willing."

Her partner spoke for her because she had a stroke. She had been a hypnotherapist. I can't recall what all else she did but at one point she was suicidal. That's before they were introduced to Reiki and Healing Touch.

When I had my first session with Toni, a God-awful smell came out. Oh, I don't have the words for it. It was awful, awful, and awful. I had a session with her each week. She wasn't about to give that up.

She's in Washington, DC now. She has a practice. Her partner is a radiologist. I mean, it's just amazing how the spirit heals us when we are ready and ask.

Finished With Cancer

I was in the advanced stages of cancer. They started me on chemotherapy the week after I got the news. There were some pretty harsh chemotherapy treatments to shrink the tumors. The following June, on the 19th, I went for my mastectomy. My lymph nodes were positive, so that meant not only more chemotherapy but also radiation treatments. I had 36 treatments, with one chemo a week and radiation on the other days.

We finished the radiation and I asked the doctor, "How many more chemo's am I going to have?"

"I don't know, I venture one a week for a year." He answered. And I thought, *Oh man, they're not a bit of fun.*

I had heard a little voice when I first felt the lump. I had back surgery in October, prior to being told about the cancer in February. They gave me physical therapy, intense exercises to strengthen my stomach and back. I lost a clothes size. So I bought a new bra. When I took it off, I had a sore spot. I thought *I wonder what that's all about.* Like a bobo I touched it to feel it and *oooh, it felt like sand.*

And this voice said, "See about that." After Dr. M. told me his speculation about the treatment, my husband Charlie and I were driving to Elizabethtown.

The voice said, "You're finished with cancer treatments." I repeated that to Charlie and he almost ran off the road.

He said, "Claudia, I'm telling you, you need to be prepared now. The doctor shoots pretty straight with you so you need to follow his advice."

And I thought *well okay now.* So they gave me a two week break and it was time to go see Dr. M. It was on a Wednesday at 2:30. I felt so much at the mercy of the doctors. I went into the sitting room and sat on the couch.

I lifted my voice to God and to Megan – my granddaughter who passed away. They called me CG because when I became a Grandmother I was quite the bachelorette and I didn't want to hear that granny stuff. You don't tell that on the dance floor. So I didn't have a name. Korey was about a year old and he came in and said, "Hey CG." Those were my initials in the phone book. I was a Greenwell.

I said, "Megan, would you tell the doctor that CG is finished with her cancer and she doesn't need any more treatments."

Charlie was sitting to the left of me holding my hand. Dr. M. came in and sat on the treatment table looking down at us, looking at my chart which was an inch and half thick.

He went through my chart page, by page, by page then looked up and said, "You're finished with treatments."

I thought, *Charlie you say a word and I will stomp on your foot.* Charlie just squeezed my hand.

Turn Around

Normandi Ellis:

This first story is from a trip to Egypt. We went to a market to shop, and one woman was particularly attached to an image of Sekhmet, who is the lion goddess of healing and of pestilence. In many of the temples Sekhmet appears as one of the guardians. She's also a healer and appears in a room at Edfu that is considered the perfumery, but it's probably something akin to where aromatherapy took place.

A woman I was traveling with was really attached to the Sekhmet statue.

She saw it on the shelf in the Luxor market and said, "I want that statue. That statue belongs to me."

Sekhmet is also equated with the will, the energy that comes out of the solar plexus and…umph! She was a woman who did not normally have much power in her life. The merchant named an exorbitant price, totally outrageous. So, as everyone should, she began to bargain with him. She bargained to what she thought was a reasonable, even slightly higher price. He wasn't going to give it to her –

"No!" He told her to go away.

And she said, "Don't you understand, she talked to me, she spoke to me? She said she's my statue."

And the guy said, "Get out of here!"

At that time, the shelf behind him, with the statue on it, broke, and all the stuff came down.

He picked it up and handed it to her and said, "Just get out here, just go."

She got that statue for free. That was kind of unusual.

Egypt is an amazing place. I think of it as a hallowed ground. When you go into a church at night, and it's really quiet, and there's nobody there, and you can just feel the presence of God. It's just there! It's so overwhelmingly powerful. All of our feelings of a divine, spiritual nature were pulled together in this one spot, and it created energy around it. I think that Egypt has consistently been a place where pilgrimages are made. Here humans spent 3,000 years paying attention to the question, "Where is the divinity in my life?"

To an ancient Egyptian, God is nature. I look into the sky and I see a divine being. It must have been Somebody who knew what He was doing when He made all this world. Thirty centuries of human feelings of standing inside such awesome power generated amazing energetic fields. I think if you're open to it you can draw on these when you're there.

One of the things I know is that this is not simply magical thinking, but it is almost magical. The ancients had an awareness of the properties of the natural world in which they lived. They knew which certain kinds of stones to carve their monuments from – stones that pick up resonances. In Sakkara they built a huge festival courtyard, and inside each of several concave chambers surrounding the field, they placed a singer facing into the chamber not out of it. As she sang into the stones, the sound of her voice would resonate into the stones and bounce over her head and out into the courtyard. The stone amplified the sounds. Somehow they just <u>knew</u> how to do that. They were using natural energies.

Sakkara is one of my favorite places in the world. It's the site of the oldest hieroglyphs, the pyramid text of Unas. That text is a ritual for transformation into the next life. In Sakkara Nikki and I led a trip. We chanted for about thirty minutes. We read from my book, *Awakening Osiris*. We read, we chanted, we tried to bring the energies into that place. Two or three people in our group experienced illnesses, including one who had a family member at death's door. We wanted to provide healing or solace, whichever was appropriate. A couple of people had loved ones who passed on. As we were in this space, I felt a bit out of my body. I don't know where I went, mentally. It was just the effect of words. All I knew were the words, but they didn't sound like English anymore. I felt like I was tapping into some really ancient sound. I opened my eyes to gaze at a nearby hillock. On that hill of sand I saw all these beings of light standing there, standing on the rim of the hill all around us. I thought to myself, *Man I'm really out of it. So I see these beings of light, no problem. I hope nobody else sees them.* I kept chanting, praying, doing what I was doing.

We closed the ceremony and prepared to leave. One of the guides who took us on camel stood there holding the reins.

He came up to me and asked, "Who <u>were</u> they?" It was not "What was that?" but "Who were they?"

So he saw all of them, too. He was actually convinced they were real.

I said, "They're our helpers." I didn't know what else to say. It was a very poignant time.

Sakkara is one of the real strong places where you can feel a sense of equilibrium. The sand is white, almost yellow. Where the sand ends and the fields begin is very distinct; you can stand with one foot in each. Once you get out of Cairo, the air is clear – Luxor and Aswan. My favorite place is the temple of Isis at Philae, which is outside Aswan. It is a pretty good place, very magical. We were inside the Great Pyramid and we were given visions of an ethereal or astral mirror that we created and this mirror was taking light from above. I was to direct it to different places of the world to create healing places.

Robert was the person who got me over to Egypt. I was about 22 or 23 years old, and I just graduated from college. I lived back in Frankfort, and I ran into him. Robert lived up the street from me when I was growing up. We were neighbors since I was ten years old. He was this great, beautiful red-headed fellow. I had a crush on him when I was younger. He walked through nearby fields with two Irish setters. He was a red-headed man with these red-haired dogs. I always thought he was pretty cool.

At the time he worked on tugboats on the Ohio River barges. One day

Normandi Ellis in Egypt, at the Nut Chapel, the Temple of Edfu, 1992. Photo by Scott Fray.

he and I were talking. I don't know how, but we ended up talking about mystical things.

He said, "You really ought to read the Egyptian Book of the Dead. I think you'd really like it."

It was a sort of out-of-nowhere kind of suggestion. Maybe we talked about art and language.

I said, "Yeah, I'll think about that."

And he said, "No, you really should get it. In fact, you should get it right now. It's over there in Richard Taylor's bookstore."

So we walked over and he pointed to the book over on the shelf.

He said, "That's the book you're buying."

It was Wallace Budge's translation of the *Egyptian Book of the Dead*. It had both English language and hieroglyphs in it, and I bought it.

The next day Robert came over and he brought a huge box of stuff.

"I just found out that I'm going downriver, and I'll be gone for a couple of months. I won't be back, and they're closing the hotel where I live. I had to get everything out. I sent everything to my parent's house, except this box – but they wouldn't understand it, so I decided to give it to you."

So I said, "What is it?"

He said, "It's all the texts from the Rosicrucian's."

He was studying with the Rosicrucian's. In fact he had been drafted to go to Vietnam, and before he went, a Rosicrucian man found him and trained him in assisting souls in transitions. That's how he became a Rosicrucian, through this man. I accepted the box, and I think I said, "I'll just put these away for you until later."

I went on a big trip to Colorado. I got off to take a shower and stayed for a week, then came back, and moved there. Boom – I was gone. When I was packing, I came across this box of Robert's stuff. I thought, *I really should give this back to him, but I don't know where he is. I'll just take them with me, and he knows where my parents live, and he can contact my mom, and I'll send them to him, wherever he is.* So I took it all with me. I think it was a year later, at Christmas, when I came home. I was at my parents, I opened up the newspaper and there was an article that said Robert had been missing for four or five months. Nobody knew where he was; his parents tried to call him and it was two weeks before he was to be married. And then they found his truck, by the side of a lake, with his car keys and wallet, and everything just laying right there. Four months later they found his body in the lake. They said it appeared that he knew whoever it was and he walked away with them, just like that. Now there was no way to get this stuff back to Robert. I felt really sad and sorry about it, like there was something just left undone with Robert. I didn't know what it was.

I went back to Colorado to get my Master's degree. I took a translation workshop. I worked with Spanish for a while. I don't speak Spanish well because I have a thick, Southern accent. But when we translated from one written language to another written language, I did alright. There were a lot of interesting, international students in my class who wanted to translate from their native language as well.

Half way through the semester, the teacher said, "Now start on your other language." He meant languages like Portuguese, German or Danish. And I thought, *I don't have another language.*

When I told him about my dilemma, he said, "Well, pick one that looks interesting to you."

I had the book of Budge's translation. I really liked the idea of doing hieroglyphs, because when I was a young woman, I never could decide if I wanted to paint or write, and hieroglyphs were the perfect combination of the two.

He said, "Go get a good dictionary and a couple of good, variant translations, and see what you can do."

So I translated the book, the class ended, and I was hooked on the book. I couldn't stop translating it. I did several different poems. I went through the entire Book of the Dead one time, just to make sure that all of the language and imagery were inherent in those glyphs. If you translate it literally, it just didn't come through. I realized that I had to get the imagery inside it, because it was so powerful. You can't really write it without the symbol and the metaphor. So I worked to try to get all that by going through the first pass. After that I went back and worked on the sound translation. When I looked at it a third time, I realized that there was never a place where the metaphors were written down as part of the mythology of Egypt, the way we have it with Greek and Roman stories. There was no tale that tells the whole thing, just little pieces everywhere. So I worked the image, the sound and then the narrative in order to try to translate this book. By that time, I graduated, held several jobs, married and I had a baby. I was trying to figure out how to write, have a job, and have a baby. I was getting up at four in the morning to try to write for two hours before I went to work. It was hard. There was a lot of tension in the house.

My husband at the time said, "You know, you really ought to forget that book. It's sitting in the closet. You're not doing anything important with the materials. You're just making yourself miserable. You should give this up – nobody cares about Egypt."

I finally decided he was right. All that time, I knew this was an important book, because I could feel the books in the closet. It was there when I opened the closet to get dressed in the morning. The top shelf was going nnnggggg. I just decided he was right. I was not going to drive myself crazy with this anymore. And one night, I packed up all the boxes and put them in the back of my car. I drove to the dumpster. It was at night, after a fight. There was a high charge in the air. I drove to find the dumpster so I could dump this whole box of books – all of my stuff, Robert's stuff, the notes.

I drove up the hill toward a dumpster, and before I turned I looked in the rearview mirror, and there was Robert sitting in the back seat. I knew it was Robert, because I could feel his presence. But his head was completely shaved, as if he was an Egyptian priest, and he wore a white robe. I freaked out because I had a huge fight with my husband and I hadn't slept. I thought, *I'm going gooney.* So I just ignored him. I kept driving – I was headed to that dumpster. I was going to get rid of this stuff.

Robert said, "Turn around."

I ignored him.

Then he repeated, "Turn around."

And I kept driving. Then just to make sure that he knew I was there, he leaned forward and put his hand on my shoulder. At that moment it felt like I put my finger in a light socket. I just felt this energy go rrrrrraugh, all through me! I remember I screamed but it was this weird sound, like wong, wong, wong, wong. My own voice was this weird vibration. Somehow I stopped the car, and I thought, *Holy sh--!* I look in the rear view mirror and he was still there.

I said, "Robert, don't you ever do that again! You scared the hell out of me!"

And then, right in front of my eyes (snaps fingers) he was gone, just gone. It was as if he stayed long enough to know that he got my attention and I recognized him, and then he left. I got out and looked at all the books in the back of my car. And I went back home and took them back into my house.

It was about two months later when I got a call from a man who was working at a bookstore.

He said, "I read a couple of your translations in *IO* magazine. Do you have the whole book?"

I said, "Yes."

He said, "I want to publish it."

To think I had been ready to toss the book because it was ruining my life.

Woman's Counsel

My husband and his first wife had two children, a boy and a girl. The children, who were under ten years old, were with their mother in the car when she had a wreck and died. Her children grew up without their mother; there was a stepmother before me, but that didn't work out.

By the time I met the kids, his daughter was a high school freshman and his son was in eighth grade. I also had a daughter who was eight years old, and I had a hard time figuring out how to blend these families. Gar was a teenage boy, doing his own thing, and I didn't know how to figure him out. Roxie was a pretty good writer. We were closer, I think. At least I could have real conversations with her.

It wasn't long before I started dreaming about Susan, my husband's first wife. She often came in my dreams. We sat together and talked, just like you and I are doing now. We had coffee over the table. It was as if she was one of my long-time friends, only I'd never met her.

I remember I had a conversation with her one time that went something like this:

"You know, Susan, I'm having a hard time trying to reach Gar. I don't know what I'm supposed to do. How do I let him know I care about him? He won't even let me near him."

And she said, "Well, you just have to give him a hug."

I said, "No, you don't understand, he won't even let me near him. I cannot hug this child."

And she said, "Normandi, you just hug him the same way you hug me."

"Oh…I get it," I said, and I think that was the last conversation I had with her. Now I can actually really give Gar a physical hug, but for a long time, I had to hug him with my heart that way. Her suggestion was good advice.

Seeing Back in Time

David and I lived in an old farmhouse that was built right after the Civil War. It's a big two-story house on a knoll, surrounded by old trees. I had trouble sleeping one particular night. I often have trouble sleeping. I woke up; the moon was so bright. I could see the moon outside the window. I got up to go downstairs and as I got up, I looked outside the window, and I saw a woman lying on the ground. She was lit by the moonlight, and holding her stomach, rolling back and forth and crying. I thought *what in the world*. I decided to go back to bed – maybe I wasn't going to go back downstairs after all. I lay down and slept.

When I woke up in the morning, I rolled over and looked at the window. And I remembered this <u>incident</u> from the night. It wasn't a dream. What really astonished that morning me as I looked out the window, was that the leaves of the trees outside were brushing against the window. They were that close. But what I saw during the night was a woman lying on the ground, under the trees. The trees were much farther back and the moonlight was coming through. And there would have been no way I could have seen the ground. I could not have seen it but the trees were much smaller. It was like I woke up and saw something in a distant, past time, when the trees were probably only fifty years old, rather than a hundred years old. It was a shock.

What I found out later, a neighbor told me, is that there was a woman who lived in that house, who was pregnant, and she was gored to death by a bull in the front yard. That is what I had seen.

Other things happened in that house. My friend Karen and I sat and visited in the living room. She came to visit one time, and as we talked all of a sudden both of us turned to watch a ghost woman walk by. She was wearing a long, dark skirt, very regal, her hair up.

"Did you see that?!" I asked Karen.

"Yeah!" she replied.

"What'd she look like?" And Karen gave me the same description of the woman I saw. We had no idea who she was, but both of us saw her.

I only saw that woman once. But there was another ghost near the basement steps. I was sitting watching television, in a room with a circular stairs off to one side that went to the basement, and there was a chimney nearby. The television sat next to the chimney, with the stairs right close by. I saw a yellow 'fog' swirl up from downstairs and come upstairs. So I thought, *Oh, hello*! And then it went back down.

My mother, who is actually very psychic, came up the sidewalk to visit one time. I stood waiting for my mother to come inside. I saw the car out there. She stood on the sidewalk, looking at the upstairs window, where there was a covered porch. Finally she walked inside. I asked her.

"What were you doing out there?"

"I was trying to figure out who that man is up there."

"What man?"

"That man, he just gave me the most horrible stare. I mean he really did not want me coming up this sidewalk."

I said, "What did he look like?" And she described a man with a very long beard, wearing a black coat with thin lapels. She drew a picture of this man.

"You mean there's no one upstairs?" My mother repeated her question.

"No, Mom, there's no one upstairs. It's just you and me here today."

"Well, I saw that man! And he did not want me here."

She made me take her upstairs, to the porch, so she could see where he was sitting. A couple of months later, somewhere in Frankfort, somebody told us a story about Mr. Penn, who used to own this place. It was the old Penn house. They described what he looked like, and that was what my mom saw. He was a prominent landowner and farmer.

Bad Spirit Energy

This happened in Frankfort, around 1977 or so, a year or so before I met Robert. My friend Janice and I bought a Ouija board at a yard sale and were messing with it. I didn't like what I was getting – it freaked me out, so I put it away under my bed. After that, weird things started happening in my house. I would hear scratching around inside the box, at night, under my bed. My dog would sit in the corner of the room and look at it under the bed. Sometimes he cowered then he got really upset and started barking. It was like he barked at somebody's heels that walked through the house. He growled and barked – he was just really mad.

One night when I slept, I woke up, and it felt like something was on my chest. It felt like something pushed me down so I couldn't move. All I could do was to move my head, from side to side. And the dog was looking at me again. There was something in my house. At the time I had a boyfriend with whom I was really having trouble. There was a lot of dissonant energy going around. Whenever we had an argument or fight, something weird happened. I had a picture set on the mantle, along with candles and books in front of it, holding it up. When I got really mad, the picture lifted up and slid down onto the floor. It never knocked anything off the mantle. It lifted itself up and slid down onto the floor. It like the picture was being thrown – BAM! – like that. I never knew if it was my energy that did that, but I don't think the energy that was brought in with the Ouija board was a really good one.

My friend spent the night with me and she slept on the sofa. She woke up one night, thinking the dog had her hand in its mouth. Then she realized that the dog was over in the corner again, shivering, looking at her. Somebody else held her hand; it was up in the air. I just decided that the house was too weird – I couldn't live there anymore. It was bad energy all the way around. I went downstairs to the laundry room one night and the neighbor from across the hall had his wife by the ears, beating her head against a metal pole. And there was this weird, schizophrenic guy who played Christmas carols in July, really loud, in the middle of the night. And downstairs on the other side was Mr. Motor Head, and Mr. Motor Head Junior, revving up their car engines.

Okay, I've got to get out of here. This is just too weird with all this stuff going on. So I left, just moved that summer because the energy was so distressing. And I really felt bad, because the woman who moved in after me was murdered in that apartment. I wondered if I could have done something to change the energy, but instead maybe I brought it in with the Ouija board. She was murdered in the stairwell by a trustee of the governor's who lived across the street.

I read about the murder trial later in *The State Journal*. It was after 1978. By that time I had already moved to Colorado.

Ghost Cat

From Louisville, Kentucky:

Like all good ghost stories, this story begins with a thunderstorm. We had a stray cat that came just out of the clear blue back in 1985. He was with us for 12 years and died in 1997. The dog we had was my father's dog. This was a year before my father passed away. The dog was only about a year old when the stray showed up. He went ballistic – he was hitting the window, hitting the door, all excited over something. I got up to look out the window because I thought, *Somebody came up on the porch.* There was a flash of lightning, and there was this gorgeous grey cat. I mean, it looked like it had come out of a show. It had perfect hair and beautiful amber eyes. It was sitting under the blue swing on the front porch. When it saw me, it took off.

I said, "Mom, there was a bushy tail cat on the front porch." Hence the name we gave him, Bushy.

We had him as an outside cat for about two years. After a year, mom took him up to the veterinarian for shots and he tested weakly positive for feline leukemia. Since we had an indoor cat, Mom wouldn't bring him in with our female cat. About six months after we tested him, Mom just insisted that he had to have the feline leukemia shot. He wasn't neutered at that point, and he got in a cat fight with a Tomcat. He came up on the porch and he was a mess, he was beaten up so bad. Mom took him up to the veterinarian, who said he would die – with the feline leukemia, this will kill him. But he pulled through, healed very quickly, and when the vet retested him there was no feline leukemia. So we brought him in the house.

Within a month after we brought him in the house, I came through the front door, walked through the dining room and glanced over to see something at the far corner of the hallway. There was the prettiest longhair white cat with blue eyes sitting there with his tail wrapped around him. My mother liked to collect animals so I thought, *She's brought a cat in the house.*

I started to call out, "Mom when did you?…"

And I looked back and he wasn't there anymore. I thought, *Okay…I'm not going to mention this. I'm just going to pretend like I didn't see that.*

I saw the ghost cat, on and off, for several months. I felt it walking on the bed. I couldn't see indentations where it was stepping, but I felt it. And it was very bizarre because it didn't have any weight to it. In the middle of the night, feeling a cat walking on the bed, I raised my head up to see which cat came to visit, but there was no cat on the bed. Some three or four months after I started seeing the white cat, my father came in the front door. My aunt, my mother's sister who lived with us at the time, was upstairs. My mom and I were in the kitchen, when my father exclaimed,

"Oh, for crying out loud, aren't two cats enough? Who brought this white cat into the house?!"

I didn't say anything, Mom didn't say anything, and then we heard my father ask, "Well, where did it go?"

I looked at my mom, my mom looked at me, she said, "Do you see it, too?"

I said, "Yes".

My aunt came down from upstairs and said, "Are you finally talking about that white cat that comes upstairs every time I turn around?"

So we all saw it, and we continued to see it. When we sat on a chair in the living room, it jumped on our lap. When we felt it we didn't see it. Most of the time when we saw the ghost cat it was sitting at the end of the hallway or at the end of the dining room table. Every time we saw the cat it was never in motion; it sat with its tail around itself. The only thing it might occasionally do is turn his head.

The spirit cat lived with us for the life of Bushy. We lost my father in 1990, and the animals were with us for thirteen or fourteen years by 1997. We don't know for sure how old Bushy was, because he came to us as a stray. My cat was fifteen years old. We had to put my father's dog to sleep in January of 1997. In May of 1997 Sadie, our Westy, West Highland white terrier, came to live with us. We thought we had a crazy little dog, because all of a sudden she stood and barked, yapping at the dining room table for no reason at all. She bounced all over the place, wanting to play. She came in the room and barked at the leg of the table. We wondered if Sadie was mentally challenged. So we decided she saw the white ghost cat.

After she came in the house we never saw the cat again. We felt it many times but we never physically saw the cat. There wasn't anything we could connect to why or when the cat appeared to us. It was just there. In July of 1997 my female cat was diagnosed with oral cancer. In November we had her put to sleep. The night we had her put to sleep, Bushy started walking and crying, walking and crying. She wasn't here at the house and Bushy looked for her. She began to hemorrhage when we took her out, so Bushy knew something was wrong. Sadie also knew something was wrong, even though she was under a year old. He didn't eat after that and within nine days we had to have him put to sleep.

The night we had Bushy put to sleep the white cat was very active. It was bothering Sadie. Sadie would move from bed to bed. It was just my mom and I staying in the house, since both my dad and aunt passed away. Sadie jumped up on my bed and after a few minutes, I felt the cat jump on my bed – the cat we couldn't see. It was very active walking around the bed. Then Sadie got up and went into Mom's room. She kept moving around. Sadie had us awake all night.

Finally, I got up and said to Mom, "Do you want me to close my door and keep her in there?"

She answered, "No the cat is bothering her."

She was still only nine months old, and we decided if the ghost cat bothered her that much, then we would let her move if she felt she needed to move around. There was no point in trying to close the door and shut out a cat that could go where it pleased. Sadie stopped eating and playing and laid with her head between her feet. Mom was scared to death we were going to lose her too. I took her the vet who checked her out and told us to get her a cat. Sadie was raised around the two cats and then they were both gone.

So I went out to Feeder's Supply and found a four-month-old Calico cat, which was a rescue cat. Feeder's Supply had her mother and three kittens. I stood for the longest time and watched all their cats and kittens. Even though her mother and two sisters were in the cage with her, whenever a dog walked by she leaned and watched that dog as long as she could. So she liked dogs and I figured that was a good match.

The ironic thing was that Sadie and our new cat, Ginger, were born two houses apart on Hikes Lane. Ginger was born in August. Her mother was locked in a garage. The rescuer lived two doors down from where Sadie was born. When we brought Ginger in the house, Sadie and Ginger hit it off – they were best friends. It was not very long after we brought in Ginger when Sadie and Ginger were sleeping with me. Sadie was lying with her back end against my side and back against the pillow and Ginger was on top the other pillow. I was asleep when the cat just sat bolt upright. It woke me up. She looked at the foot of the bed, when I could feel the white cat walking on the bed. Ginger started growling – a real, little low sound. She was only four months old. She took great offense that the spirit cat was there. Ginger turned around and nudged Sadie a couple of times, getting down between Sadie and the pillow, going back to sleep. I didn't think any more about it.

A couple of weeks later, my mom and I sat in our living room chairs. Ginger liked to lie in my mom's lap. Suddenly Ginger sat up straight, looked to the middle of the floor, jumped down and attacked something that we could not see. Ginger had fur flying, she was screeching, she looked like she was wrestling with something. It nearly scared both of us to death. She then stopped; her tail was a big as it could be, all bristled out. Next she went flying to and jumped on the dining room table. The fighting started again. I had some schoolbooks on the table – she knocked those off. We had a white lace tablecloth, which she pulled up. She knocked off a flower arrangement.

Mom said, "I'm going to get Sadie out of here, because I'm afraid she's going to attack her."

My mom picked up Sadie to walk past the table when Ginger stopped. She looked at my mom and then quickly looked toward the front of the house. She bolted right for the lower front window and hit that window so hard I thought she was going to go through it. She ended up spread eagle on the window and still she looked outside. She ran to the front door and looked out. She came back and started cleaning herself. That was it. Her tail went down. She got up on my lap. She was trained as a kitten to be kissed on top of her head. She'd put her head down and butt at you.

Mom said, "Don't do that. Something's wrong with this cat."

But I kissed her on the head, and she curled up and lay down.

The next day I took her to the veterinarian. After I explained what happened, he said, "Well, your cat is having seizures."

I asked him, "Are animal seizures like people seizures?"

He said, "Yes".

But then I replied, "These were not uncontrollable movements. She was at my dining room table, sitting up and boxing something."

But he repeated, "Well, that was a seizure. We won't medicate her now, but you need to watch her. If she has a couple of episodes, then we can determine what is causing them and medicate her."

Well, about that time Jasmine, their office cat, came through the examining room and Ginger went crazy. She hissed, spat, screeched. The technician had to pin her on the table.

I said, "That's the way she was acting!"

He put Jasmine out of the room and said, "Well she doesn't like cats. Could she have seen her reflection in a mirror or in the window at night? Did she see the cat on the TV in a commercial?"

But I didn't want to tell him, "No, she saw our ghost cat!"

But I firmly believe that she chased the ghost cat out of the house that night. We haven't seen or felt the cat since, and that was ten years ago. The ghost cat came with Bushy. Bushy died on November 29 and the cats fought in mid-December. There's no other explanation. The white cat wasn't here before Bushy came in the house. I think she fought it and ran it out of the house, not because it was bad but simply because Ginger doesn't like cats. She loves dogs. But when she sees the cat across the street, she goes nuts.

Girl With Watering Can
"Susan", Louisville, Kentucky

This happened at my brother-in-law's house, "Andrew's" brother. He lives across the street from us in Lake Forest. It was March 13, 1991. That is the date of my sister-in-law's and also Andrew's mother's birthday. Andrew's mother was killed in a horrible car accident the previous June, in 1990. It was our first celebration for "Cindy's" birthday without her. Cindy invited several family members to our dinner party.

When we went over, there was horrible snowstorm that weekend, in the middle of March. It was horrible, the wind blowing and everything. The Mountain Parkway in eastern Kentucky was closed down. It was just an unbelievable blizzard. Andrew's sister, Terri, Andrew and I and our two children, my sister-in-law, her husband "Burt" and their two boys were there.

Some of us were in the living room and dining room. We were in a center area but we could see out the dining room window. The windows went to the ground and there were a few shrubs. It was dark but we could see outside where the snow was blowing. We were talking, getting ready for dinner, having drinks and appetizers. Some of us were around the house mingling. I wasn't drinking, yet.

I looked out the window and said, "Somebody's looking in the window."

And how their house was situated, we could see the full body of a girl about ten or twelve years old. She had on a white, gauze kind of dress, blowing in the wind. It was antique-type clothing. She had long hair, it was blowing, and she was holding a green plastic watering can. She had her face up to the window, looking in. She didn't have a coat or any other cold weather clothes and the temperature was below freezing.

We all started saying, "Somebody's at your window! There's a little girl at your window."

Everybody ran to the window and the snow kept blowing her hair and clothes. We left to go get the others to show her the girl and by the time we got back, she was gone. We all ran outside in the yard and looked for the girl. There were no footprints in the snow, which was several inches deep and drifting in places. We should have seen tracks right up at the house. But the watering can was blowing back and forth outside the window.

Now the significance of that green watering can is that Andrew's mother and father, even though they lived in Louisville, had a country farm near Flemingsburg, in Poplar Plains, Kentucky. They loved that 80-acre farm. They had an old green watering can that had been in the family for years, since this farm had belonged to relatives. It was a tobacco and cattle farm. The watering can we found outside the house that night was the same kind as the one from the farm. And Burt and Cindy didn't have a watering can. So now there are two, and we have both of the watering cans.

Later on, I was going through the drawers of a piece of furniture we inherited – it was a "secretary" – I found a photograph of a little girl who turned out to be Andrew's grandmother, or maybe his mother. It was the girl who was looking in the window. We saw the ghost on her birthday.

Dad's Spirit in Our Home

Unexplained things happened in our home over the week when Andrew's father died. His father had been in the hospital. He had surgery, but nothing that would have killed him. I was working as a dietician then. His father got out of the hospital. One day he died. Things didn't go well and they had to get up and walk him around. This would have been maybe 1982 or 1983. Our daughter, Wendy, was little at that time. She was born in 1979. The week that his father was in the hospital weird things started happening in our house. All of our parents were still living, and we were worried about his dad. His dad had surgery but it was not even major surgery. We visited him at the hospital and then came home.

Once when we returned a La-Z-Boy chair had been totally changed. It was moved across the room over in front of the fireplace. Nobody had broken in. We weren't there; we didn't move it. On another day, Andrew and I were at home sitting at the kitchen table and listening to the radio. The radio was by the opposite cabinet and nobody else was in the kitchen. Andrew and I looked at the radio as it totally spun the dial to the other end. It went to a completely different station. And he and I looked at each other. We had actually been talking with each other about all the weird things that were happening.

This was the week before Easter. The week Andrew's father died, Wendy and I went to visit him. Before we left I did laundry. The clean clothes and bed sheets were in a basket in the family room. I pulled the sheets off the bed and I hadn't yet put them back on the bed. When we came back home, the beds were made and the clothes were all folded. And the night his dad died, about midnight, when I was back from the hospital, I saw our clock fly off the wall at the same time he passed away.

Civil War Spirits

Lois Madden, New Richmond, Ohio

A number of years ago, during a visit with my brother and his family in Vienna, Virginia, I had an amazing, recurrent, otherworldly experience. They were living in an apartment complex located on an old Plantation site known as Ashgrove House. The complex was close to Tyson's Corner in Virginia as well as near to Washington, DC and by many other Civil War battle sites.

During our visits it was my routine to rise early and walk the complex grounds. The area was a fascinating mix of retail stores, restaurants, office complexes, a sub-division, a wooded area with walking paths and several of the Plantation's historic buildings smack dab in the middle of it all. A couple of the Plantation structures were under renovation. I love history and was fascinated that all these people were now living in apartments/townhouses on what was once a working Plantation.

Midway through our visit, I awoke one night to the sound of horses neighing and hooves pounding the ground, not concrete or blacktop, but dirt. I also heard the sounds of metal clanking and the low murmur of men's voices. I couldn't believe what I was hearing! I thought to myself, *What in the world?* I looked over at my husband, who was sound asleep. I got up and looked out the window, the street was perfectly clear – no horses or people to be seen anywhere up or down the lane. I just couldn't believe what I was hearing. I was totally immersed in listening. Later, I went back to bed and eventually drifted into sleep listening to those haunting sounds.

The next day I told the family what had happened during the wee hours of the night. Not surprisingly, no one else heard anything remotely like the sounds I had heard. My sense was that I had heard the sounds of an active Civil War encampment during the night. The very first time I awoke to these sounds I heard them every night during that particular visit. On later visits only occasionally did I hear the ghostly sounds of men, metal and horses. It was an awesome experience. My early morning walks took on an entirely new dimension!

Grandpa's Stormy Spirit

The second event involving Grandpa's spirit took place when I was a teenager. We'd driven from Cincinnati to Somerset, Kentucky for Decoration Day/Memorial Day. We went to the family cemetery located on a small hill off the Tick Ridge Road. We'd gone to tidy up around the gravesites and put flowers on the graves. I was with Mom, my stepfather and my maternal grandma. It was a clear day, perfect for cleaning up around Grandpa's and Great-Grandma Mam's graves.

As a kid, I always thought Grandpa's gravestone was really weird. It's one of those big double stones, which also includes Grandma's name and birth date, with an empty space for her death date. It was strange seeing her name and birth date engraved on that stone. In fact, it's still surreal! As I was standing there, looking at the gravestone, it got really dark outside, like a bad storm was coming. It got dark! It was black as pitch. The wind started blowing and it got really cold. It felt like an incredible frontal system descended on us. It was almost as if someone had flipped a switch. It went from being a really pretty day to just a horribly stormy day. The wind was blowing and howling.

I was standing on Grandpa's grave, unable to move. I tried, but *I could not move*. It felt like something was holding me there. I was terrified. I got that horrible feeling again, that mean feeling. I was so frightened and alone; I couldn't see any of my family. I was glued to that spot. It was like somebody was holding my feet. I could not move. That's what I remember, that's what was happening to me. The next thing I knew – I don't know how much time transpired – I was back at my grandma's house, safe and sound. I was sitting in her kitchen, in a chair, and everybody was looking at me like I had two heads. I don't have a clue what happened. I have no memory of anybody leading me out of the graveyard. I have no memory of getting in the car. I have no memory of the trip back to the farmhouse.

Everybody was really reluctant to talk to me; however, it was obvious they were very much aware that something had happened to me.

The only thing I really remember them saying is, "We led you to the car."

I don't think I collapsed. I don't think I was picked up off the ground and carried to the car. Someone probably just came and put their arm around me and led me back to the car and we left. I remember trying to share my bizarre experience.

Again, everybody was in total denial about the whole thing. The adults were grasping at some plausible explanation, maybe there was something medically or psychologically wrong with me. From their perspective, nothing had happened in the cemetery, except my weird behavior!

Now, the interesting part of the story is that recently I learned of the mysterious circumstances surrounding Grandpa's passing. It was common knowledge on the Ridge that he was a big drinker. There is some speculation that he took drugs – what kind of drugs, I don't know.

I've heard Grandma say many times, "He was a mean man."

He was a violent man. She must have felt that his drinking and possible drug use made him behave that way. On the night of his passing…he left earlier that day…Grandma said she felt really strange all day. She was really afraid. Things were coming to a head. She felt very strongly that something was going to happen, that day. Grandpa kept guns in the house, so she gathered them up and hid them in one of the rooms. As the day wore on she got Mom and they barricaded themselves in the room where she'd hidden the guns.

Grandpa came home really drunk. He beat on the door to the room where they were hiding; he wanted to get in. She wouldn't unlock the door. They heard him looking for something, probably his guns. He came back and became verbally abusive. Grandma said she and Mom were terrified. She made Mom get under the bed in case he somehow broke into the room. She could hear him out there just tearing the house apart. After a while it got really quiet. Grandma guessed he'd just passed out somewhere. They weren't about to come out of that room to find out.

She said, "I was not coming out of that room for anything! For all I knew he was sitting on a chair on the other side of that door."

The next morning, not hearing anything, she opened the door and ventured out. She found Grandpa in bed, *dead*. He died sometime during the night. There was no sign of violence, nothing like that. He'd gone to bed, had a heart attack and died. There's some history of heart disease on Grandpa's side of the family. The cause of death was determined to be heart related based, on his family history more that anything else.

A few years ago I asked Grandma, "Grandma, what do you think happened to Grandpa?"

She said, "I think God took him because he was just mean. He was mean and God took him."

That's what she said. She felt safe after he was gone. She was relieved the Lord had taken him.

Another interesting tidbit, relating to my cemetery experience, was recently revealed. Mom shared a detail, unknown to me, about the day Grandpa was buried. She just adored her Dad; his death was very hard on her in so many detrimental ways. It's impacted her whole life and it influenced the way she raised her kids. It was around Decoration Day, in May 2007, that Mom and I drove down to Tick Ridge and spent the night in Somerset. We shared a hotel room, something we never do. The three of us, Mom, Grandma and me, went to the cemetery to put flowers on Grandpa's grave. It was the first time, since my cemetery experience, that we'd all been there together.

Later that evening, after we'd gotten Grandma settled in for the night, Mom and I were chatting over dinner at Ruby Tuesday. She reminisced about the day Grandpa was laid to rest. One of the worst storms they've ever had down there occurred that day. The way she described it, it was very much like my gravesite experience. *Frankly, it gave me chills!* That's the first time I'd ever heard that bit of information. All I ever knew, up to then, was that he'd died during the night in his bed. And I was always aware of Grandma's sense of relief after his passing.

To this day I don't know what motivated Mom to tell me about the weather the day Grandpa was buried. My experience, as I stood on Grandpa's grave those many years ago, seems somehow validated since Mom provided that piece of the puzzle. Sadly, I've never felt as threatened as the two times Grandpa chose to visit me. I wish our encounters had been more positive and I truly hope his journey took him to a loving, peaceful place.

Grandpa's Icy Visit

My maternal grandpa passed away when my mom was a teenager. I didn't know him, nor did I know much about him, other than his name and that he'd died in his sleep. However, I will say that I've always felt there was a very strong connection between him and Mom.

I've had a couple of experiences involving my deceased grandpa. One occurred when I was a teenager. My family was visiting Grandma and her husband at their farm on Tick Ridge in Kentucky. We'd often drive down from our home in Cincinnati, Ohio and spend time on their farm—I loved it! My grandma had remarried after Grandpa passed and bought this wonderful farm on the ridge. My grandpa never actually lived on this farm. My family always slept in the three bedrooms on the second floor when visiting. This particular trip I was given the smallest of the three rooms. Wow! I thought it was pretty cool having my own room. Little did I know how 'cool' it would be!

One night, during our stay, I went to bed and fell asleep. I woke up feeling cold, *very cold*. I started looking for the quilt, at the foot of the bed, to pull up over me when I felt, then saw, a male presence standing not far from my bedside. As I mentioned, the room was really small. There was a twin bed and a dresser separated by only a few feet of space. Due to the smallness of the room, the presence seemed overpowering. This man wasn't anyone I recognized, physically. That said, I knew him – it was my grandpa!

I started screaming and he slowly melted away. The feelings the experience evoked were somehow more frightening than seeing him standing by the bed. He wasn't doing anything threatening. He wasn't trying to hurt me in any way. I just had an overwhelming sense of evil. I just felt he was mean – I don't know any other way to describe it.

Needless to say, my screams woke folks up. I tried telling mom what I had experienced but my telling fell on deaf ears. She insisted I'd just had a nightmare. Once I'd settled down, everyone went back to their beds, leaving me awake in that room for the remainder of the night. It was one of the longest nights of my life. It seemed morning would never break.

I know Grandpa's icy visit wasn't a nightmare or night terror. I was wide-awake in that frigid room in the presence of my grandpa's spirit. I refused to sleep in that room ever again. I very seldom even entered the room unless someone was with me. The trauma of that event remains with me to this day.

As an adult I had nightmares about my grandpa during stays on the Tick Ridge farm. One of the last nightmares happened while visiting Grandma with one of my younger brothers and his wife. I woke them as they slept in the next bedroom, screaming in my sleep.

I awoke to my brother shaking me and saying, "Wake up, wake up – you're okay, you're okay!"

Mam's Lasting Gift

I was nine years old when my great-grandma, Mam, passed away. She was born in 1882 and died in 1964. She lived and died on Tick Ridge in Kentucky, a place that's helped shape the person I am. I visit her gravesite whenever I make it back to Tick Ridge.

Mam was always very old in my eyes. She wore pretty dresses and always wore her hair in a bun. I have fond memories of her rocking in her favorite rocking chair. She's my role model for aging. I've always said I want to be like Mam when I get old. Mam was deaf and practically blind. She lived on the old home place on my mom's side of the family. She just lived alone in her house and made do.

Mam always held a special charm for my cousin and me; we adored that woman. It's not a stretch to say I worshipped the ground she walked on.

We always heard tell she had 'the sight', which of course added to the mystery of Mam. She always knew when we were on our way to visit. We always found a plate of cookies and glasses of milk on the kitchen table after walking through her kitchen door. She didn't have a telephone, so nobody called to tell her we were headed down the road for a visit. Often she didn't even know that my family was down from Cincinnati. Mam was a joyful blessing in our lives and she was our best friend.

Great-Grandma Mam

We were devastated when we lost her. Her passing was my first experience with death and funerals. I stayed at my cousin's house the night before Mam's lay out and funeral; we found comfort in each other's presence. That night we were lying in bed facing the bedroom window. We cried, reminiscing and talking about Mam. We really had no concept of where she was or what happened to her. We just felt an overwhelming sense of loss and sadness. Our world was empty without Mam in it.

I remember feeling really strange, that's when I noticed something in the window. **It was Mam!** She was so real. It was Mam as we knew her in life with her hair in a bun, just watching us. I remember looking at my cousin and wondering if she was seeing Mam, too.

I wondered, *Is this some sort of a trick? How did you do that?* I looked at her and asked, "What do you see? Look at the window." And I remember thinking, *Don't tell her what you see because if you do, you're giving her the information.*

She was looking at the window as stunned as I was…and I asked, "What do you see?"

She answered, "I see Mam."

We both experienced Mam's ghost outside that window. However, that wasn't the end of our shared visitation. We both received the same wordless message from Mam. I guess it was telepathy. I don't know what else you'd call it. Her mouth wasn't moving. She wasn't speaking to us normally nonetheless we were able to understand her meaning clearly. She told us she would be with us all the time and not to be afraid, that she was okay.

I remember getting a sense from her of "I'm okay, I'm not gone, and I'm still with you and always will be."

And then she just very slowly faded away. To this day I get chills just thinking about it. Mam gifted us with peace, acceptance and the ability to heal. The next day, at the funeral, as I walked by the casket I remember pausing to look at her in wonder. Despite seeing her the night before, I felt her loss very deeply. My cousin and I would miss our horseback journeys to her house to visit. I'd never be in her space again. However, with the loss came a warm sense of comfort, like I was being hugged. Because I knew she was there, guiding me through the ritual of death. There's never been a doubt in my mind or heart that she was standing there with me. Mam helped me get through that long day and many since.

Mam is with me each and every day. I keep two photographs of her in my bedroom and I talk to her all the time. I enjoy sharing my life with her. From what I understand, she is the person who most likely gave me the gift of song and music because she loved to sing. Most of my family doesn't sing, they're just not musically inclined.

I've often heard family members say, "You got that from Mam".

Her gift of music has always been with me and I cherish it.

As sad an experience as Mam's passing was for me, it was also life-changing and empowering. I've never been afraid of death and I've never been afraid of talking about dying. I'm always sad when someone I know and love passes but I'm not overcome with any sense of dread or fear. I feel calm and appreciate the opportunity to celebrate life and wish the person that's crossed over a good journey.

Thank you, Mam, for the gift of knowing, without a doubt, that there's something more for us after we cross over.

My Kentucky kinfolk are very strong Southern Baptists, allowing for little or no discussion about ghostly encounters. I grew up Baptist as well, but I've always felt more spiritual than religious. I remember, as kids do, wanting to share our experience with the grownups.

When I blurted out, "I saw Mam last night", everybody looked at me like "What?"

I don't remember if my cousin spoke up or not, but I distinctly remember my sense of disappointment when nobody believed me.

"Oh, you're just seeing things; you're upset."

I understood Mam's appearance much more than I did family not being receptive to the possibility that we **had** seen her. Even at that young age I remember thinking *what's up with these people?* Why don't they get it?

As my cousin and I grew up, we grew apart. We never really talked much about our ghostly encounter so I don't know what she took away from the experience. She still lives on Tick Ridge in the same house that she lived in when we visited Mam. My dad has since passed and she's lost both her parents. We've never talked about our losses. We're two very different people who once shared a profound experience.

Ꮪhe Message

I met Jennifer Jones in early July 2007, at the Highland Methodist Church, Ft. Thomas, where I was storytelling. I told a variety of stories, but I finished with a number of ghost stories requested by popular demand.

When I finished, a few folks were interested in talking about true ghost stories. Jennifer told me that she was visited by a spirit, and here is what happened.

Jennifer:

This occurred about eight years ago. I had two children and recently suffered two miscarriages. I awoke in the middle of the night and saw a woman standing next to my bed. I cleared my eyes, thinking I was still sleeping or dreaming. At first I couldn't identify the woman. I only knew that she gave me a feeling of calm and peace. She was luminous and ethereal. I originally thought it was my sister Diane, who has a very calm presence, but quickly realized, and I'm not sure how, that it was my cousin Monica. Monica was born two months before me in February of 1962. She was married and had three little boys. On December 10, 1995, after a few hours of Christmas shopping with her mom, she went upstairs to go to bed early because she was so tired. Her littlest boy found her "asleep on the bathroom floor". She died instantly of a ruptured heart due to total blockage in several main arteries.

That night she spoke to me without words. I understood her thoughts in my head. She told me, "Everything will be all right."

I soon found out I was pregnant again and thought *great, everything would be fine with this pregnancy.* However, I lost that baby and four thereafter. I realized later, however, that Monica was telling me not that *that* pregnancy would be all right, but that "everything" would be all right. It was a message of faith. She knew what lay ahead for me and offered me reassurance. When I am unsure I remember that moment and gain strength from its message.

My Nanny the Witch

Lisa Renee Myers, Louisville, Kentucky

I was born in Connersville, Indiana. But I lived and was raised all my life in Waco, Kentucky. When I was growing up in Waco, we always had a family reunion. Nanny Bette Hensley was always there. My mom's mother's brother married her daughter. She would always invite me every summer break to stay with her in Richmond, Kentucky. That was about ten or fifteen minutes drive from Waco.

She was just a very interesting little old lady. She was 5 feet and 3 or 4 inches tall. She always wore the old-time, flowery granny dresses. She had gray, salt and pepper hair and big, thick black glasses that pointed out on the ends. They looked like witch's eyeglasses. She always claimed to be a witch. But she said she was a good witch. Her younger sister, Stella, lived in Florida. She claimed to be a good witch. They both said they were the good witch and the other sister was the bad witch.

Stella always said, "The oldest is the meanest."

I never got to meet Stella and I don't know if she is still alive.

Nanny Bette lived to be 103 or 104 when she passed away.

At family reunions she would ask, "Why don't you come spend the summer with me when you get out of school?"

I was always intrigued with her. I thought, *yeah, I'll go stay.*

And I asked my mom and she always said no. So I walked back to Nanny Bette and told her, "Mom said I can't go spend the summer with you."

Nanny Bette answered, "You can come. I'll talk her into it. I want to teach you to sew without holding the needle and how to make brooms walk."

She told me how she could make pictures move on the wall without touching them. She told me that there were certain rooms in her house I couldn't go into.

"If you promise you won't go into those rooms then you can come and spend the summer with me," Nanny Bette said.

I always made that promise, but I never got to go.

Finally, when I got older I asked my Mom, "Why would you never allow me to go to Nanny Bette's for the summer, because I always wanted to go there?"

So she proceeded to tell me stories that happened to her because she got to go to Nanny Bette's home and spend summers. They quite frequently went to visit her because my mom grew up with her cousins who are Nanny Bette's children.

My mom was best friend with Betty Hensley, who was Nanny Bette's granddaughter. My mom said one time after church they went on a picnic at Lake Reba. Nanny Bette would always bring a bushel of apples from her apple trees. They would go down there to peel the apples to make them ready for apple pie or fried apples for the next day. My mom and Betty were playing near the lake.

Nanny Bette hollered at them saying, "Why don't you all come up here? I want to show you something." They ran up to her.

Nanny Bette asked, "Don't you want to play with the ducks?"

Mom and Betty said, "Well there's no ducks."

Nanny Bette insisted, "Sure there are. See this bushel of apples?"

The girls answered, "Yes."

Nanny Bette told them, "There's ducks in there with the apples."

Mom said she and Betty moved their hands around amongst the apples and there were no ducks. She said Nanny sat back and just flipped the basket over and little yellow ducks crawled and ran out from under the basket and there were no apples. Mom also told me that they once were playing with sticks at Lake Reba.

Nanny Bette told them, "Put the snakes down. Don't be playing with snakes."

The girls told her, "There aren't snakes here. They're sticks."

Nanny Bette repeated, "You put the snakes down."

And the sticks in their hands turned into snakes!

My mom said one time she was in Nanny Bette's house. She and Betty were playing by a table that she did not want the children to be around. Maybe she was afraid the kids would scratch it or break something on it. Nanny Bette asked them to get away from the table, but being young girls they didn't listen.

She said, "If you do not get away from the table, then I'm going to move it."

But the girls never moved away from the table.

The table then *walked* from one side of the room where it was by a window across the room to under the opposite window. So Mom, of course, never went around the table again! That was a scary experience for her. It was not long after that my mom never went back to Nanny Bette's house. My mom's father was a minister. I'm sure when my Mom went back and told them stories he would not let her go back.

No one in our family really knew how she was related to us, but if she didn't like you she would set a curse on you. She said if you don't leave me alone bad things will happen to you.

"I'm going to make you get hit by a car," or, "I'll chop your head off."

She would say those things but nobody ever took her seriously. They just thought she was an old crazy woman. My little brother Rodney loved to harass Nanny Bette, every chance he could get. He was just like my dad. If my dad or brother could find something wrong with you they would aggravate you with the most irritating laugh. They'd get under your skin. This is a true story. I know because I always sat next to Nanny Bette and ate with her.

One time Rodney walked over to Nanny Bette, saying, "Hey old witch! Give me those green beans."

Rodney was then about 22 or 23 years old.

She said to him, "You get away from my food."

She always brought her own metal fork. It was the dullest fork in the whole world. She must have used it for years and years. It was worn out down to the stub. Rodney tried to take a green bean and she hit on the table like she was going to stab him with the fork. He would die laughing.

She looked at him with the meanest look and said, "Rodney Cain, you get away from my plate. I don't like you."

Rodney patted her on the back and said, "Nanny Bette, why don't you like me? I like you."

But she stabbed back at him with her fork to try and get his hand. When he kept agitating her she took the fork and flipped it and it stabbed right in the picnic table although it was the dullest fork you've ever seen it stuck straight up.

She then said, "If you don't leave me alone I will chop your head off."

But Rodney kept on aggravating her and aggravating her.

Nanny Bette said, "I'm going to tell you what – you'll have a warning this time tomorrow. And if you ever bother me again it will not be a warning."

It was about 1:00 in the afternoon. So the very next day at the same time in the afternoon, my brother and my little nephew who was about five or six years old, were in the car as they drove down Eastern Parkway in Richmond. They stopped at a red light. He kept trying to get past a car in front of him. But he couldn't get around them. He was directly behind this car and when the light turned green that car took off. But a car coming the opposite direction did not stop and T-boned this car. The driver's head was cut off and their body hung out of the car. My little nephew saw that. When they came home and told us about the accident, Rodney was shook up. He never again bothered Nanny Bette, never ever.

He told me, "She said she'd cut off my head and the next day at the same time I'd be warned."

Those could be coincidences…

I would always get Nanny Bette to tell me stories at the family reunions. She loved anybody who was interested in her. And I was never afraid of Nanny Bette. I don't know why – I just never was.

I told her, "Tell me stories about what happened in your past, things you've really kept in your memory."

She told me that years and years ago when she was raising her children, she had a neighbor who had a beautiful lamp that sat in her front window. She said you could see it from the road. It was beautiful. It was the old type lamp that had the big, huge ball on the top and was really decorative at the bottom. It had crystal prisms hanging around its edge.

They were really good friends, like best, best friends.

She told me that, "I just took such a liking to that lamp."

One day Nanny Bette went over and told her neighbor, "I want to buy your lamp."

And the woman said, "It's not for sale. It's been in my family for generations."

Nanny Bette insisted, "I still want to buy the lamp."

Her neighbor repeated, "Nanny Bette, the lamp is not for sale."

Nanny Bette came back with, "Okay, then just give it to me."

The woman replied, "What part do you not understand? It is not for sale and I'm not giving it away. It will go down into my family for generations."

Nanny Bette told me, "That just made me so mad."

Nanny Bette looked at her neighbor and said, "If I can't have it nobody can have it. Expect it to be gone at midnight."

The neighbor asked, "What do you mean? You're not going to come in my house and steal my lamp!"

Nanny Bette repeated, "No, I'm not coming to steal it, but if I can't have it then nobody can have it."

So I asked Nanny Bette, "What did you mean by that?!"

And she told me, "You just listen to the story."

Nanny Bette told me, "I knew my neighbor was not going to sleep that night." And she added, "I never stole anything in my life. I will never steal anything. Before I left my neighbor's house, I just walked over to the lamp. I rubbed the side of the lamp and said if I can't have it nobody can have it. And I left."

At midnight the lamp blew up.

I asked Nanny Bette, "What do you mean it blew up?"

"It blew up into the smallest pieces that it could never be glued back together."

I asked her, "Why did you do it?"

She said, "When I want something I get it one way or the other. If I don't get it, you don't get it."

But still they never scared me. I just thought they were stories. Until I became an adult and I had my daughter. Her name is Virginia Marie.

I took her to a family reunion and Nanny Bette loved children. She loved babies. She wanted to hold my daughter. Naturally I went over to Nanny Bette and let her hold my daughter.

She loved up on her and she said, "I want your baby."

I said to her, "What do you mean you want my baby?"

She said, "She's a beautiful girl. I want her. I want to teach her everything I know. I said you can't have her but when she gets older I promise to bring her over and you can teach her everything."

I insisted, "Nanny Bette – you can't <u>have</u> her! But I tell you what … I'll bring her by when she gets older and you can teach her everything you know."

Nanny Bette answered, "You promise?"

I said, "I promise."

But I remembered her story about when I want something and if I can't have it nobody can have it. I thought about how if I promised her something or if I told her I'd do something then she always knew I would do what I said I'd do. As my daughter got older Nanny Bette wanted every year to hold Virginia and I let her.

When she became about three or four years old, Nanny Bette said, "Now's the time that she can start learning everything."

I asked, "What do you want to teach her?"

Nanny Bette told me, "I want to teach her everything I wanted to teach you but your momma wouldn't let me."

I said, "Well, tell me what you want to teach her."

She replied, "I want to teach her to sew without using her hands. I want to teach her to make brooms fly without touching them. And I want to teach her how to decorate her house without ever lifting anything."

And I said, "Wow, that would come in handy!"

Nanny Bette said, "Yeah it does."

She added, "But I'm going to let her go into those rooms I told you I would not let you go in."

So I said, "Okay, I tell you what, why don't you talk to her daddy and see when could we bring her over? I don't have a car and I can't drive. I can only bring her whenever he'll bring her."

I laid the ball in his court, because I didn't want to get into trouble. That kept me out of getting in trouble. And he always made it to where we were busy and couldn't go over there. But my daughter would always play with her. She never seemed to mind. I don't know if it was because she trusted me. But Nanny Bette's granddaughter heard Nanny Bette asking Virginia and me telling her I would come.

Betty got me off of the playground and she said, "Lisa, don't ever go to Granny's house."

And I said, "Why not?"

She answered, "Because she's very evil. She'll do things and she'll teach Virginia things that she'll never forget and that will scare her. Lisa, my children have *never, ever* been in my grandmother's house."

She would not let her own children go into her grandmother's house. I knew then that I would never let my daughter go there. So she never did go. I saw Betty maybe a year or two ago. I was very intrigued with Nanny Bette and I wanted to get some stories from her.

She said, "Don't ever say her name. She's dead and gone and that's where she'll stay. I'll never tell her stories."

Nanny Bette's daughter and son-in-law lived next to her. She put in a doublewide trailer next to her house. Betty grew up all the time in and out of Nanny Bette's house. As soon as Nanny Bette died Betty had the house tore down. Now, there's an apartment house complex there. I have many times wondered if there are stories or things going on in these apartments.

Nanny Bette said she never stole anything. But all the times growing up when there was a family member or friend who died we had to put up a watch for 24 hours around the clock. She robbed graves. She took the bows off the flowers and made pillows to sell them. She stuffed the pillows with bows from graves and people didn't know she was doing it. She made quilts all the time for sale. She would appliqué the satin bows from the graves into her quilts.

We always watched the graves for 24 hours because we wanted the flower arrangements to stay there. We saw her many times. As soon as the funeral was over we went down the street and watched her take all the bows off. She even picked off flowers to take home for the centerpiece on her table. The things she did were really weird. But she never stole anything her whole life. She just robbed graves. If there was a pretty basket or wreaths she took those, fixed them up and resold them in a yard sale.

Nanny Bette Hensley never married, but had one daughter, Barbara. She never married. Betty the granddaughter knows and saw a lot but will not talk about her. The granddaughter had the home tore down. My mom told me that when she was there brooms flew all over the house all the time. Things were constantly flying. She moved pictures back and forth through the air. If she didn't want a table somewhere it walked. My Mom said it did not slide across the floor, it walked.

Everybody older than their sixties can tell you plenty about Nanny Bette. My dad, who is my stepfather told me that if it wasn't for Nanny Bette he would not have had a Christmas. His family was very poor. She would always bring toys and clothes to the children at Christmastime. Nanny Bette always liked my dad. So she had that good side. She was only interested in teaching the girls, never boys. My firstborn was a boy and she never wanted to fool with him. He was cute, she said, but she never asked me if he could come.

She went to church, she always talked about Jesus, she talked about God and she always talked about doing the right thing, but she was always known as the witch. She was Nanny Bette the witch; everybody knew it. She was never seen outside her house. When we drove by she was never outside. The only time she was ever outside was at our family reunions. I never saw her in the grocery store or gas station. I never saw her in a vehicle. I don't even know how she got to the family reunions. She was there when I got mom there; we stayed until late and she was there when we left.

She had the prettiest flowers but I never saw her in her front yard, not watering them, not nothing. She always stayed in her house. It was just weird. In Waco and Richmond when I grew up there was only one grocery store. Back then it was a Winn Dixie. There were little Mom and Pop grocery stores. It was easy to get food but nobody ever saw her walking.

My grandmother's brother married Nanny Bette's daughter. My mom's uncle's mother-in-law was Nanny Bette. She was no blood kin in my family at all. Her daughter married into my family. Her daughter married a Cox. Betty the granddaughter's maiden name was Cox, daughter of Barbara Cox.

Papaw On the Hill

My Great-grandfather Preston Van Winkle, who lived in the late 1800s, was a dreamer. He was my mom's dad's father. He never dreamed unless it came true, no matter what. She had a little baby boy also and they lived in Richmond, Kentucky.

When Preston was four or five years old, he got up one morning and told his mother, "The horses and the wagon are coming for Tommy."

She said, "No they're not! And don't you say that no more!"

But he repeated, "Mommy, the horses and wagons are coming for Tommy."

The very next morning the horses and the wagon came for Tommy, because he died. The only time the horses and wagons came back then was to pick up the dead.

He always dreamed of all kinds of stuff. He had apple trees and he would be under an apple tree cutting apples to feed to the squirrels. He put little apple pieces or nuts up on his leg and the squirrels crawled up and ate. They ate right out of his hand, but not for anybody else.

I said, "Papaw, tell my about your dreams," because I always dreamed.

His dreams were everything I was told by my mom or by my grandfather, his son, of things that really happened. These were things in their past that happened.

I told him, "Those aren't dreams. You're telling me about Papaw's life or Mom's life or Mammaw's life – when Mammaw was a little girl."

He replied, "I know, but I dreamed it before it happened."

So when I got older we always called them Mammaw and Papaw Van Winkle. They were Preston and Marie Van Winkle. They both passed away now. They lived up on a hill. We all as kids called them Mammaw and Papaw on the hill.

When they phoned we said, "Mom, it's Mammaw on the hill."

To us it was a huge deal and now it's not that big a deal at all.

When I got older I asked, "Papaw, tell me about your dreams."

He answered, "You know I don't usually dream, but when I do dream it comes true."

I asked him, "How did you get that? How did that happen?"

He said, "My father gave it to me before he died."

I told him, "Really? Would you give it to me before you die?"

And he said, "No."

I asked him, "Oh you can't give it to your great grandchildren? You can only give it to closer family?"

"No!" he said. "It will die with me. I won't give it to anybody. It's a curse."

It was handed down in his family from generation to generation. He said it was always handed down right before they died. You could give it to whomever you wanted to.

I asked him, "How do you get it to them?"

He said, "There's a certain sentence that you say over the person. And they get that. My family has always called it a gift. But I've called it a curse."

He told me it was a curse, because when it started he always tried to wake up but he never could wake up. He dreamed the whole thing and he always knew what was coming up.

He knew every time before any of his children died. He outlived almost all of his kids except for three. He buried three or four of his children, but he always knew before it happened.

So I don't know if that's how Nanny Bette got her whatever it's called. Or maybe they studied and trained for it. It could have been something that her mother or grandmother gave to her before they passed away. Because she always seemed very determined when a new little girl was born in her family to give it to her. I don't know if she ever did get her grips on somebody. I don't know if she considered me family.

Everybody knew she was a witch. Nobody questioned it, not ever. All of the people with whom I experienced the ghosts are now dead. Michelle was with me at the barn and she's dead. I experienced the babies crying with Tammy who was with me at the well. So I'll have to get rid of the curse!

It's really weird that the types of things I experienced with those people – Nanny Bette's dead, my grandfather's dead – they're all gone.

My great-grandfather, we very rarely saw him smile. When we hugged him he sat still and never hugged us back.

When we said, "I love you" he would say, "well thank you."

He never said he loved us ever. He was really a different person. He only hugged me and told me he loved me once. That was about a year or less before he died.

I could have been both a witch and a dreamer. I wanted the dreamer. I never really desired to be a witch, good or bad. Maybe if I had witnessed and been around it more it might have been different. I believe we all have powers beyond the ordinary. The mind is so powerful. We can move and do things. But there's also that evil power as well as the good power which people can focus in on.

Obviously there's nothing good in turning snakes into sticks in little girls' hands or blowing up somebody's lamp because you want it and can't have it, and then there was that person who died with their head cut off. Those things are selfish and scary. But I never experienced that one on one with Nanny Bette. I was never afraid to be around her. I never sensed it. I have a very good intuition about spirits and people. Maybe that was only brought out being around specific people when she felt intimidated.

There are certain places I go if I feel the evil auras then I'll stay away from that person or group. There are certain things I see and feel which I don't think everyone else can see or feel. Nanny Bette though could put that on others. I haven't been to see her grave, but I know where she's buried. She was just the sweetest thing to me. But Nanny Bette Hensley was very intimidating with her looks. She died about eight or ten years ago. It may not even have been that long ago.

Runaway Ghost in Car

There's a road called Hwy. 52 East. It's a terrible thing, because we called it Hershey Hill and that's where all the blacks lived when we were growing up. Somewhere there in my bunch of pictures I have pictures of Nanny Bette's house and her.

Growing up we heard a ghost story in Richmond. If you get on Hwy 52 and head toward town, there was a fairground on Hwy 52 and right across from the fairground was the Armory Training Center on the hill. There was an old barn across the street up on the hill. The story was if you ever drove by and parked in front of the barn, the passenger side door would open and you could see the seat would go down like someone was sitting on it.

There was a family that lived there and the man went crazy. He was very jealous. He married a woman who was much younger than him. He would never like her going out anywhere. People looked at her and she was very pretty. She was never allowed to leave the house. She went out to town once and when she got home he got so angry at her he took her to the barn and beat her up. But she had to go out to go to the store and to see family. The last time she went out he took her to the barn and chopped her head off.

Every night at midnight she would try to get into someone's car parked there to get away from him. It seemed that she was trying to run away, but he would always find her. So that was her spirit trying to run away. When I turned sixteen I got my driver's license. My girlfriend Michelle and I parked there at midnight. The door opened and the cushion went in. Nothing bothered us, it's just that the door opened on its own. It looked like somebody sat on the car seat. The door never closed. We had to close it to take off. It was not anything that I ever wanted to do again.

Dead Baby Ghosts in Well

I used to go on a road called Bend Road down in Waco in Madison County where I grew up. I had a friend who lived at the end of Bend Road. My friend lived where the locks were at Kentucky River. Their neighbor, who lived a couple blocks up from them, was Mr. Suell, our bus driver. I would go spend the night with her all the time. I stayed at their house. Her name was Tammy.

I went and spent weeks with them. We had a blast. They had a huge farm. They raised chickens. That's where I learned to wring the necks of chickens. We had their head in our hands and their little bodies running around. That's where I ate my first frog legs.

We had to walk up the road early, early in the morning because we were the first ones on the bus. At four in the morning we had to walk up to Mr. Suell's house to catch the bus, because there was nowhere for him to turn around at their house.

We got up at two or three in the morning, we didn't really go to bed. As we walked down the street at 2:00 a.m., I heard these babies crying. We walked northeast and off to the left I heard babies crying. There was an old church and a well behind the church.

I asked Tammy, "Do you hear the babies crying?"

She said, "No, let's go!"

I told her, "No, there are babies crying."

I was in middle school, probably twelve or thirteen years old.

I said to Tammy, "I want to go over there and check it out."

She said, "We don't have time."

I answered, "Tammy, we have an hour and a half before we have to leave on the bus."

We took our blankets and the bus driver let us take a nap in the back of the bus. So when he got in to drive he just went off as we slept. She didn't want to go over there.

Finally we went to school, came back home and I went back home with her and I asked her mom about it.

Her mom said, "In the 1700 and 1800s, if any of the young women were pregnant out of wedlock, they would have to take their babies to the minister. He sacrificed them by throwing the babies alive down the well."

On certain nights or early in the morning they always heard the babies cry. I don't know if the church is still there. It's been a long time the last time I was there I saw the windows were knocked out. But the stone well was still there. It was a wooden building with a spire, painted gray. There was a cap on the well but we slid it off to look down inside. But the sound was so terrible we had to put the cap right back over the well. It was so loud it would literally make you want to go down there – we felt like babies were down there. I believe it was the worst thing I've ever experienced in my life. It was a sacrificial well not for water but to avoid bringing a reproach upon the church for children to be pregnant and have a baby. I don't know how much of the history is true, but I can tell you I heard the babies crying way too many times.

Dead Man With Axe

There was also a guy who walked up and down the road at midnight with an axe on his shoulder. They said he chopped up his family into small, small pieces. He killed his children, wife, mother-in-law and mother – everyone who lived with him. They said he was crazy and he was only seen at midnight. He only walks from that church to where his house was.

Most of the time I could never get Tammy or her mom and dad to walk at midnight. I was always the little curious one. *I want to see it for my own self.* I finally did see him. We got a bunch of us and we went walking one night. She had a big slumber party. He just walked and we could walk right with him. It was not like he was a shadow or that you could see through him.

We saw everything about him. He wore old bib overalls, red-checkered shirt and brown cap with a long handled axe. The axe was always pointed up toward the sky – never down. He was six feet tall, old and dirty – dingy, dingy, dingy dirty. It was really weird, really strange. I spoke to him the first time because I thought he was real.

My friends just said, "He's dead. That's the ghost we told you about."

I saw him one other time. He never looked at me. He never responded. He kept walking, staring straight ahead.

God Wears Shiny New Pajamas

This story begins with my collegial friendship with storyteller Cynthia Changaris. Cynthia, who is a wonderful storyteller and outgoing, positive person, lives in Louisville and has a Bed and Breakfast in Bethlehem, Indiana, called the Storyteller's Riverhouse Bed and Breakfast. It is very close to the Ohio River, and Cynthia and Mary Hamilton have quarterly storyteller weekend workshops there. Cynthia tells stories from her own experiences, folktales, and sometimes tells a tale which was shared with her by one of her friends. This is her friend Linda's story, which Cynthia told to me. She later encouraged me to contact Linda directly and see if she'd share it for my book. Linda cared for Cynthia's children when they were young.

Linda Moore, Charleston, South Carolina:

Our son's name is Joshua and at the time he had this experience he was fifteen years old. He had a series of brain surgeries to help reduce the effects of epilepsy, or severe seizure disorder. He had two operations in 1990 in Augusta, Georgia at the medical college of Georgia. Joshua lives with us and he is 32 years old.

Joshua had frequent hospitalizations since he was eleven months old. At four years he tested at a normal IQ. Due to the medication and the numerous seizures, Joshua experienced more and more mental delays. He is now classified as mentally challenged. Joshua has a very sweet and innocent spirit. He works in a sheltered workshop for the disabled. He has always been brought up in the faith of Christ. When we were naming our infant son, Joshua, as in the Bible, we didn't know that he would have his own "Wall of Jericho."

When he was a very young child Joshua had conversations with God. One night I saw him talking to Jesus. We let Joshua and his sister, who is a few years older, camp out indoors. Joshua was sitting on the end of the sofa bed in the den. I saw him talking back and forth with someone, but no person was visibly present. I heard his half of the conversation and saw him look back, saying 'yes' or 'no'. He was silhouetted by the fire in the fireplace as he spoke with God, and I sensed a spiritual presence.

Joshua calls the Trinity "God, Jesus and Lord". And I heard him address Jesus. The center for speech in his brain is damaged, so I often interpreted for him. He used to stutter, but that is now miraculously gone.

In the first brain surgery the doctors put probes in brain to try to find the focus for the seizures. The results showed that there were three foci. The removal of brain tissue was not recommended. The surgeon then decided to partially sever the hemispheres of the brain in order to lessen the severity of the seizures. One of us was always with Joshua. We never left him unattended, since he can't take care of himself. Since we left him in the care of the doctors and nurses in the intensive care unit, for the first time we couldn't be with him. We tried to prepare him for this situation. We talked with him before his operation and told him we were not allowed to stay around clock. I worried that he might be scared.

Then when he was back out of the hospital, we got home and talked at breakfast one morning. Joshua told me, talking about how the doctors removed part of his skull,

"They took my head off," he said.

"You know, Josh, I'm so sorry you had to be by yourself and they didn't have room for Mom and Dad. I hope you weren't scared?"

And Josh answered, "I not by myself."

I thought of course, of the hospital staff, and I replied, "Well the doctors and nurses were there with you, Josh."

And Joshua said, "No Jesus, God and Lord were with me."

Then I asked Josh, "They were? What did they say?"

Now I must say that the staff set a TV at the foot of Josh's bed to give him something to watch during his recovery.

"They said, 'That is a good Price is Right show.'"

I looked at him and exclaimed, "That's good Josh! Did they stay with you?"

And Josh replied, "All the time" he said, "At nighttime, they took off their bedroom shoes and got in the bed with me."

Well, I was thinking of that small hospital bed, so I looked at Josh and smiled, "O my goodness! The hospital bed is kind of little. They all got in with you?" Joshua had a funny little smirk on his face, realizing too how small the bed was.

Mrs. Moore, Mr. Moore and Joshua.

I next asked Joshua, "What does God look like?"

And Joshua answered, "God had red hair and a beard. Jesus was brown like Mrs. Miller, and he had brown hair and a beard."

Mrs. Miller is a teacher who Joshua had in middle school. She is African-American. So I understood Josh to be describing Jesus as having olive skin.

Then Josh added, "Lord (the Holy Spirit) had red hair, but no beard." We have red hair in our family, and Josh has strawberry hair.

Next I asked, "What did they have on?"

Joshua answered, "New pajamas"

So I asked Josh, "They had new pajamas? How did you know?"

And Joshua repeated, "They were just new."

So it was a bit later when Joshua and I had another conversation about God, Jesus and Lord visiting him in the hospital. I happened to be wearing a long robe, a 'MuMu'.

Josh spoke up, saying, "God, Jesus and Lord had on pajamas like you."

So to clarify what their clothing looked like, I asked Joshua, "Josh, were their pajamas shiny?"

And he answered, "Yes."

I was curious if, since seeing God, Jesus and Lord in the hospital, maybe Joshua had seen them again? Josh said no. I asked him to tell me whenever he might see them again.

I know that Joshua walks close with the Lord. He prays for people all the time. I am a high school math teacher, and I have youngsters come to my home for tutoring. Joshua tells them that he'll pray that they make 100 on their test.

And when the kids return they thank him, saying, "Thanks Josh! I did really well on that test!" We are really blessed to have Joshua in our family.

Jesus is Holding Your Baby

Ashley Campbell, Louisville

I was 25 weeks pregnant when I went to the doctor.

The doctor told me, "Something's wrong. I'm sending you to the hospital."

I went into the hospital and they ran tests. I had arrived at 2 PM. At 6 PM they came in and said, "We're going to take the baby."

I immediately went into the operating room and they took Jocelyn. She was born at 25 weeks and one day. She weighed one pound and eight ounces. They had actually told my parents that neither one of us would live until midnight. They told them to prepare themselves because we would both die. I woke up from the anesthesia at 11:30 PM. I was in a hospital room in

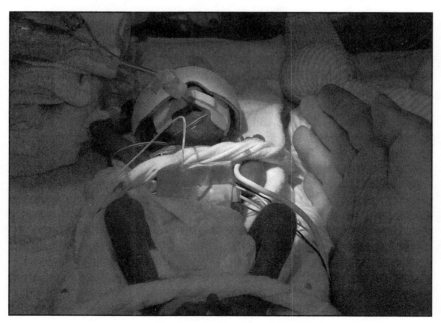

Newborn Jocelyn Campbell.

a different part of the hospital from Jocelyn before I got to see her. She was born on a Thursday and I got to see her late on Sunday.

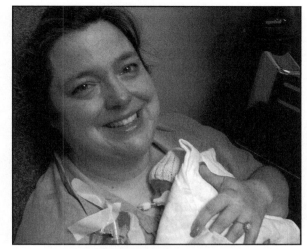

Ashley and Jocelyn Campbell.

When I got there to see her, honestly, I thought she was going to die. She weighed a pound and a half. Although she was twelve inches long she looked like a newborn puppy. She was just the size of my hand.

The doctor expressed his disapproval of my going over there, through the nurses, as he kept calling my room and I wasn't there.

But I told them, "If my baby is going to die then she's going to die with me standing next to her."

I sat at her bedside the majority of the time.

A friend of mine came in on Monday after she was born on Thursday. We are Christians. I had sat on the Habitat for Humanity board and I had emailed to tell them that something was wrong and to please keep us in their prayers. They sent an email all around the world for people to pray for me and Jocelyn. My husband John's company is international and so he talked with his boss and they sent emails out all over the world too.

On that Monday my friend Leanne came in to visit. She is not a Christian, although she believes there is a Higher Being. But that's it.

She walked into the NICU (Neonatal Intensive Care Unit) with me and she said, "Jesus is here."

I was surprised to hear her say that.

We walked over to Jocelyn's bed and she said, "No, Jesus is here and he's holding her."

It gave me goose bumps. For someone who doesn't believe in Jesus or God to believe that He was there, holding my baby and keeping her safe, taking care of her…It's just amazing to me! She does past life regressions for people. She does see visions. She told me that He was sitting there holding her. So if she saw that or some spirit told her that – I don't know.

After that she didn't <u>immediately</u> get better, but she steadily got better. Her health condition never regressed. When she was born they put her on an oscillating ventilator. The ventilator shook her so her lungs could open up and take in air. Her lungs weren't developed enough for her to breathe. After four days they changed to a regular ventilator, which forced air into her lungs. When she was born her eyes were still fused. To protect the eyes they are fused together until a certain week. It was nearly two weeks after she was born when her eyes became un-fused.

Since babies put fat on their body in the last six weeks, Jocelyn had no fat. She was literally skin and bones. You could see the blood in her body – she was a bright red. We took a picture with my hand next to Jocelyn and my hand is twice as big as she was. It's pretty amazing.

The miracle girl.

I never even questioned Leanne telling me about what she sensed or saw. I just thought *yes, He's here.*

Not a week after Leanne told us Jesus was holding Jocelyn I got an email about the little girl smelling the rain.

In the story the girl says, "I smell Jesus."

She was a premature baby who survived her early birth and years later commented that the smell of the rain reminded her of when Jesus held her when she was an infant.

The Gift of God
Dorothy Kress

My birth name is Dorothy Ellen Alsup. I was born in Ogden, Utah. I have two sisters and a brother. I'm the oldest. I was born August 27, 1960. I lived in Utah until I was 17 years old. It's in the Rocky Mountains.

We saw a lot of UFOs. We lived by Hillfield Air Force Base, so who knows what was ours or what was otherworldly. The Dugway Proving Grounds were not far away from Ogden, where they test experimental aircraft. I know they were flying experimental craft because I saw a Harrier in 1968, before anyone knew about it. I was eight years old at the time.

My Dad worked for the Navy. He was a Chief, and was responsible for pushing the button in the case of a nuclear war for the Western half of the United States, if the President was unable to. He started out working in ammunitions, loading the airplanes with ammunition and bombs.

I was a wild child, not in terms of partying but I was really independent. I wanted to be an interior decorator, photographer, artist and journalist – everything. I did it all when I went through high school. I actually designed a house that was built. One of my sisters was wild in terms of hanging around with biker gangs, and my other sister was pretty much quiet and reserved. My brother was the "good guy". By the time he came around my Dad had given up on having a boy.

My Dad taught me how to fix cars, repair the house and took me out to go hunting but that quit when my brother came along. I was kind of glad. I hated being the surrogate-son. I was kind of raised like a boy.

The houses we lived in were always haunted. My parents always seemed to manage to buy haunted houses. I learned early on I had 'special' talents. For example, our house in Bear River had a big septic tank. The guy they hired to come out and look for it couldn't find it. He was supposed to be a water witch. Remember, this was before they had ground radar and such, so he used metal dowsing rods.

I asked, "Could I try?" I was eight years old. He passed the dowsing rods to me. I found the septic tank on my first try.

Once, when my great-grandmother was dying, we were at the hospital. I was eighteen years old then. I saw a lady sitting in the room with her. I asked my family about her, since I didn't know who it was.

They replied, "What lady?"

I said, "The lady holding Great-grandma's hand by her bedside."

They said, "There's nobody in there." And there wasn't when we went in there.

My family asked, "What did she look like?"

The person I described – they told me – looked like my dead aunt. She died of ovarian cancer before I was born. Her name was Vera. She looked to be in her

Dorothy and Great-grandmother.

thirties with shoulder-length, curly light brown hair. It looked like she had a dress that women wore in the 1950s. My great-grandmother was in a coma by then so I don't know if she saw her, too.

I had a premonition that she was going to die, so I asked my family to go and see her in the hospital. She died the following Sunday.

We had a family tradition that the first-born daughter of each generation was born with what was called "The Gifts of God". We even had a relative that was burned as a witch. She lived in the Black Forest of Germany, near Nuremberg. She was actually an herbalist and midwife.

The house we lived in, in Bear River, Utah, had a tendency to catch fire. We were constantly putting out fires. One time it caught fire and my parents blamed it on my brother. He was only two years old. They said he kept playing with matches. It almost burned down after we moved out but was rebuilt. I don't know why that happened, unless there was somebody who had lived and died who was fascinated with fires. One fire happened in the bathroom where there wasn't really anything to catch on fire. When the calendar on the back porch caught fire they blamed my brother as well. We were on a farm in the middle of nowhere.

My mother was psychic but was afraid of it. My mom was 5'4". I think being psychic was part of her problem. My mom went nuts when I was eight years old, after having many failed miscarriages.

The farm in Bear River was about five acres. We raised stuff for ourselves, such as vegetables, chickens and pigs. One year, my mom picked up an injured turkey, which was in a crate that fell off the back of a truck. She nursed it back to health. When it got time for turkey dinner for Thanksgiving, my dad killed the turkey but told us kids it was a different turkey, since we thought of the turkey as a pet. He said he traded with our neighbor for his turkey. I really hated the pigs. The pigs got out a lot and headed to the neighbor's house. I hated to go get them back. It was a two-mile walk each way. I was very happy when the pigs went to the butchers!

There were noises, knocks, voices and things all the time. My mom thought I was the source of the talking and noises. We lived there for four years. When I was twelve we moved to the next house. Before we went there we spent two months in California because my Dad got transferred. Then we moved in with my uncle back in Utah until we got a house. I was there over the summer between school grades. The home in North Ogden was about 8-10 years when they bought it. It was brick. It was in a well-to-do neighborhood up against the side of the mountains. I always wondered how they lucked into it and that maybe it was because it was haunted! Nobody wanted it. We had to pay only $12,000 for it. Other houses in the same neighborhood sold for $45,000 back then. The sellers didn't tell us it was haunted.

Within one or two months after we moved in strange things started to happen. Our bedroom was in the basement. I shared it with my younger sister. It was a pretty good size room and we had two big double beds. The first time I felt someone sit down on the bed by me, I just thought I was dreaming. I was used to our farm house and dismissing all the odd things. Two nights later my door opened and closed all by itself. I heard the door from my sleep and thought *oh that must be my mom*. Then something grabbed my arm. I opened my eyes, figuring it had to be my mom. This guy was standing there. He was in his late twenties. He looked fairly dirty. He was dressed in a dark suit. He had on a dark hat and a beard. He looked like a pioneer. Then I screamed and covered up my head with the bed covers. I realized I couldn't see what he was going to do so when I pulled away my covers he was gone.

My sister woke and told me, "No, you just had a bad dream."

It got worse. One night I was laying in bed reading. I was a night owl and often couldn't get to sleep. My shelves, behind me on the bed, picked up from the backside at the wall and everything spilled down on me. I had antiques that my great-grandmother gave me. I was angry. Then later I thought *how did <u>that</u> happen?* It was pretty constant after that – people saw things out of the corner of their eyes.

My sisters and brothers thought I was nuts. We all were watching TV. Then all of a sudden the television picked up. It moved around the room like someone invisible carried it and landed back on the table where it was sitting.

Shelf that fell down.

Alsup family home in Bear River, Utah.

I looked at my sisters and brothers and said, "Did you see that? Am I really nuts <u>now</u>?" They sat there with their jaws dropped open. That happened in broad daylight so I knew I didn't dream that. The TV had those rabbit ears on top of it, which didn't fall off but still it unplugged itself.

Most of them don't remember their childhood because it was beaten out of them. I don't want to dwell on that because that will hurt the family.

My dad doesn't know about the abuse because he was gone a lot in the Navy.

My mom babysat a little girl. I wasn't in the house at the time and she saw another girl in the bathroom.

My mom told her that I was at school. The girl shook her head and said, "Uhuh, Dorothy's in the bathroom." The little girl was scared and my mom realized she'd better make up a story.

She told her, "Oh you probably saw me and thought I was Dorothy."

There was a little boy ghost too. He looked like he was about three years old. He had blond hair and blue eyes. I saw him once. I was in my bedroom listening to my radio and doing my homework. The door was open and for some reason I looked up. For just a fraction of a second I saw a little boy there. I saw him a few more times after that. When we plowed up part of the backyard to make a little garden, we found an old tractor toy buried in the ground. It was a pioneer era toy tractor, like one the horses pulled. It was fairly rusted.

They looked like a little pioneer family. There were three of them, the little boy, the lady and the man. I think the family was killed by Shoshone Indians on the site where the home was built. The ghosts hated Indians. One time we had a foster boy come to live with us, who was Native American. He was slugged in the stomach by one of the ghosts. They were very active ghosts.

I didn't like going to church when I was a teenager. However, one time I decided to go with my mom, because it was Easter Sunday. I came home with my mom after church and went downstairs to change.

My dad asked, "How did you get dressed so quickly?"

"What are you talking about? I was at church with Mom. I thought it would be nice to go."

He said "No you didn't go."

I said, "Yes I did."

He retorted, "No you didn't. I saw you walk from the bedroom to the bathroom and back."

"I was at church, Dad," I insisted.

He turned really pale and said, "Oh". It scared him real bad.

My family thought I was possessed due to the ghosts and my abilities. They arranged for an exorcism on me. My Dad came to get me, because he said we had to have a family meeting. I should have realized something was up, since my sister went to the same school and he didn't come get her too. I was really suspicious, *what's going on?*

The first I know when I walked in the door, the Mormon missionary pointed at me and said "Out Satan!"

"What are you talking about?" I didn't realize they were talking to me at first. I started to laugh because I thought it was a joke.

I said, "You got to be kidding me!"

Then I realized they were serious, and I went down in my bedroom and closed the door. The two male missionaries followed me in.

In the Mormon Church there are six degrees of priesthood and the missionaries are supposed to have a direct link to God. I have no idea what they saw in the bedroom. I just know that they turned heels and left and refused to go back downstairs after that. They didn't stop until they were outside. I don't know what they saw. I was in shock because I realized they were serious!

Then I got mad, telling my family, "Take me back to school you guys. You bring me home for this crap?" I must have been about fifteen or sixteen years old then and a lot of the activity in the house centered on me. I guess they thought I did it all, the voices, stuff being moved and weird sounds.

My husband never believed in ghosts before he went to my old house in North Ogden. We went to Utah to get married. We planned to stay at my parent's house. He decided he wanted to go downstairs to take a nap. After a little while, we heard a scream. It was my husband. When he came up, he said someone he couldn't see had sat down on the bed next to him.

"Oh my God, oh my God, oh my God" he said. "I'm not going back to that bedroom. We're going to a motel." It creeped him out badly.

I said, "Richard we can't really afford a motel."

So we went up to a campground and spent the rest of the nights in a tent. I think he preferred rattlesnakes to ghosts. I think that is stupid. A ghost might hurt you but rattlesnakes could kill you. He still won't stay there to this day.

I had a party there one time and my girlfriend spent the night. She sat on the bed across from me, looking at the shelf behind me. She stopped talking mid-sentence and her jaw dropped.

I asked, "What's the heck's going on? You must have seen something."

She answered, "Your doll moved."

I told the ghost, "Leave my shelf alone, damn-it. I already told you that once!" The doll then slid back into the place where it was supposed to be.

She would not stay with us and she went home at 2:00 AM.

By that point I was so used to that kind of thing happening. It happened all the time. The time I was most freaked out was when I heard heavy breathing in the bathroom. It sounded like someone was on a microphone, breathing in and out. I finished going to the bathroom, went up and got my Dad.

I said, "Dad you got to hear this, something is weird in the bathroom, come down and fix it."

He asked, "Fix what?"

"There's some ghost down there getting his jollies off while I'm going to the potty." I said.

"What?" He asked again.

"Someone or something is doing a lot of heavy breathing."

So he went down there to check it out. He heard something and it freaked him out. But he said it was the water in the pipes or some such thing. He ended up tearing out part of the wall to 'fix it'. He couldn't handle the fact that it must be a ghost.

Alsup home in North Ogden, Utah.

In fact, the last time I went back home, there were some of the holes in the wall still there. It makes me wonder if Dad is still looking for the sounds in the pipes!

My dad still lives in the house.

My Dad reported, "I was at the top of the stairs. Then it felt like someone took their foot and kicked me in the back and I fell down the stairs."

Home with Ghost Babysitter.

His shirt had a footprint on it, like somebody stepped in dirt before kicking him.

I went back last time and told the ghosts, "If you touch my dad I'll get rid of you. You leave my dad alone." I talked to the ghosts and tried to get them to leave. I don't know why they won't leave. Maybe they're afraid of crossing over.

Dorothy's son with mysterious image.

It was about three years ago when my mom died. My mom's ghost was there for a while. I saw her when she died and she appeared in the car next to me as I was driving.

Dad said she used to crawl in bed and sleep with him after she died and he missed that.

I told him, "You're holding her back from crossing over, Dad."

He said maybe she should take the other ghosts with her. It was the first time he actually openly admitted that he believed in ghosts.

The day after I graduated high school in 1978, I went to live at a commune in Fort Morgan, Colorado. Fort Morgan is about an hour's drive east of Denver. I was seventeen at the time. It was a back-to-nature kind of place. We had goats and gardens. It used to be an old boy's school. The school was haunted.

One time I was in my bedroom, which used to be the principal's office. I was the only one sleeping in the school building. There was another building that the others lived in. I heard music at the other end of the building. I thought *someone left the radio on.* I walked out to find no one else was in the building. Then it dawned on me; there was no electricity in that building!

One time I heard kids on the playground. However, the commune was all adults. Not a lot happened there – I wasn't there that long. Mostly I was in Denver and I went to the commune on the weekends. I ended up getting knocked up on my 18th birthday. I didn't really know about birth control or even that it was possible to get pregnant on your first try. I ended up going back home. When my baby was two months old I moved out to an apartment building. That's where I took the picture of the ghost. I didn't get any bad feelings about that picture. It was like the spirit was being very protective of him – almost like it was guarding us.

White Cloud wolf dog watches orb.

My kid had a ghost babysitter. When he was really little, only a month old, my sister and I were getting ready to go out for dinner. My son was in one of those beds that attach to a baby's swing set. I had it swinging so I could get ready then it wound down and stopped. My son started to fuss a little bit.

My sister said, "I'll go wind it up." Right then we heard the wrrr, wrr sound of it being wound up, then click, click he was swinging again.

It freaked me out a little bit, but at least it was being helpful. Other things happened all the time. I would hear the bottle fall out of his crib. He'd start to get fussy and when I walked in the bottle would be back in his hand.

My son used to talk about "the lady who helped him". He learned to talk really young. He had a pretty good vocabulary for a six-month old.

When he was nine months old he would say, "Hi, how are you I'm fine!"

The spirit stayed with the house when we moved away. One time my roommate's boyfriend came over drunk. He dropped my roommate's baby on purpose. Although he weighed 300 pounds, I picked him up and threw him out of the house. Something in me snaps when I see someone hurting a child. I took the ghost picture that same night. I think the spirit helped me get him out of the house because I picked him up with one hand and I opened up the door with the other hand. I wouldn't have been able to do that by myself. I've never been that angry, so I don't know for sure how that happened.

As I grew up, I kept getting premonitions of things that would later happen. I would get flashes. Every once in a while I would hear they came true. I was in my twenties living near downtown Chicago in Roger's Park at 31st and Wells Street. My kid was in school. I was going to go shopping. I went out to the car, but something made me go back inside. I was able to catch a phone call. It was the school calling to say my son fell in the bathroom. He slipped on some water on the floor and cut open his face.

I dreamt that a school bus was going to get hit by a train. But I didn't know any details – where, when or anything like that. So I kind of ignored the dream. Then I was at a friend's house. She had on the TV news and a reporter mentioned that a commuter train had hit a school bus. It hurt a lot of people including a lot of kids.

When I get premonitions, the events usually happen within three days. I usually am sleeping but I had a few waking premonitions. I once had a dream that an airplane from Air Canada was going to crash. But I didn't even know there was an Air Canada. I dreamt the flight number, time of arrival in Chicago, how many people were supposed to be on the plane and that it was going to happen due to hydraulic pressure failure. We lived by O'Hare Airport. I called information. I asked for the phone number for Air Canada and they gave me the number. I debated with myself about calling and then I thought, *what's the worst they can do to me – lock me up?* I thought if I got someone to check things out then maybe some people won't die. I asked to talk to someone in charge. They got a man on the line.

I told him, "One of your planes is going to crash."

The official asked me, "Is this a joke?"

I answered immediately, "I swear to God."

He then asked, "Is it going to be a bomb?"

I said, "No it's going to be hydraulic pressure failure."

I told him it had 118 passengers and was scheduled to get to Chicago at such and such a time. It was supposed to take off from Montreal and land in O'Hare.

"Somewhere around Minneapolis it's going to crash."

He asked, "How did you get the flight number? We don't even announce it until shortly before we list the flight."

I said, "I dreamt it, I didn't get it."

The official then asked me, "Do your dreams come true?"

"All the time" I answered, "but this is the first time I got enough details to be able to call and warn someone.

He said, "Within how long will the crash happen?"

I answered, "Three days."

The man said, "That flight is scheduled to leave tomorrow."

"Then check for a fluid leak" I insisted. He promised me he'd check out the plane. He hung up and I thought I'd never hear from him again.

Next thing I know, about four or five hours later I got a phone call.

"Oh my God" he said.

I asked him "What?"

"You were right! Their plane had an oil leak and they would not have discovered it. It was bad enough that they probably would have lost hydraulic pressure."

Then he added, "Thanks for calling and if you ever have any more dreams like this feel free to call." I don't remember his name. I don't know if they even have it on record.

That was one I felt good about.

I had another premonition of an airplane crash. I acted on it, calling the airlines but they didn't believe me. The plane crashed. But I didn't have enough details in that dream. It was the same year or the year after the Air Canada dream. This time it was an American Airlines flight. I dreamt that a plane was flying in the mountains but they were in the wrong valley. They didn't realize they were in the wrong place. As they were flying down the valley instead of turning up toward the airport they swerved to miss a Cessna and plowed into the mountains.

I called American Airlines and I spoke with a man.

I asked, "Are there any of your flights that are going to be going through mountains? Verify where they are, make sure they know where they are and talk to your pilots to watch out for a little Cessna.

And they just kind of laughed at me. They wouldn't listen. And I told them to call Air Canada if they didn't believe me. "I get real warnings."

The plane crashed. It was a flight in Columbia. There was a TV show about it. The plane was going in for a landing but the drug lords had taken out the transponders planes use to navigate the mountain passes. The pilots thought they were in one valley but they were actually in a different one. And they don't know why the plane suddenly veered and crashed. But I knew it was because they were avoiding the Cessna. They thought it had something to do with air guidance control. It happened in late 1995. It was so remote that it took them a while to get up there for rescue and recovery.

Our current home is not haunted, but we took a photo of our dog watching an orb.

I saw Resurrection Mary before I knew about her story. We lived in Justice, Illinois not far from the cemetery. Since there was no school bus, I had to drive my son to and from school. I went to pick him up at school. It was later than normal, because my son got detention for being unruly. It was after dark when I went to go get him.

We were driving home and I saw a lady walking along the side of the road, in a nightgown. It was snowing, so I thought she must be cold.

I thought *I better stop to see what is going on and if she needs help.* So we pulled over. My son opened his door to go ask her and I looked into the rearview mirror. She was nowhere to be seen. The street was wide open. There's nowhere she could have gone. There was a cemetery wall on one side and open fields on the other side. There is no way she could have gone anywhere! There were no cars and nobody to be seen down the street.

I didn't know about Resurrection Mary until three or four months after that happened. I was talking with someone and he started to tell me the story of a ghost called Resurrection Mary. Then it clicked, that maybe I've seen her. There was another lady I knew who might have seen her too but it wasn't as clear as when we saw her. I was told that people looking for her don't see her but we didn't know about her and maybe that is why we saw her.

There is a legend about Resurrection Mary that a man picked up a young woman who was hitchhiking. Richard Crow tells about it in his Richard Crow's Ghost Tours of Chicago. The driver took her dancing and to dinner, then drove her home. She got out of the car and went to her house. The man suddenly realized she had left her sweater in the car.

He took the sweater and went to the door and knocked. Mary's mom came to the door.

He said, "Your daughter left her sweater in my car." He noticed the woman was upset and asked what is wrong? She replied her daughter had died a year earlier.

I have seen a lot of tragedy in real life. Once I was driving on the highway and it was foggy. I was taking a friend home after she came to eat dinner with us. It was foggy and I heard a muffled bang. We came up out of the fog and around a turn. I saw that a car crashed into the metal barricade in the center median and was on fire. I found out later, as he came out of the toll-booth, he somehow got on the wrong side of the highway without realizing it. The paper said he was drunk and that the children in the back seat were about three and seven years old. I didn't find this out until later.

It's kind of hard to talk about. Anyway, I pulled my car over to the outside emergency lane and stopped. When we first got there, only the engine was on fire. I tried to cross the highway to help, but my friend kept pulling me back. I almost got hit by traffic a couple times. We could not see far due to the foggy conditions. I knew there were people in the car but at that time I didn't realize there were kids in the back seat.

Suddenly the car exploded and all three of us heard screaming, but not physically, it was in our minds. That's the one time I prayed to God to let people die, so they wouldn't suffer. I don't know how to explain it, but I felt them die and then they were at peace.

I heard a voice ask me, "What happened?"

I told them their car had crashed and caught fire. Then the voice got scared and said he was at fault. I explained it was an accident and to look for the light. I felt his joy, happiness and peacefulness and felt all of them go. It was just overwhelming to watch three people burn to death. I really felt sorry for the parents who lost their two children and their nephew, but I knew the people who died were okay. I still get sad when I pass by the accident spot.

Me, my husband, my son, my mother and father all went to Nauvoo and Carthage, Illinois. Carthage is the town where Joseph Smith – founder of the Mormon religion – was assassinated by an angry mob. There is a place on the floor where his brother Hyrum's blood stained the floor. You cannot see it with your eyes but they tell you where to put your hands and a photo shows a bloodstain on the floor. They tried to strip the wood but the stain is still there.

My mom was sad because this was where the founder of her Mormon church was killed. After we climbed the stairs, my Mom wasn't feeling well, so she sat down in a chair. What happened next was that I looked up and before the tour guide even started to speak, I saw three men in the room. One man was sitting on the bed, one was at the window looking outside and one sat at a desk. They were being held in that room on the second floor, instead of a regular jail cell. The guy by the window was Joseph Smith. He heard a noise and turned around to look at the door. They all heard the mob coming upstairs. His brother Hyrum ran to the door and braced himself against it to hold it shut. Somebody shot through the door and hit him in the head. He fell down on the floor dead.

The door burst open and they shot Joseph Smith, who fell through the window to the dirt below. The third man dove under the bed and was not killed.

I saw all that happen. Both my Mom and I had emotional reactions before the tour guide started talking.

The tour guide said, "You must be relatives."

I asked her, "Why is that?"

She answered, "Because only relatives see the scene of his death."

Apparently Joseph Smith was my great-great-great uncle.

I <u>never</u> heard what happened before that vision, only that he was killed there. My mom saw the same thing happen. I took photographs in that building. One picture of the kitchen showed a towel flying in mid-air that was not there when I took the photo. Other pictures came out with weird streaks of light. But the pictures on that roll of film before and after that building were perfectly fine. Every single picture from there had something unusual in it.

Back in Utah I took part in a psychic contest, which was sponsored by *Omni* Magazine. It was a test of people's ability to do remote viewing. It happened in 1981 and was run through their magazine. We each paid $5 to participate. I did it just for fun because I was bored. They projected an image generated on a computer. We were asked to sit, clear out our minds and draw what we saw. There were five categories of pictures. The one being broadcast at the time I chose was land and water interfaces.

It turned out that the image I drew matched the computer-generated scene. I saw mountains with a thin strip of land in front of them. In front of the thin strip of land was lake and in front of the lake was another strip of land. I also saw a triangular shape to the right I drew as a pine tree. My drawing almost identically matched the photo they sent me, except the triangular shape was a fishing net in the water. They told me that the percentage of those who matched their chosen category was very low. I found out later that it was the government's way of finding out who had remote viewing abilities, which they could use for espionage. I heard another guy who participated in the test was so good at remote viewing he went into a government program. I don't know why they didn't ask me to participate, maybe because I had a child and was a single mother.

I participated in the Pan-Pagan Psychic Olympics in the 1990's. Some friends of mine ran this contest. I later won first place. I still have the plaque.

They said, "You say you're psychic. Put your money where you mouth is."

They actually hired me as the caterer to cook food for the event.

I had food in the oven, trying to cook dinner and I said, "I hope it won't take too long."

We were in a campground in the south side of Chicago near the Indiana border. They tested us on five types of psychic abilities – pychometry, precognition, telepathy, telekinesis and dowsing. A friend administered the test and enlisted other folks to participate. He was involved with the Paranormal Institute in Chicago. I don't know if they had the Psychic Olympics again.

There were about 20 of us tested. The other people had good psychic abilities too. The lady who took first place in the dowsing took second place in the other four categories. I didn't really know her before then.

In the telekinesis contest someone rolled six dice and we were asked to make them come up all ones. But I had a block against rolling ones from playing Yahtzee for so long I couldn't do that.

I told the tester and she said, "Well, pick a number besides one then." So I chose six.

It then came up with six sixes, five sixes, four sixes and six sixes. They then averaged my scores.

For the dowsing contest they marked out an area into a grid of 12 squares. They told us what was buried, but they didn't tell us which squares. There were 12 items but not all were buried. We had to then dowse over each square to find out which had buried things. I matched two squares and the other lady matched six. It turned out they buried things in eight of the 12 squares. I only did a little bit of dowsing, just for fun, before that.

For the telepathy contest they took us to some outside picnic tables. We were asked to see which cards a man inside a trailer was looking at. They used a double deck of the ESP five-symbol Zenner cards. The symbols include a circle, star, square, cross and wavy vertical lines. I got a bunch of matches averaging 80 percent correct.

For the psychometry contest we touched various items then walked over to give them to the person they belonged to. There were watches and other things they had on their person for a long time. They randomly went around and got the things from the people who were administering the tests. I got every one right. I suggested that they instead test with name and photo not the person standing there because I can read body language.

That's why when I later did psychic readings at various functions for people, I told them not to say a thing at the beginning. I only did readings for friends until a friend who was a reader got sick. This was about 1993 in Chicago. That was the first time I did readings at an event where people paid. It was a Richard Crow Ghost Tour and we were on a boat. It was kind of windy, so the boat was rocking a lot and my rune stones kept sliding around, making it tough to do a reading. I used a hand-painted set of my own rune stones.

There was one lady who went to every single one of the psychics. Then she came to me and asked me to read for her. I asked her, "Why are you going to every psychic?"

She said, "They said they can't read for me and suggested I come to you." I told her I'd try and when I cast the runes I said, "This can't be correct." So I threw them again.

I told her, "I guess I can't read for you either, I am sorry!"

She asked me, "What does it say? I don't care if it is wrong, just tell me!"

I reluctantly told her, "It says you're going to marry a woman."

"How in the hell did you know I'm a lesbian?" she exclaimed!

At this point I knew the reading was correct, so finished it for her. She had been married before to a man and didn't know how she was going to tell her kids.

I asked her, "Are they adults?"

She answered, "Yes."

I told her, "Well, it's your life!"

Every time I threw the runes they came out in the same pattern. It was really kind of freaky. I've also used the Mother Earth Tarot and the Native American Indian Medicine Cards.

A friend, who didn't even know I did readings, bought me a set of the Indian Medicine cards. I do that too – I'll see something which I know is not for me and I'll hold on to it until that person comes into my life to give it to them.

I took a course in Hindi in college. I had trouble learning classical languages and only knew little bits of Greek, Spanish and French. We had so much rain and Chicago was flooded. The night before I stayed up all night because I knew somebody was going to go in the creek. Early the next morning, just as the sun was coming up, a car missed the bridge and went into the flooded creek. There were volunteers holding the car to keep it from sinking and they pulled the kids out through the windows. The passengers didn't speak English. I suddenly remembered the Hindi I learned. I asked the woman how many were in the car. She said eight but we saw seven survivors. I told the rescuers there was one more in the water. I happened to turn around and look downstream. Just then I saw a woman roll belly up from under the water. Oh my God, she is pregnant I thought, and started running towards her. I thought I was running quickly down the slope to the water to get the woman but someone went by me like a streak. They got her out, did CPR and managed to get her breathing. The baby she was carrying died but she survived. For some reason the little kids didn't get pulled out of the car by the floodwaters but the pregnant lady did.

If I hadn't talked to them in Hindi she would have died. So sometimes, we do things for later use. I don't believe in coincidences. It seems like God puts me wherever he needs me.

This kind of thing happens all the time. If I have a day go by where somebody doesn't ask me for something it's a miracle. It's almost a game now. People will walk up to me and tell me their life story as if I am a close friend.

One kid in a game I was playing was pacing back and forth, and I asked, "Are you okay?"

He said, "No."

I asked "Why not? What's wrong?"

He answered, "I'm thinking of killing myself." I spent the following three hours talking to that kid. Last time I played the game, he was still playing.

In 2005, I was living in Tennessee when I got a call that my mom had a stroke and my dad suffered a massive heart attack at the same time. I drove out there, thinking one of them would be alive. I didn't think my mom would be. I had to get to them in Utah but I couldn't fly. The plane changing altitude is not good for my heart. It took three days to get there and I went slowly so I could adjust to the higher altitude along the way.

Driving into Wyoming near Cheyenne, I came near one of the highest mountains in America. I hit fog and whiteout conditions. Then my mom appeared in the car in the front passenger seat. So I knew she died.

She said, "I'm sorry for everything I put you through."

I answered, "Well Mom, we're in whiteout conditions. I can't talk with you right now." I thought *it's kind of dangerous. I might die and join you!* So she left and anyway I turned back to Cheyenne because they closed the roads.

Right after she left my eyeglasses broke at the bridge of the nose. I had them for only five months. There was no pressure that broke them. They just fell off my face. I tried to drive holding up a piece of the eyeglasses up to one of my eyes – that was not fun. So I went to an optometrist in Cheyenne.

I told them I had to drive to Utah, "How can you help me with this?"

They tried to fix them but the glasses didn't hold together. They told me my only chance was a place down the road. Now I have a severe astigmatism, which normally means a two-week wait for special lenses to be shipped. This other place just happened to have the lenses I needed and they had a two-for-one eyeglass price special.

I told them, "I think my mom just died and I need to get there as soon as possible. Are you going to be able to help me? I can't sit around and wait for them to be done."

They didn't have time to custom grind the lenses. But I found a frame that worked. I wanted one of the pairs to serve as sunglasses and I tried to figure out the best shade for that purpose. I heard my mom's voice say *get purple.* I thought *purple – why would I want purple glasses? That would make everything look a weird color.* But the feeling just got stronger and stronger and I thought *Okay – I'll do it!* I rolled my eyes and told the person I chose purple.

They said, "Why are you getting purple tinted glasses?"

I answered, "I have no clue."

"You don't like it?" he tried to clarify.

I told him, "Well, purple was my mom's favorite color. Maybe it will be an honor to her."

I bought the glasses and he only charged me for the eyeglasses and not the exam and the purple tinting.

I returned to my drive up through the mountains and they opened the roads. It was no longer snowing but there were still whiteout conditions. I still couldn't see with the glare, so I pulled out the purple sunglasses, hoping it might help. Immediately I clearly saw the road as if there was no more glare. When the drivers behind my car realized I could see, they kept following right behind me to also get through the mountains and the snow glare. I drove through the mountains and back down again in plenty of time. And it turned out that the time I saw my mother in my car was the time of her death – almost to the minute.

In July 2005 a friend and I traveled to Savannah, Georgia and stayed in the Eliza Thompson House. We asked for one of their most haunted rooms. There was a slave quarters behind the house and our room was located out there on the third floor. After we checked in and got to our room my friend went to the bathroom to take a shower. I saw a boy bending over looking into the courtyard. He was dressed in a child's sailor outfit like the children of the 1800s wore.

Seeing him lean way over the railing I said to him, "That's not smart."

He looked up and then ran down the walkway. He passed behind a little section of wall and never came back out. I thought he was a real boy and I panicked, thinking he fell. I looked around for him but found nobody.

That night in our room the television came off and came back on by itself. My friend thought I was playing with the remote control.

I told her, "No, and it's right over by you on the nightstand."

Later we turned off the TV and left, locking our room to go to dinner. We walked over to the downstairs courtyard to get into the main section of the house. From there we happened to glance back at our room. The door was wide open, the lights and TV were on. I walked all the way back to our room.

I told the ghost, "You can play with the TV and lights, but leave the door closed and locked. I don't want my stuff stolen!"

We returned from dinner to find the TV back on and the bed turned down. The hotel manager told us he'd leave chocolates on the bed but we didn't find any.

The next morning I asked, "Why didn't you leave any chocolates?"

He told us that he did leave extra chocolates but – it happens a lot – the ghost likes chocolates and takes them instead of the guests. Then at night when we tried to sleep we heard footsteps walking in the room above us. I thought *whomever that is I wish they'd stop doing that so we could sleep.* Then I suddenly realized there was no room above us, since we were on the top floor!

It was September 9, 2001. I went outside in my yard and I was looking at the dogs playing. All of the sudden my vision clouded and I saw a plane hit a wall and another plane hit a wall. Then a plane seemed to hit a nut (like a bolt) in the ground and a fourth plane hit a field. And then I saw fifth plane but I didn't see it go anywhere.

I went in and I told my husband, "We're going to go to war."

He told me, "You're crazy. We're not even fighting with anybody."

I repeated, "No. We're going to be at war really soon and I don't know why. I had the weirdest vision that I know is going to lead us to war."

On September 11 when the first plane hit the World Trade Center my dad called.

He said, "You need to turn on the TV."

I asked, "Why?"

He answered, "Just turn on the TV. I can't talk." I turned on the TV and they were talking about a plane hitting the World Trade Center. Then I remembered my vision and thought *Oh my God there's going to be another plane!* Just about that time another plane plowed into the other tower.

I called my son first and said, "Turn on the TV."

He said, "Wake up, you're dreaming."

I answered, "I wish I was." And then I understood my vision. I called 411 and got the FBI in Washington, DC. I asked for an investigator.

I told them, "There are five planes and you've got to get them all on the ground."

They said, "Oh yeah right sure. We think it's just an accident." About the time he told me that, the third plane hit the Pentagon.

I said, "Now you listen to me, damn it. You get those planes to the ground; there's still two more missing."

He said, "Oh yeah right, sure. How do you know this anyway?"

I told him, "I saw it happen. You've got to do something."

He finally said, "We'll check into it." And he hung up.

After I was watching TV for a while they mentioned the fourth plane, which went down in a field in Pennsylvania. I thought *I wonder if that's related or not, I'm not sure.* Well I forgot that Pennsylvania is so close to Washington, DC. They didn't mention a fifth plane.

I called the FBI back and said, "There's still a plane missing!"

He said, "They're all grounded now. Everything's down."

I said, "Okay. But there was supposed to be another one."

He came back with, "We'll handle it ma'am."

Then he hung up. I was watching the tower burn and I just knew it was going to collapse. I watched a TV program before on the World Trade Towers. I learned what kind of building it was. I suddenly <u>knew</u> – not only intuition but – based on the fact that it was a suspended-floor type of design for the building. That means the only support for a floor is the walls! I thought *if the walls were damaged it's not going to hold, no way in hell.* There's no support for the floor then.

So I called the guy back and I said, "The buildings are going to go down."

He was angry, "<u>Ma'am</u> we're handling it."

I insisted, "The buildings are going to go down."

He patiently explained, "Ma'am those buildings are designed to withstand high heat."

I retorted, "Not that kind of heat. A jet fuel fire will melt steel, because it burns hotter. And the outside walls are starting to lean. I can tell. Get the people out!"

I went on to try to explain how a suspended floor building is designed. But he wouldn't listen.

He assured me, "We will take care of it."

And he hung up again. I got really frustrated. Of all the guys to talk to I felt like this guy was an idiot. And each time I called I kept getting the same guy. When I asked for someone else, he said no one else was available. He had a simple name like John Smith, so I can't really recall it.

When the first tower collapsed I called back and said, "See? Now get the people out of the other tower."

The man told me, "I can't talk to you right now. I'm really busy." He hung up.

Then after a while he called me back and asked, "How did you know there were five planes?"

At that point I started worrying about getting arrested. I heard later they arrested the guy who was going to fly the fifth plane. They just didn't talk about it anymore, who knows about it now?

I asserted, "You can call Air Canada and they'll tell you about how I saved one of their planes. You can verify it with anyone who knows me that I get visions of things that happen." Apparently the FBI had a whole bunch of people calling with psychic warnings. I can't really tell you how I know that.

One other plane crash that I should have warned but I didn't. I dreamed that Air Force One plane was going to crash. I told my friends about the dream. I just knew there'd be a crash and I didn't get any details.

They said, "You can't do anything about it."

I asked them, "Why not? I could try and prevent it."

They told me, "You can't because it will be seen as threatening the President. You could get arrested."

I mentioned, "The President doesn't travel alone. He goes with advisors, journalists and staff workers on the plane with him. All of those people will die if I don't save them."

They came back, "You can't do anything about it."

I said, "If I call, maybe it will prevent it from happening."

But I didn't call and Air Force One didn't crash but Air Force Two crashed in 1996.

I almost got to the point that I hated to go to sleep because of dreaming of things that would happen. If I can get to the phone to call someone to warn them I don't mind. Otherwise, I don't like it. People say the Gift of God is a blessing, but I see it as a curse.

Angels

Angels, divine messengers and servants of God, may be the spiritual beings who guide us to the next plane of existence. So angels may be what ghosts eventually see, when they go to the light. Angels have a noble and noted legacy in scripture and folklore. Angels may have a commanding, gentle or urgent presence, but they lead us to divine love and light.

In these stories, angels save lives, provide loving reassurance, and offer companionship and protection. We like to think, in our doubting moments, that angels come to our side and bolster our faith. We hope angels are present to protect our children or aged relatives. There are some stories about deceased relatives who almost appear angel-like, with bright spiritual garments, and acting as ever present guardians. And thus the quote, "Our own acts our angels are", by Paracelsus.

It is a precious gift to see, hear or feel an angel nearby. At the very right moment, angels can step in to give us hope and remind us that God cares about our fate. We are not rescued at all times, and we may not be rewarded for testing divine mercy. But angels demonstrate that a complete and usually invisible order of spiritual supremacy is just out of sight.

Our faith leads us to decide whether a miraculous event was truly angelic help or mundane synchronicity. It may be a tribute to the subtle workings of our angels, that many times we are simply unaware of their assistance, thinking instead that we had a good turn of luck. Angels are ever present, available and willing to act on God's command to bring safety and comfort.

My Angel Was a Good Ol' Boy

Thomas Freese

On Thursday, June 12, 2003, I was in my last semester of full-time graduate school, and my work of over three years was nearing completion. That day, I interviewed at St. Margaret Mary Elementary School in Louisville for a counselor position. I was excited to work in the field of art therapy and figured a job with the Catholic schools would be a good match for my background and talents.

After the interview I went to class at the University of Louisville, College of Education and Human Development. I stopped by the Education and Resource Technology Center, where I had just a few months left to work as a graduate assistant, and joined employees celebrating a manager's birthday. After that, I drove home, following my usual route to merge on to fast-paced Interstate 65 north. I drove a 1990 Honda, which was a gift from my Mother. But as soon as I got on the busy expressway, I heard a loud noise coming from my car. It seemed something was dragging from the bottom of the car. It was my muffler, and I was very concerned about pulling over on the narrow shoulder with speeding trucks and cars inches from me.

I kept driving, entering "Spaghetti Junction", where I-65 interweaves with two other Interstate highways, I-71 and I-64. I curved along the ramp to merge onto I-64 westbound, evaluating my options and praying that sparks from the dragging metal wouldn't start a fire. I hoped my way past the downtown exits, past West Louisville, and cringed as the muffler noise grew and I approached the Sherman Minton Bridge over the Ohio River. There was just not a good place to pull over, and I wasn't sure what to do anyway. My auto repair skills are near the bottom in terms of practical life knowledge. I just wanted to get home, where I could call friends about muffler shops from the quiet safety of my rural 70 acres in Georgetown, Indiana.

But as I crossed the busy bridge, westbound lane above the eastbound, I knew it was too risky to keep driving up the long hills past the Knobs. So I kept right and turned off the first exit into downtown New Albany. I didn't think about it then, but now I certainly know that people heard me coming from a few blocks away. I turned right into a quick stop/gas station. It wasn't a mechanic's service station, so what could I do anyway? I turned off the engine and as I walked around toward the rear, I noticed a friendly man just walk up to look at the muffler.

These are the things that people mull over later. Who was this person, where did they come from? Why were they there and how did they already know exactly what to do? It all seems easily explained away. But when I was reluctant to get dirty, with my nice clothes from the job interview, this man just somewhere produced a wire coat hanger and trussed up the fallen muffler. I remember him looking like he was a country guy, slender about 5' 7", short hair, and maybe 45 years old. I'm not sure I even thanked him, or if or why I might have looked the other way, but after he fixed up my muffler so I could safely drive back home, he was simply gone. I didn't watch him walk to a truck or go around the corner – a pedestrian who chanced by, knew what to do, and didn't mind helping.

But I was thankful, whoever helped keep me safe that day. It's interesting to look at my entry in my desktop calendar about that event; the next day was a Friday the 13th!

What amazes me is how very personal the nature of help from the Universe can be, as that help is defined as synchronicity, God, angels, or good luck. There are many others who talk about a stranger who helps in a time of need, when anything from the small to the severe threatens our well being.

Baby Angels

Janet Marlin:

I can relate to having two angels. The first one was a baby boy that our daughter carried for 8-1/2 months. He died in utero. How sad it was to watch the parents go through losing a baby. They had two other boys that were healthy. Why this happened remains a mystery. The little boy was named Benjamin and was baptized. A picture was taken of his little body.

Approximately two years later there was a baby, but it died in utero at 6-1/2 months. Again, the cause of death was a mystery. She was a little girl. She was named Cameron. She was baptized and a photo was taken of her also. As grandparents we grieved with them. When we were given a photo of each of the "angels", I put the pictures in a locket, which I wear almost every day. I wear it close to my heart. The brothers will every so often speak of what might have been part of the family. I look at their photos quite often wondering what they would be doing at their different ages.

Guardian Angel

Virginia Gilpin:

I had many experiences that I believe are angelic experiences. One that came to my mind immediately was a time in the early 1990s. I was driving a 1991 Ford Explorer, coming home after working a full day at the factory. It was in the wintertime and we had an ice storm the night before. I made it to work that morning with no problems. The sun was shining most of the day and melted the icy roads...or so I thought.

On one of the back roads that I took to get home, I rounded a curvy stretch where the sun had not shone and hit a patch of black ice that sent me into a spin. No matter how I turned the steering wheel, I couldn't straighten the vehicle back into control. I took my hands off the steering wheel and called for God to help me. It felt as if the vehicle was picked up in the air and landed on a bed of cotton.

When I looked again, I went off into a wooded area and my front bumper was kissing a tree. I got out of the truck, thinking I was going to have to walk to the house down the road to call my husband. I heard a voice telling me that I could make it out onto the road and head on home. I turned around and looked at my vehicle and saw in my mind how it was possible to put the truck into reverse and back up the ditch line into a driveway and pull back out onto the road. That's what I did, and was able to make it home before I finally let go of the tears I was holding back.

When I checked out the truck, I only had a minor scratch on the front fender. I feel it was an angelic presence that helped me at that time...one that drove my truck to a soft landing and also spoke to me to help me get back onto the road. God is good and has sent me wonderful helpers in the most trying times. I have learned to "Be still and KNOW". God helps me and ALSO I have to do my part by LISTENING and being aware that I am not alone. We all have angels and spirit guides to help us on a daily basis. I am so grateful for the help I have been given and the spirit guides who work with me.

Mystery Lady

Michael Dennis:

I was the lanky, big eyed, thirteen year old boy, who cowered in the corner, my hands over my ears. I tried to block out my parent's screaming and yelling. When the noise died down, I slowly got up and walked to the door and opened it just a crack. I quickly shut it again when my mother passed by. I shut my eyes, afraid to look. Would it be a black eye, bloody nose, or would she fall down and go unconscious? It was my fear for so long, that my father would kill her. The bathroom door closed.

"At least she's still alive," I sighed, rubbing sweat off my forehead.

I waited until I heard the bathroom door open before looking through the crack again. My mother went into her bedroom and shut the door behind her. A few moments later my father joined her. I quickly put on my jacket and shoes, grabbed a book and tiptoed out.

"Don't anybody move," I said, "please God, let it be all clear until I get outside." There was a crisp breeze, which blew the book cover open. It felt a bit too chilly for mid September, but I figured I'd read a few chapters of *The Grapes of Wrath* before evening began to set. Maybe then, my parents would be passed out, sleeping off the alcohol.

I curled up against a maple tree by a fence, which separated the backyard from the big field in back. I tried to read, but I just couldn't concentrate. So I lay it down and looked up at the clouds.

"Well, at least there is church tomorrow and tomorrow night," I said aloud. "Yippee, I'll get away from here for a whole day. And next Saturday night is our big gospel singing. That will be fun."

Then a wave of sadness came over me.

"Why do they have to be like this? Will it ever end? I'd like to get away from this place for good. I wish I was old enough to go to college."

I looked at the dancing clouds and blowing tree branches.

I thought *it must be nicer up there. Wherever you are up there, it must be better than here at this crazy house in Shepherdsville, Kentucky.*

I closed my eyes and drifted off to sleep. Fifteen minutes later I awoke and saw a bright light beside the big gas tank on the other side of the yard. *What is that?* I saw a golden swirl with silver strands on the edges, like big taffy candy. The swirling slowed, and then stopped. I saw a ball of golden light about the size of a basketball.

"I'm dreaming!"

I shut my eyes but couldn't keep them closed. When I again opened my eyes, I saw the ball of light was transformed into a form. The light was brighter now, and I had to squint. *Oh, goodness, I'm starting to have hallucinations. They'll take me to the mental hospital the next time Mom goes.*

I got up and ran around front, hoping to see my neighbor Daniel. But there was no trace of Daniel. I slowly made my way around back again, finding my book on the ground. I also noticed the ball of light was still there. For some reason, I had a sudden urge to approach the ball of light. My heart pounded, and my hands shook, as I walked towards it. I walked until I was about ten feet from the light, and then stopped. I no longer felt the autumn chill. Lovely warmth emanated from the light. I made myself look at it, while I hoped my brothers didn't get back early to find me standing still staring into space.

The ball unraveled into small strands, which darted out in different directions. I closed my eyes again and stood there frozen for some time.

When my legs began to ache slightly and I felt stiff, I took a few steps forward. I opened my eyes wide as I beheld a radiant angel. Her golden hair was long, and she wore a snow-white robe. Her eyes looked silver!

She swayed slightly. I put my hand over my mouth. I was too terrified to run or say anything. A smile came over her face then she waved her arm in the direction of the big gas tank. *She wants me to sit down.* I jumped up on the old tank, and folded my arms. Then I found the courage to speak.

Michael Dennis

"Who are you?" I asked softly. She grinned and looked at me for several moments before speaking. I felt she could read my mind.

"I heard your prayers," she began softly, as she crossed her hands over her heart. "You have a very tender and good heart, young man. You have many talents and abilities you do not know about yet. You are going to help many people in your lifetime. God is watching over you as he does all his children. He has many ways to reach and make contact with them. The degree depends upon their faith, capacity, and abilities to receive Him. Be open to the many ways that God can reach out to you. I promise you He is already doing so daily.

"Though your heart has been wounded by all that you have seen and experienced at home, your spirit is still strong. You hunger to know God and the ways of goodness, and you have faith that you can know and even befriend, God, your Heavenly Father. Perhaps this is easier since your earth father gives you little time or attention, and is certainly not the loving, caring father a boy needs to be able to count on and look up to. That you read His Holy Words and talk to Him daily gives him much joy. If only all His children would talk to Him like the simple, loving parent He is.

"You pray with earnestness and expectations. You yearn to get away from your parents and this town and you want to go to college. Though part of you fears you might never get away and find a better life, another part of you dreams and hopes, and more importantly, expects and knows. I am here to strengthen your hopes and to remind you that your dreams are real and that God knows each of your wishes. Remember your grand faith when you face the obstacles and difficulties that Life will bring.

"You will go to college and you will get away from here. You will doubt and even try to deny this visit, but don't ever forget it. Think of what happened here today when you are feeling low and want to give up, and your faith will be renewed. It will help get you through the trials you will face ahead. I must take leave now."

Her image slowly faded. "When you call out to God or think of me you are halfway to heaven. You are much stronger than you realize, and you are loved as are all God's children," she whispered, then disappeared.

"Please don't leave," I called out, but she was already gone.

The angel's prediction that I would doubt and try to deny her almost immediately came true. More importantly, I think, was her prediction that I would never forget her visit. That one came true as well. And yes, all her other words came true. Less than a year later I moved to my first foster home. Five years later I was attending Berea College in Berea, Kentucky, where I went on to complete my studies in Psychology, Religion and Theology, French, Spanish, German and Voice.

The trials and tribulations came as she said they would. I struggled with chronic depression, low self-esteem, and other dysfunctional maladies that came from spending what I call a lousy childhood. And when in the throes of the doldrums, pain, and rage, I had a tendency to block out and forget anything good that happened. "Out of sight out of mind" definitely fit me, with one exception – the visit by the mystery lady. I have the memory in my mind and it will never be lost. I prayed, pleaded, and even pouted, hoping she would pay me another visit, but she never came back.

The journey is different for everyone. But the power within us is a spark of love and magic given to us by our Creator. This Light burns away our fears, pains and doubts and manifests our hopes and dreams. We all have the spark. It cannot be extinguished or we would cease to be alive. Norman Vincent Peale calls it the Life Force, which animates and sustains all life on the planet. This "Plus Factor" is a special manifestation of the Light, which, if we come to understand and reach out for it, can do remarkable things in our lives.

Twice Saved From Death

Ann Richer

Back in the early 90s I was saved from a certain death when I accidentally fell four hundred feet off a cliff while skiing.

I was training to be a ski instructor in the Cascade Mountains near Seattle, Washington. Since the skis I had were short and light, I was flying over the moguls (snow bumps). My instructor said I was spending too much time up in the air and not enough time on the ground, so he encouraged me to get a longer, heavier set of skis. The instructors took a group of us trainees really high up the mountain. On the top, we were on a ledge at the top of a 400-foot cliff. We had to side step along the ledge, and do a kick turn to turn the corner. A kick turn involves kicking one ski up into the air and swinging it around to face the other direction. Then the other leg is pulled around to match the first leg's new direction.

I forgot I was using the new, heavier and longer skis, so I didn't make the extra effort to kick my ski high enough in the area to turn it around. I caught the end of the ski in the snow on the ledge and toppled off the cliff, which was a near-vertical drop. I screamed (for the first time in my life) and saw my life flash before my eyes. My body hurtled rapidly toward a grove of trees at the bottom of the cliff. About five feet before I hit the grove, I felt something wrap around me. I saw what looked like angel's wings. They wrapped around me and lay me gently into the side of the mountain, in the snow. I was able to pick myself up and ski back down the mountain, with no injuries at all. But if the angel hadn't caught my fall, they'd still be scraping parts of my body off the tree bark. I wouldn't be here today if it wasn't for my angel rescue.

I was very scared, relieved and awestruck. I was amazed that I was saved, when seconds before, I knew I was a gonner. There was nothing physical that could have kept me from hitting that grove of trees. When I met with the others down at the lodge, the ski instructors were absolutely horrified and amazed. When they saw me fall towards the trees, they were certain that I wouldn't survive. I told them about my angel wings and how I was saved. Some of them thought it was really cool, and others just blew it off.

I was driving in downtown Cincinnati on a bright, sunny summer afternoon in 1994. I was doing errands, parking and running to a number of places. At one point, I drove under a freeway overpass on a street that went under the freeway bridge for about a block. Even though there were no pedestrians in sight and no other cars around me, I suddenly stopped the car, but didn't know why. It felt something just take over the lower part of my body and "make" my leg step on the brake. I was going about 25 mph. My car came to a complete stop, and as I wondered *why in the world am I stopping in the middle of the street?* A huge chunk of concrete the size of half of a barrel, fell down off the bridge underside and landed right in front of my car.

If I hadn't stopped the car, it would have landed on me. There was no one else who saw what happened. I drove on to my other errand, where I called the police so they could send a crew to pick up the fallen concrete. By this time, I had enough experiences to know that I was saved by angelic intervention. At my first opportunity, in meditative prayer, I gave thanks for my angel's help.

Mosh Pit Angel

Brooke Raby, Lexington

When I was sixteen or seventeen, I went to a concert in Nashville with a classmate that I had tutored. It was a day long festival, five or six bands I think, and she and I had both been fairly close to the stage all day, as the bands that had played earlier in the day weren't particularly raucous. I guess, too, that there hadn't been enough time for everyone to drink enough either.

Later in the evening, my friend and I got caught in the mosh pit with all these HUGE guys and some seasoned mosh-pitters. She was a small girl, but a basketball player and real scrappy, and I was about the size I am now, only about 15 pounds lighter, but just as fearless and, frankly, stupid. We did not belong there at all. It got particularly intense, and neither of us was afraid to throw punches or elbows, and we did, honestly, but it was just all too much. It may have been the closest I've ever come to fainting; it was like when you're in the ocean, and the riptide is stronger than you expected, and you can't manage to pull yourself up out of the water to the shore.

The next thing I knew, I felt an arm reach across my shoulders from my right to my left, and effortlessly pull me out of the middle of the mosh pit, and when I looked, Eva, my friend, and I were both well outside of the danger zone, so to speak. I looked around, trying to find whoever had helped me, but there were no likely candidates in sight; no one that even looked in my direction or as if they had just come from where I was.

When I told Eva about it, she said that she felt like the exact same thing had happened to her. Clearly, someone does not think I am rock and roll material. A few years later, I saw the same band, but time had pretty much killed their star, so I had no need for a mysterious rescuer there.

Angelic Intervention
Deena Madison, Louisville, Kentucky

At this time I was going through a separation and divorce. I drove a red van, which I was driving behind St. Matthews Mall near Brown's Park. This is the intersection where Brown's Lane changes into Hubbard's Lane. While I was sitting in the van waiting for the red light to turn green, something flashed into my mind *watch it, this guy is going to run his light and turn in front of you*. This was first guy at the opposite set of cars. When the light turned green and I started driving straight into the intersection, the guy cut in front of me just like that! This guy was not supposed to turn until after I passed.

I swerved away from him, but that took me toward the line of parked cars perpendicular to my right. So I swerved the wheel and my car went left off the side of the road and downhill toward trees. The next thing I knew, I was up on the other side of the hill – I turned to simply get back on the road again. I knew that section of road and after my near accident I wondered *what happened back there?*

I wondered how I got up the opposite hill because when I went downhill I thought for sure I would hit one of the many trees. The trees weren't huge, but they were big enough to destroy my car. So I went back and looked and saw my tire tracks come down the hill toward the trees. I saw the space between the trees was not wide enough to let my car get through. The tire tracks just stopped and then continued <u>on the opposite side of the trees</u>.

I said to myself, "How the heck can that happen?"

I know I didn't dream the accident, because not long after that I had to replace the van's tie rod from the off road banging the van went through that day. And if I hadn't had that flashed message run through my head before the light changed I don't think I could have responded quickly enough to avoid a collision with him or the parked cars.

Cat Angel

Debi Magnes lives in Louisville, Kentucky. She is a life coach and motivational speaker.

Not long ago, I had a dream. I saw a huge, brown moth on the ceiling. I thought *let's get that thing out of here!* In my dream, I got up from my bed and opened the door to let out the moth. But instead, the moth flew toward me. I was slowly starting to wake up, but I still saw the moth, which moved toward me.

Some pretty lights appeared in front of this very large moth. There were four colored lights; they looked like jewels in a brooch. I reached out to slap away the moth, but then I fully awakened. I looked to my side, and saw it was not a moth but rather a small angel. The angel hovered next to my bed. It looked a bit hazy, and its wings beat very fast so that it could hover in place.

Then the angels face became more defined, and it appeared as the face of a cat. The body went downward in a simple cone shape. I smiled at the cat angel and reached up to touch it, but my hand went through its form. The angel then faded away.

I wonder if the cat angel appearance is linked to my experience having several cats. My husband had a cat when we met, and Coco lived with both of us after we married. She was a mix of some gray and browns. But she disappeared for three weeks. I felt she would return, and she did, but not long after she started having seizures. I spent a lot on the veterinarian bills, but she eventually died of her sickness. I was very devastated. Since Coco died, many times I felt the cat. She was in our house in spirit, jumping on the bed. I saw the paw indentations on the covers as she walked on our bed. Now a lot less seems to happen after we got our dog, Mr. Wilson. Maybe Coco came to say goodbye and to let us know that she was our angel now.

Family Angels

Roberta Simpson Brown is a storyteller and author. She tells scary stories, ghost stories and also has been active with her husband Lonnie in the Louisville Ghost Hunters Society. They live in Middletown; before they married Lonnie arrived in the area in the 1950s and Roberta came in the 1960s. Lonnie and Roberta are both authors, and Roberta has published many books of both fiction and nonfiction ghost stories. But I was intrigued to hear about their family stories of angels. It appeared that the angels were most active when someone from the family

Roberta Brown and Pudgy, Russell County, Kentucky.

had taken ill. Lonnie's grandmother, Zona Rooks, was a full-blood Chero-kee. Roberta told me about what happened when Lena was young. This first story took place not far from Columbia, in Adair County, Kentucky.

Little Cripple Angel

Roberta:

My mother-in-law, Lena Mae Brown, was a little girl when this happened. Her grandmother got very ill and sent for Lena's mother. When she arrived, her grandmother said that she wanted to tell her about what she saw.

"What was it?" Lena's mom asked.

"Well," said the grandmother, "Last night, I saw a little crippled angel come and dance in the doorway."

Lena's mother said, "Why, Mom, I guess that means you are going to get well soon!"

"No," the grandmother answered. "I think it means just the opposite."

The grandmother died two days later about the same time at night that she had seen the angel."

Roberta noted that "Leeni" had dark hair. She was half-Cherokee with high cheekbones, flashing dark eyes, and pretty dark hair. She described her personality as "outgoing like other little country kids." Lonnie added that there was someone Lena and her family knew who died a few years before this incident. There was a crippled girl that passed away, and that's why his great-grandmother knew the little girl was coming for her, since she preceded her in death. Lena told this story, now and then, of the little cripple angel. She described her as glowing with a light different than a ghost. It does make one wonder; do some people die and become angels?

Years ago, Roberta was curious to find out more about angels, when she walked into a bookstore in Columbia. She asked the lady working there if they carried books

James Milton and Zona Mae Rooks.

about angels. Roberta was taken aback when the woman asked in return, "Do you mean the real ones that were so mean?" Roberta said the woman became very animated about how those angels had cast other angels out of heaven.

Roberta:

"When my dad was real sick, Emily, a friend of my sister, told us, 'I hate to tell you, but I don't think your dad is going to live for much longer. He's got two angels standing behind him'."

There was yet another time when some animated spirit, possibly an angel, visited their family.

"My mom was very sick and I was sitting up with her praying *somebody please help her through this illness.* Then I noticed a little light appear on a picture on the wall. This was a picture of some horses by a pond that my mom brought to my sister's home. The little light started dancing across the picture. I got up right way to look outside to see what was causing that light, but I saw no cars or people with flashlights – nothing. It seemed then that Mom had an easier time dealing with her illness.

"Sometime later they took her to the hospital and she never came home again. I wondered if I was asking her guardian angel to help her. The funny thing was that the picture was a bit of a joke between my mom and my dad. There was a reflection of the horses in the pond. Dad didn't notice when he hung the picture. She always laughed at him about that picture because he hung it upside down. Dad has passed on by then, but maybe his spirit returned to let her know he was there and waiting for her when she crossed over."

Roberta related one more story, and this one seems likely the most fascinating. It again involves her mother-in-law, Lena.

Angelic Children

On New Year's Day, 2006, my mother-in-law got very ill. She lived in Okolona, in Louisville. Years before she dealt with the effects of strokes. But now the doctor said there was fluid around her lungs, but he did not put her in the hospital. He just gave her some medicine and sent her home. Since she was almost 93 and was obviously not able to take care of herself, her children and her daughters-in-law took turns sitting with her. None of us had much hope that she'd come through this alive.

One night I was sitting by her bed and she looked at me and smiled. Her voice was weak, but her mind was clear. When she spoke, I leaned over to see what she was saying.

"You don't have to sit with me all the time if you need to do something else," she told me. "Ever since I got sick, two little angel children have been with me. One is a little boy who stays behind me. He sleeps at my feet at night. The other is a little girl who stays on the front of the bed or on the floor beside me."

"That's great!" I said. "What do they look like?"

"They've got dark hair and they are wearing dark clothes. The little girl has a ruffled petticoat!"

"Do they talk to you?" I asked.

"No," she said, "but when I was reading my Bible one night, the little girl nodded at me." She continued to see her little visitors until she recovered! I asked her about them the last time we were there.

"There're not here now," she told me. "They just stayed as long as I needed them."

Then Lena became ill again.

Roberta reported that Lena and she were sitting at

Lena and Lucian Brown

the dining room table, when Lonnie went out to pick up lunch. Lena asked if Lonnie was picking up some fish. Then Lena said, "You know my little angels are back. Do you see them?"

"No," Roberta replied, "but that doesn't mean they're not there."

Roberta wondered if, since Lena loved children so much – she had six of her own – perhaps that is why her angels showed up as children. "She certainly wasn't scared of dying or crossing over. Whatever it had been that came to visit was a comfort to her.

"When I visited her once I took one of the tools we use as ghost hunters. I brought along an EMF meter on the suggestion of a friend. When I got to her apartment, I got a reading around Lena. I checked my meter to see if it would pick up something from the light socket – nothing. But by her on the sofa, or with her into the kitchen, the meter picked up some kind of electronic field."

Dad's Visitor

El Wanda Horsley

In March of 1977, my sister Neline and I went to visit my father in his hospital room. We visited Dad just before 7:00 PM on the night before he died. He was in intensive care, and every visitor had to scrub and wear sterile gowns so no germs would be carried in to him.

As we approached the room by the nurses' station, I suddenly saw through the wall! Dad was lying very still on the bed and a figure that was a few feet off the floor was bending over him! I could see all of that clearly.

The figure was wearing a checked top with colors of green and blue, like shirts Dad used to wear. I couldn't see a head or face because of an extremely bright light where they should have been.

I said, "Hurry up, Neline! Something's wrong with Dad. Somebody's in there with him."

She said, "What are you talking about?"

I tried to explain as we hurried to the nurses' station. Neline asked if anybody was with Dad, but the nurses told us there was nobody there. They added that Dad had been very quiet. From the station, we could see through a window in Dad's room, and there was nobody there. Nobody could have come out without our seeing them.

We scrubbed, pulled on the sterile gowns and went inside. I was frightened about Dad when I saw the figure and the light. But once in the room, I saw nothing in the room, not even a night-light. And the room was filled with a feeling of calm. I wasn't worried or frightened anymore. We were with Dad when he died early the next morning. I am certain that what I saw was an angel by his bed that had come to comfort him and help him cross over.

Flooded Car
Jackie Atchison

There have been two times in my life where I was compelled to turn around to help someone while driving. The first was on a cold wintery morning after a tremendous rainy spell in Central Kentucky. I was driving to work from Horse Branch into Hartford. It was very dim, very gray and snowflakes were beginning to fall. All of the fields on my left and right were flooded; I was driving down the middle of a lake.

As I passed one intersection, out of the corner of my eye, I saw head-lights in the water.

As I kept driving, I heard myself saying out loud, "If anybody can get him out it's you." I pulled my Jeep Wrangler over at the next safe spot and turned around. When I got back to the intersection the lights on the car were off. You couldn't even tell there was a car there if you were just passing. The old man behind the wheel was waving to me where his car had died where the road dips. The water was up to his windows. I gauged where the road was supposed to be by keeping my eyes focused on the dry land behind him and pulled up beside him.

When he rolled down his window I asked, "Do you want to climb in to my car, honey?"

"If you can push me up to the hill I think I can get her started," he said. It didn't seem like a good idea, but neither did trying to get a heavyset old man to climb from his flooded car to my Jeep. I took a deep breath and focused on the dry road in front of me and started driving, the water lapping underneath the floorboards. When I got to the top of the hill and turned around I again lined up the Jeep with his car, popped the gears into Grand-daddy Low and headed back into the water.

"That's a good girl," I said to my Jeep, "You can do this, you can do this."

When I got up to his bumper I ever so slightly pressed on the gas. It took him a few seconds to realize that I was actually going to push him to dry land. He fumbled with the gears of his own car to get it into neutral. I knew he had to be wet because water was coming into the Jeep and I sat a bit higher than him. I revved the engine a little more and then finally let loose the clutch. The wheels gathered power that I didn't know they had and the big four-door car started to move up the hill slowly, both of us trying to focus on where the road was in relation to the stop sign in front of us at the top of the hill. We pushed him to the sign. The Jeep idled a few seconds before I slid her into reverse to pull up beside him but the old man's car rolled back into me.

"Put your break on, sweetie," I yelled out my window to him. He waved and put his car in park. When I did pull up beside him I got out. He was shaken but dry.

"Why don't you come with me into town and I'll have someone drive you back out to get your car, honey," I said.

"You're an angel," he said, "You're an angel. Thank God you stopped."

I took his hand that was resting on the open window, "Come with me into town."

"No, I think she'll start in a minute. I have to go see my wife in the nursing home," he said.

"Come with me anyway, I can't leave you out here in this weather, the snow is coming."

"I know she'll start in a few minutes," he said while turning the key again.

"Then I'll send someone out when I get into town," I said. There was no arguing with him. It's hard to win arguments with tough old farmers, no matter how serious their situations are.

"You're an angel," he said and cranked his engine again, that much closer to starting.

I kept an eye on him in the rearview mirror as long as I could as I headed into town. *Nobody would have even seen him if I hadn't*, I thought. I stopped at the little gas station in Beaver Dam and told them where to check on him and where to reach me if they needed to. They only called to tell me that there was no car at the stop sign by the time they got there, so he had obviously gotten to where he was headed. I was relieved and grateful for being in the right place at the right time. I never really felt like I was an angel, but I do think he had a great guardian angel looking out for him that day.

Dog Daze

The second time I felt compelled to stop in the same manner was years later coming back from Hanover, Indiana. I had just come out of the Louisville Spaghetti Junction and onto I-71 on a very hot July day. Right as I passed Zorn Avenue, I saw a man sitting on the side of the expressway with a German shepherd on the end of a rope. The man looked tired, but the dog was done. At 70 miles an hour, I didn't have much time to react and pull over while I mulled the whole situation over. I found myself thinking, *if anybody's going to stop it's going to be you.*

There are no exits between Zorn and Brownsboro, which is off of the Waterston Expressway. So, when I finally got there I swung back around and got back onto I-71, got off of Zorn Avenue, looped around onto I-71 North again and pulled up alongside the man sitting on the guardrail. I got out of the Jeep, opened the back and gestured for him to put his dog in.

The man just sat there dazed. He had been writing a letter, to whom I never new but he didn't move.

"I can't leave my dog," he said still holding the pen.

"That's why I came back," I replied. "Get him on in the back."

He lifted his road-weary dog into the back of the Jeep, frayed rope and all and I closed the door. After he got in the front with a brown paper bag containing a change of clothes and some dog food, I put the Jeep in gear and asked him where he was headed.

"Richmond, Kentucky, where my uncle lives," he said.

"Well, I've got to go home and feed my own dogs, let's go look at a map and decide from there," I said. He just nodded and held onto his bag. His dog lay quietly in the back, panting from heat but grateful to be off of the road.

After a long quiet he looked over at me and said, "You're an angel."

"No, I'm not," I said. "I saw that your dog couldn't take one more step and it's too hot out here for man and beast."

"A couple people stopped but said that they couldn't take my dog. They said to leave him tied to the guardrail. I ain't going to leave my dog," he said, tears welling in his eyes. He crossed his feet; he only had sandals on, and leaned back in the seat. "I ran out of insulin and food. I just have food for him, that's all that matters. He's a good dog and I ain't going to leave him."

"I know," I said. "That's why I came back."

I took them both to my house, made a big dinner while the man took a shower and then watched the two of them get comfortable and fall asleep. The next morning I asked him where he needed to be.

"I 'spect I should go home and take care of some business," he said.

"Where's home?" I asked.

"Richmond, Indiana. That's where my girlfriend is. You see, she took my car and…"

I held my hand up to cut him off, "Then that's where we're going," I said. Richmond, Indiana was a good two-hour drive from Louisville, so I loaded up the car with water jugs, his dog, my dog and finally the man himself.

"To Richmond," I said and pulled out of the driveway.

I didn't feel like an angel that day, but I am sure his guardian angel was glad I was taking him and his dog home where they belonged for whatever reason or reasons.

Lord Giveth and the Lord Taketh Away

Cora Alyce Seaman lives in Evansville, Indiana. She is married to Don Seaman, who also contributed stories for this book. Cory Alyce authored a number of books, including *Emily's Quest* and *Keeping the Promise*, published under her maiden name, Alyce Godbey. She is a founding member of the Midwest Writers Guild.

Cora Alyce is very supportive of other writers, hosting meetings in her home. She is frank, but also very supportive of others, offering encouraging comments and keeping busy helping friends and family. Although Cora Alyce and Don slept through the Newburg tornado, she nevertheless heard many stories about the terrible loss. Both she and Don drove past many miles of devastated countryside.

Cory Alyce:

On November 6, 2005, there was a tornado that went through our area. There were a total of 21 people killed that night. It was quite devastating. A friend of ours lives out on a country road. She's lived out there all of her life. She is about 83 years old. She never married and has no children. She worked for the telephone company for many years in the old days when they had the plug-in switchboards. Madge of course has been retired for many, many years and lived in the family home all these years. She has quite a collection of antiques and many nice things. When the tornado came through, it destroyed a twenty-mile wide swath of land and properties. It came through the area where her house was located. Her niece and nephew live across the street from her.

Madge's nephew related this story to us. The tornado hit at 2:30 in the morning. It took the top off of his family's home. But he realized, after he found that his family was all unhurt, that he needed to check on his aunt Madge. So he went across the road to see where she was. Of course, there was no power and he used a flashlight to look for her. When he went in to her house, he found her still lying in her bed. As she related what happened, she said she remembered hearing the glass break and the wind coming through.

She heard a voice say to her, "Just lie still, just be still".

She said she felt the hand of the Lord on her face holding her down. She felt her big antique bed moving. We laughed, because she wanted everyone to know she had a big antique bed. She felt the wind – she was cold – so she pulled the covers up. The nephew later told us that when he found her she was still lying in her bed and under her body were plaster, broken glass, wood and debris. But she was still lying in her bed. The truth was, when her nephew revealed it to her, the bed didn't move one inch. But the entire house moved sixteen feet off its foundation. She was found alive, unhurt, and still lying in the bed. She was astounded to realize that the hand of the Lord kept her safe.

We suspect that the tornado must have lifted her off the bed by at least two or three feet for that much debris to have been blown under her body. The debris was not under the mattress; it was literally under her body. The house was damaged beyond repair and later was demolished. She moved across the road to another house also owned by her family. When we talked to her about all this, she said she had two antique dressers.

"In one of them I kept my linens" and she related in detail about her table-cloths, napkins and pillowslips that she

Cora Alyce Seaman

ironed and carefully placed in this chest of drawers. Then she said,

"In the other chest of drawers I kept my 'undies'". She was very modest and began to speak in a whisper.

She said, "They never found that chest of drawers, so I don't know where it is."

I told her "Your undies are scattered all over Warrick County!"

She said in shock, "Oh I certainly hope not."

My friend lived out near Degonia Springs. The power went out and he went to his garage to get his generator working. They had a split-level home with three areas – basement, stairway and living area, and the third story. Their son called them from Chandler and said,

"The tornado is on its way and you've got to do something." Well, he was out in the garage working on the generator when the tornado hit their house broadside. It threw him up against the tractor where he cracked a few ribs. The tornado literally blew away the house while leaving his wife and daughter standing in the hallway between the basement and living area.

There were many things found months later, up in southeastern Indiana. Some hunters were outside in the Madison area, looking for deer, when they found pictures scattered all over the fields. They returned some of those pictures, which happened to be photographs from Carolyn's family. There was a picture returned of Carolyn's daughter when she was three years old. There were framed photos in the hallway; three remained but two disappeared with the tornado.

Sam and his son Danny heard that the tornado was going to hit when they were in the downstairs of the house. Of course, it was two in the morning. They called upstairs, and actually Bette went upstairs to get the two boys. They were groggy-headed and half-dressed when she wrapped a blanket around them. As soon as they got downstairs they heard a loud sound. The top of the house and all the roof joists were lifted up. One of the windows, above the bed where one of the boys was just sleeping minutes earlier, shattered and a large section – half of the pane of glass – stabbed through the mattress like a spear.

Out in Degonia Springs, there was a house that the tornado deposited in the middle of the highway. And around the corner there was a church called the Baker Chapel Methodist Church. It was there for many years. Over the years, we watched that church grow. Although it was a small country church, on Easter Sunday so many people would be at service that they parked up and down Highway 62. You couldn't get into the parking lot; there was such a large congregation. Before the tornado struck, they were getting ready to initiate a building program. But the tornado completely blew away the church – nothing was left standing, except the three steps that went up to the front door. It too was deposited all over southern Indiana.

When we went out there to look afterwards we saw that someone had found a flag, a banner, which was hanging in the church. It read "He is Risen"…they draped it over the surviving front steps. Within the last two months, ten months after the tornado event, 20 firemen from New York City, from 9-11's ground zero, came and spent a weekend rebuilding that church. They reported so many people helped them at the 9-11 disaster that they wanted to return the favor. A couple of the Amish craftsman from Montgomery came down, and along with volunteers and the fireman, they accomplished more in a weekend than most of us would hope to do in weeks.

My Angel Smells Like Vanilla

Claudia Thurman, Sonora, Kentucky

I know my Angel smells like vanilla. Her name is Iris. When I'm really pondering something I'll call out "Iris…I need a little help here."

Then the scent of vanilla will come to me and I know exactly that she's there. It happens anywhere, in my car. It's not like I'm always in the kitchen cooking surrounded by kitchen spices.

Camouflage Angel

One weekend last June, I put on faux-period clothes and joined the merry folks at Henry County's Renaissance Festival. I went to sell a few books and see how a Renaissance Festival goes. I enjoyed making new friends and one woman, who bought my books, told me she might have a story for my new book.

Pam Ford, Auburn, Kentucky:——

We moved to a 130-acre farm in 1989 when I was still married to my son Wesley's dad. After we divorced, about a year after we moved, I decided to stay on the farm with my three children. Before the following events occurred, the girls were grown and were no longer living in the farmhouse.

I worked in Bowling Green in 1995. The commute involved long hours and long drives; it took about an hour and a quarter one way. I was very unhappy about leaving Wesley with a babysitter so much. I began to complain to God all the way to work and again all the way back home.

One morning, while complaining, I heard in my inner spirit: "Why don't you just quit?"

I answered out loud – "I can't quit!"

But the idea played around in my mind for several months and finally I just knew I had to quit. I felt an inner urgency that I could not deny. I finally quit in November of 1995, but only intended to stay out until the end of the year. That break turned into about six years.

When I told Wesley I was quitting, he asked me, "Does that mean I can come home after school?"

It broke my heart, because it seemed so important to him to just be able to come home instead of going to the sitter's. He had a wonderful sitter who was very good to him. I am quite confident that I would have serious health problems or be dead by now if I had not taken the time to heal and to allow the Lord to show me how to let myself be healed. I really had no one to turn to during this time because no one I knew had ever experienced what I was experiencing. My guess is that most people thought I was crazy. It wouldn't be surprising, since I thought I was going crazy at times. The Lord was my best friend and the only one I could turn to.

Around the first of the year in 1996, I felt prompted to home school Wesley. I did not know anyone at the time who home schooled. I gathered information, talked to Wesley and made the decision to teach him at home. I ended up going to court with his dad over the decision. The first three months I tried to teach him at home as a regular student in a regular classroom. That did not work. He was going through emotional turmoil from things that had happened prior, during and after the divorce. He had outbursts of anger and other emotions.

I decided to let him experiment, which was extremely difficult for me, and he spent about three months reading about airplanes and gliders. He made airplanes and gliders and parachutes. He threw stuffed animals with parachutes off the outbuilding. He also wrote stories, developed characters, researched names and their meanings. And I just observed him. He spent hours outside with his dog, Chloe, going off in the woods or fields where I could not see or hear him. I believed this was necessary for his growth, so I prayed that I could just hear the dog bark or hear his voice and then I wouldn't worry. Wesley and I began the process of learning to depend on the Lord and trust Him for everything we needed.

Our finances were tight. On paper, there really was no way we could manage, but we did. There were many times when I paid the bills and I would have ten dollars left to make it through a whole month, and we made it through. I cannot explain how we managed, but we did. We never missed a meal, had meat and milk every day, and cannot really think of anything we ever went without that we needed. We both started having spiritual dreams, visions, and experiences that we had never heard of before.

In 1997, when Wesley was twelve, we moved to a smaller farm in Auburn.

He came in the house one day and asked me, "Do angels wear camouflage?" I said I guess they wear whatever they want to.

I asked him back, "Why?"

He said he sat down under a tree in the woods and looked up. He saw a man wearing camouflage sitting up in the tree. He said at first he was afraid, but then a great peace came over him. When he looked back up, the man was gone.

Around the same time, he dreamt he was in a huge army. They were on the front line fighting another huge army. The other army had strange creatures with strange weapons. His army had all the latest weapons but they had no effect on the strange army. It just kept coming. Then he heard a noise from behind him that sounded like helicopters. When he looked up, he discovered the sound was angels arriving. These angels landed in front of Wesley's army, forming a line between his army and the strange army.

I immediately thought of the scripture II Corinthians 10:4, which reads, "For the weapons of our warfare are not carnal."

And I also recalled a verse in the book of Ephesians 6:12, which says, "We wrestle not against flesh and blood, but against principalities, against powers, against the rulers of the darkness of this world, and against spiritual wickedness in high places."

Our experiences and growth seemed to slow down for several years but once again, we are feeling drawn to listen and wonder what the Lord will do next.

An Angel's Warning Call

Helen Nave, Rossville, Georgia

My husband Charles Nave was working on a construction site to build a church. He parked the crane right up against a concrete and block wall. This wall was built just a few days before then.

As he waited for instructions to swing over material to the workers, he heard a voice say, "Move the crane!"

He looked around everywhere to see who spoke, but he saw no one. He continued to sit where he was, against the building.

Five minutes later, he heard the same voice loudly speak in his ear, "MOVE THIS CRANE NOW!"

He hurriedly got out, removed the outriggers from around the crane, got back in the cab, and moved the crane away from the wall. As soon as he turned off the motor, the entire wall collapsed; it fell just three inches from where he parked the crane. He was hit by flying debris, but was lucky to have only one small cut.

Everyone heard the collapse and ran around the building. They feared he was dead. Charlie told them someone told him to move the crane, so he did. At sixty-one years old, Charlie never gave much thought to the existence of angels. But after that day, with his escape from death, he did believe in angels.

He had a few more close calls since that day, but he still felt someone was watching over him.

I'm An Angel!

Jan Carter

When I lived in a small town on Lake Michigan, I worked and traveled with a lady named "Anna" for several years as her caregiver. Anna was an Alzheimer patient. Her condition was steadily declining and I had just been informed that they were going to let me go, as they wanted to hire professional nurses to care for her.

I had become very attached to Anna and was sad to be leaving. The day after receiving this news, I was sitting across the room from her as she took an afternoon nap. Suddenly, her snoring woke her up.

With a startled look on her face, she pointed her trembling finger about five feet above my head exclaiming, "THERE'S AN ANGEL!"

It felt as though she was seeing a very large being behind me.

And then, with her eyes still wide in amazement, she looked directly at me, still pointing and excitedly stated, "YOU'RE AN ANGEL!"

She then proceeded to give me a very lucid "reading", saying, "Don't worry. You're going to be fine. You're going to get everything you want."

Hearing these words brought tears to my eyes. There was no way that she was consciously aware that I would be leaving soon. Generally, she was not able to formulate more than a three-word sentence and any type of conversation had to be continuously prompted. There was a calm caring authority coming through her. She helped me let go and see that there would be more good things on the horizon. In recollecting this story, I am reminded of having several dreams years ago of being called an "Earth Angel".

The Quilt and the Angel
by Oleeda Bolton

One day in the summer of 1998 I was sitting in my doctor's office, looking through a magazine when I ran across a pattern for a blue jean quilt that had photographs on it.

I immediately thought, "I have to make this quilt for Bobby."

I had seven grandchildren and Bobby was the middle grandchild. I asked if I could have the magazine to take home with me and the receptionist said I could. I began to collect blue jeans from any and everybody, some faded, some fairly new and began the project. I enlisted the help of my daughter, Connie (Bobby's Mom) when it came time to adhere the photographs to the jeans. I must have broken at least 20 needles on my sewing machine but finally finished "The Quilt" in time for Christmas. It had photographs of Bobby's cousins, aunts, uncles, Mom, Dad, Granny, pictures of him when he was very small and several of his little daughter, Summer. When Bobby opened the present he was so pleased he had a smile from ear to ear.

I didn't know at that time why I felt such an urgency to make a quilt for him, because usually when I do things like that I start with the eldest. In May 1999, Bobby was killed in an auto accident. The family and I were all very distressed.

My daughter kept saying to me, "Mom, if I only knew he was okay."

I knew in my heart he was okay, because he had made a profession of faith at an early age and always went to church with me on Sunday. He was very steadfast in his faith. One Christmas he memorized the entire chapter of Luke 2 and quoted it at our church Christmas service.

One day in the summer of 1999 I came home from the grocery and saw a young man mowing my

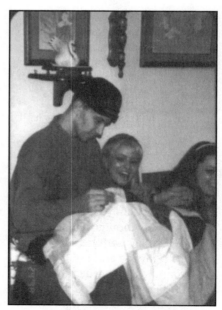

Oleeda's Grandson, Bobby, Christmas 1998.

222

back yard. He had on a cap with the bill turned around backwards and a "muscle shirt" just like Bobby always wore. I thought to myself *who is that mowing my yard?* I jumped out of my car and ran to my back gate, but there was no one there. I went back to my car to unload the groceries and there was a young man going down the street with shoes on just like Bobby wore. They were teal green and white. I never saw that young man in my neighborhood before and have never seen him since that time. A couple of weeks later, Bobby appeared in the back seat of my grandson's car. He told his cousin that he was so happy but he missed his daughter, Summer.

I later saw Bobby in a dream. He was sitting at a table with a smile on his face. So I know he is safe and I will see him again some day.

I really believe Angels appear to us if we just look for and believe in them.

Angel's Voice

"Donna", Evansville, Indiana

When I was somewhere around the age of nine or ten, I laid down in the backseat of the family car. I guess there weren't any seatbelt laws in the late 70s, early 80s, with my mother driving and my brother riding shotgun. I don't recall exactly what I was doing. I might have been looking up at the sky from the window – I did that often. I heard a man's voice, which sounded incredibly kind and deep.

He said, "Donna, sit up."

This voice was so amazing! The only way to describe the feeling that came with that voice was a sensation of pure, unconditional love, like a warm blanket wrapped around me, surrounding me with peace and love. I just laid there for a moment, and the man's voice told me a second time, only with a loving fatherly sternness, "Donna, I told you to sit up."

I sat up after he spoke the second time. Just a few seconds later, our car was hit by another vehicle. My mother had turned left into the path of an oncoming car. My lip was a little bloodied, but I'm positive my injuries would have been far worse had I not sat up. The other car hit close to where I was lying down. The memory of that voice and the unconditional love that it gave me carried me through many terrible moments in my life. I'm so blessed to be given such a gift.

I actually remembered the same voice when I was much younger, maybe five years old. This sounds incredibly silly, but at the time it meant a great deal to me, and I guess it still does. I was lying on my canopy bed with my eyes closed. I don't remember being asleep. I very, very much dislike spiders now, but as a child I was TERRIFIED of them, and we had some very large scary ones in our older house. As I was lying there, I heard the man's voice tell me to open my eyes. When I did, I screamed as I rolled off the bed onto the floor with a loud thud. A very nasty spider was about to drop onto my face as it slid down its web. I know, it's very silly, but it's true and I'm so glad for the warning!

Invisible Protector

Lahna Harris, Clarksville

I was in a hurry. All of my co-workers left the building in downtown Louisville where I was employed, and I stayed an extra half hour to finish up some tasks. It was 1976 and I had a one-year old son to pick up at the babysitter's house.

As I left the building located between 4th and 5th Streets on Liberty Street, I noticed that it was turning dusk. It was a clear, warm day in early fall, and I had some fleeting thoughts about the upcoming season before I noticed that my car was the only one left in the large parking lot across the street. The lot looked barren, almost abandoned. On a normal day it served as a home to at least a couple of hundred other cars. This day turned out to be anything but normal for the parking lot.

I continued walking quickly, crossed the street to the lot, and noticed a few people walking along 4th Street. It was rare to see anyone along that stretch of the street during the mid seventies. What once was the place to go for shopping or for dinner and a movie outlived its glory days and became a rather rough area of town. The splendor of the popular, ornately decorated theatres had faded. The locally famous Rialto, Mary Anderson, Ohio, Kentucky, and United Artists all closed their doors to patrons and shut down their projection rooms. The excitement once generated by nicer restaurants sadly dimmed and was replaced with dives.

The next thing I noticed were three young men who had apparently also noticed me. They stopped walking for a few seconds, spoke briefly among themselves, and then began walking toward me. Of course, I picked up my already fast pace toward my car. They picked up their pace, too. As I got what seemed to be a little closer to my car, they seemed to get a lot closer to me. It was obvious that they had malevolent intentions, and I was so afraid.

My actions did not match my thought. My actions were that I reach my car, quickly get in and speed off just before they reached me. My thought was *there is no way that I will make it*. My body moved fast, my heart raced as fast as my thoughts, yet what followed then seemed in slow motion. During the peak of my fear, I heard and felt someone walking up behind me – coming to my right side. I thought it must be someone who was still in the building, saw me leaving alone and decided to be sure I made it safely to my car. *Thank goodness*, I thought as I turned my head to the right to see who it was.

I saw no one there. But I felt someone there. In that instant, the three young men transformed from would-be perpetrators with malicious expressions on their faces to pale-faced boys who appeared to be scared out of their wits. They wasted no time turning to run in the opposite direction, each looking over their shoulders as they ran like mad.

Whoever came to protect me was not visible to me, and I still wonder what persona this guardian angel took on for the hoodlums to see. My guess is that all three of them still talk about that day, as do I.

Ruthie's Angels

Jackie Atchison, Grant County, Kentucky

When I was down in the deep south of Murray, Kentucky, I took care of a few old southern Belles. One was Ruthie, or as I called her The Bird, a well to do widow and a "pillar of the community." I called her The Bird, because I fixed big meals, which she just 'picked at' like a bird. Her son and a husband were both named Jack, and she spoke of them often. She lived in Murray her whole life along with her cousin Desiree and a few of the neighborhood girls. They all grew old together, very old. Ruthie was 95 when I came to her household. I worked with her for about two years and as her health gradually failed I worked extra hard to keep her safe, comfortable and out of a nursing home.

As a perfect southern democratic lady of stature and respect is want to do, she had me drive her to the court house on Election Day one chilly November so that she could pull the lever for the straight democratic ticket. But then she proceeded to have a stroke. By the time I got her home I could no longer understand a word she said.

After her stay in the hospital she returned home. The Bird was never the same and grew very weak and agitated. She was bed-ridden and the decision to keep her home for good was made. Every day I would make her breakfast and lunch, leaving dinner to the night nurse who came in. During my time in the kitchen I would hear The Bird talking. I assumed she was talking to me so I went in to her room.

Ruthie looked around, very confused, and asked me, "Where did Jack go?"

"I don't know," I would respond.

On other occasions she asked me, "Where did that little girl go?"

I responded every time, "She had to go home."

One time, after the little girl had visited her in her room she again asked where she went. When I told her that she had to go home again she said that she wanted to go home herself.

"I cannot drive you, Ruthie. You have to go there by yourself."

That evening she had developed a small cough and by dawn she was gone. Hopefully she was holding the hands of the little girl she had grown up with and her husband and son.

Nanna Heard Angel Music

Nanna was my husband's grandmother. She was very religious her whole life. The wife of a farmer, she left a lot up to the Lord throughout the years. As her health started to deteriorate, but not her sense of humor, she went to stay with her daughter. They had a strained relationship and were coming to terms with the love they had for each other as the days passed.

I bought Nanna a book on angels for Christmas that year and every day her daughter read her a story while they watched the boats pass by on Lake Barkley.

Nanna closed her eyes and said, "Isn't that music so pretty?"

When her daughter asked what music she would reply that it was organ music or people singing gospel. She heard music until the day she died. On her deathbed her daughter said that when she took her last breath all of her wrinkles disappeared and her withered, arthritic hands finally relaxed.

Ginger, My Angel Dog
Jackie Atchison

I got Ginger when I was in college; she was an older dog of about five. She was a man hating, child despising, chocolate loving, forever protecting of women dog. Ginger was a Carolina dog, one of the oldest breeds in the Americas that came with the very first explorers to this continent.

I moved from Murray to Hartford to Horse Branch to Carrollton to Pewee Valley finally, with Ginger. Her health started failing when she was about 17 years of age. When she died, I was there, just me and Ginger. I buried her on the edge of the property by the woods with a warm blanket and a chocolate bar.

Later that summer I noticed a small clump of St. Johns Wort grew from her grave. I was collecting St. John's Wort for quite a few summers, but it only grew across the creek in a large field. There was never any trace of it in the yard until that one clump from Ginger. I took it as a message to not worry, be happy and not to be sad. It meant a lot.

Swirling Pillar of Light
Dorothy Kress

In the winter of 1984, I was living in Chicago, on Wells Street. Just before my grandfather died, I was asleep in bed. I was awakened by a brilliant white light. It woke me up out of a dead sleep. It was swirling in a pillar, kind of like the Ten Commandments movie, and I knew that my grandfather was going to die. It didn't say anything, I just knew. Then it disappeared. I figured I had to be dreaming, but I was wide-awake.

A couple days later, my grandfather came to me in a dream and told me he died. I argued with him in the dream, and said, "No, the family would have called me."

He said, "Be quiet, I don't have much time. Take care of Grandma. She will die not much after me, and take care of Mom. I love you."

And then he disappeared. Just then the phone rang, it happened right when he went away. It was my family calling to tell me my grandfather just died. I really don't know what the pillar of light was.

Spinning Tires
Diana Szerletich

About 27 years ago, when my oldest son was in kindergarten, I took him every day to the school in our neighborhood. This meant I also loaded up my two younger children. One morning there was a very dense fog, which made it impossible to see very far. I backed the car to the end of the driveway and stopped to look for traffic. I couldn't see any headlights, so I tried to continue backing up. Only the car would not move.

I could hear the tires spinning as I tried giving it gas. Our driveway had a slope at the end, so that ordinarily all you had to do is take your foot off the brake and the car would roll into the street. Just then a car flew down the street and as soon as it passed my car rolled out of the driveway. If we had rolled out before then there would have been no way for the other car to avoid hitting us. As I sat there shaking and trying to figure out what just happened and why we were saved, I heard a voice in my heart say that we were going to have another child. She was born eight years later.

Angels on the Lookout

"For he will command his angels concerning you to guard you in all your ways; ..." Psalm 91:11(NIV)

Glynnis Whitwer, Glendale, Arizona

I woke up at 4:00 AM on a Saturday. No noise disturbed my sleep. No dog licked my faced; I just woke up. There was no prompting to do anything special, so I just got up and started my day early. Around 2:00 PM, I started to fade and stopped to rest on the couch. My son Robbie snuggled up next to me and we enjoyed a few moments together. To explain my exhaustion, I mentioned to Robbie how early I awoke.

"That's weird, Mom," Robbie said. "I woke up at 4 o'clock, too."

"Why didn't you come downstairs?" I asked. "We could have spent the early morning together." He got very still and silent with an odd look on his face.

"I was afraid to get up," he replied. I looked fully at Robbie and asked what frightened him.

"I thought I saw a man sitting in the chair beside my bed," Robbie answered sheepishly, a little embarrassed in the daylight of what scared him in the dark.

In a moment of divine revelation and without a pause, I responded, "Robbie, I'm not surprised you saw someone sitting by your bed at night. I've been praying for angels to protect you every day. And since you were a baby, I've prayed for God to send His biggest, strongest angels to watch over you and your brothers. Robbie, I think you got to see an angel this morning."

Relief flooded his features and together we grinned in delight at what God allowed Robbie to see. Emboldened by my belief in his story and in God's protection, Robbie proceeded to share another sighting – one that involved what looked like a man dressed in battle fatigues on guard at the back window. He told me he hadn't said anything before, because he thought people would make fun of him.

I told Robbie that for generations, angels scared almost everyone who saw them. Who wouldn't be afraid at someone appearing where he shouldn't be? Just look at the Christmas story. Zechariah was "gripped with fear" when the angel Gabriel appeared to tell him he would be the father of John the Baptist – the prophet who would tell about Jesus. Mary was told to "not be afraid" by the angel who told her she would bear a child. The shepherds were "terrified" when they saw an angel and heard of the birth of their Savior Jesus.

Heavenly messengers, our protectors and worshippers of God – angels have many roles. The Bible says they are created beings (Hebrews 7:7) and that we have probably seen and entertained angels without realizing it (Hebrews 13:2). But the Biblical description of angels that brings me the most personal comfort is that of protector. Psalm 91 speaks of God's care for us in this manner, *"For he will command his angels concerning you to guard you in all your ways; they will lift you up in their hands, so that you will not strike your foot against a stone" (Psalm 91: 11-12).*

As Christmas ends and I prepare for the New Year, I thank God for angels. Just as they appeared to Zechariah, Mary, the shepherds and others, they still appear today. In fact, I believe they appeared to a 12-year-old boy at the response of his mother's prayers for that boy's protection. Miracles still happen!

Flames of Light, Flames of Love

I met Dale Epley when I worked at the Spirit Earth, Spirits of Light Psychic Fairs. I enjoyed Dale's positive attitude and her focus on giving readings. Dale became a reader in 1993 when she started out learning to meditate. She eventually noticed her inner "still, small voice" and developed her ability to do clairaudient channeling. Dale hosts groups of interested individuals in her home for classes, teaches at local colleges, and conducts workshops to assist people in developing their intuitive talents to receive messages from their spirit guides and angels.

Dale Epley

Dale Epley:
A few years ago, I was teaching a class at a friend's house. The class was made up of very spiritual individuals, including numerous healers. Toward the end of class, I asked everyone to relax and see if they felt the energy of the angels as I asked them to enter the room.

I was amazed that not only did we feel their energy, but we also saw numerous small flames enter through the windows and walls. The angelic light danced around the room. After a few minutes, the angel flames left as quickly as they entered.

My Guardian Angel, Damien

My Guardian Angel, Damien, appeared to me numerous times in the past. Usually, I don't realize that it is Damien until after the experience. Two times stand out in my mind. The first happened many years ago when I was sitting in a Starbuck's in Austin, Texas. I looked up from the book I was reading to see a young man with dark curly hair peering at me from behind one of their sales racks. I smiled, and then looked away for a second. When I looked back in his direction, he was not there. In fact he was nowhere in the store. Later, in my spirit communications, Damien verified for me that he gifted me with his manifested presence for that moment in time.

The other occurred just a few years ago when Jerry, my husband, and I were traveling in Florida. While traveling on a turnpike, we stopped to have breakfast. As we left the restaurant, a medium-aged black man approached me and asked for a dollar for gas. It surprised me, and I hurriedly caught up with my husband and we got into our truck and left.

As we left the area, I felt this had not been an ordinary experience and asked Damien if that had been him, and he replied, "Yes."

There are three reasons I felt this was not a mortal being. It cost $10 to enter the turnpike. Typically, a person in need of money will avoid a costly turnpike. The combination restaurant/gas station was in the median of the turnpike and not on an ordinary street where someone might be panhandling. Lastly, the black man was clean and very well dressed. He did not look at all like he needed money for anything.

Floating White Feathers
Kim Owens, RN

I didn't believe in angels, certainly not the stereotypical ones with wings. When I was certified to do healing Reiki work, Marilyn Fischer guided us in a meditation at the end of the Reiki class. She asked us to try to visualize our guides. I visualized what seemed to be typical guides and I didn't know whether to really believe in them or if it was my imagination. I "saw" a young American Indian woman, an older American Indian woman, and an Asian man with a Fu Manchu mustache. I also saw one or two other figures. Marilyn told us to imagine our guides leading us up a path. Next, our visualizing took us to the top of a mountain. She suggested on that mountain top we could feel the unconditional love from our guides.

Then she said, "Visualize your angel."

I didn't necessarily believe in angels, but I saw a HUGE image of an angel! He was male, at least nine feet tall, and he had a huge set of wings. At that time, I hadn't heard of angels being so large. Then Marilyn asked us to receive a gift from our guides and angel. I visualized my angel handing me a white feather. This gift was symbolic to me, because of what recently happened. Before I started nursing school, I was in the unemployment office. I wondered if I should become a nurse, which involved a lot of sacrifice. I was a single mom and it meant two years of living on student loans, with a mortgage. Plus I didn't know if I could be a nurse, and give someone a shot, UGH.

In the unemployment office, I asked myself, "Do I really want to be a nurse?"

Just then, I opened up a magazine. On the page where I opened it was an advertisement for a nursing program. The picture showed a ceramic figurine with a nurse bending over as if to help someone.

It said, "Nurses are God's angels on earth".

I decided to start nursing school. Later, I took Reiki to help me to do more healing work. Now, back to the meditation with Marilyn – she went around the room and asked each person to share about their meditation. When it was my turn, I confessed that I didn't think my images were real. I told the group that it appeared that everything I saw was so predictable. I thought my mind made up stuff since I was told to visualize guides and an angel. But Marilyn assured me that I saw what I was supposed to see.

Laura Dunn is one of my friends who was also there getting her Reiki certification. So she heard everything I said and later we talked over our experiences. We did a lot of spiritual growth together and were understood each other's journey.

Not long after the Reiki workshop, I was on the phone, talking to a girlfriend of mine named Ann. We were roommates a few years earlier. She knew I did energy work even before becoming Reiki certified. She asked how the Reiki certification went, and I told her all about both the workshop and meditation. When I got to the part about my angel handing me the white feather, I had a phone number show on my call waiting. I told Ann to hold on, so I could see who it was. It was Laura Dunn. I switched back to Ann, and told her it was Laura. I said I'd call Laura right back, since I HAD to finish telling Ann about my angel and white feather.

I told Ann, "I am just not sure whether to believe it really happened."

I kept thinking it was my brain making it all up. When I finished talking with Ann, I called back Laura. Laura said she tried to call me to tell me that a white feather landed on her out of nowhere. She got the thought, that very moment, to call me and tell me what just happened.

When I didn't answer, Laura thought to herself, *oh, maybe she's talking to someone about it now, and telling them she doesn't know whether to believe it or not. I'll call her back.*

I couldn't believe it! Then I told Laura about my conversation with Ann.

I said, "Well, NOW I believe!"

Laura had white feathers fall on her out of nowhere two other times, and she called me those times too. We believe that the white feathers are symbolic for both of us. What a great gift! Needless to say, I also called Ann right back and told her about Laura's experience. It gives you SUCH an awesome feeling when something like that happens and you know that

God and your guides and angels are touching you in such a personal and obvious way.

Mom's An Angel Now

I met Willie at the Mid-South Paranormal Convention in late September 2005, in Louisville, at Waverly Hills, where I had a vendor's table. I was selling my first book, *Shaker Ghost Stories.* Willie had a steady line of people at his table all day, as folks sought him for readings. Since then, I've been impressed by the good references I've heard about Willie and his skills.

Willie "Windwalker" Gibson lives in Valley Station, Kentucky, approximately ten miles north of Ft. Knox. He lives with his wife of 20 years, Schmon. Willie is of Irish and Cherokee decent. He is a known as a Paranormal Consultant, dealing with matters that lack the normal means of explanation. He is an Ordained Minister and Shaman.

For those of you who ask how one can be both shaman and minister, Willie explains, "Ministers look to God and Shamans look to the Great Spirit. The Great Spirit is the supernatural being who made us all. We practice the same things, and we just take different paths. I Corinthians 12 says that there will be people who will have the gift of healing, ministry, discerning of spirits, speak in tongues, and prophecy. That is what I do. Whenever there is a paranormal problem and someone requires my help, I do my best to solve their problem for them."

Willie "Windwalker" Gibson is the author of the Book *Windwalker* and has a television cable access show called "Spiritual Gifts and Wonders". He has also done a FOX News and CMT Network special on the Paranormal. In addition, he reads medicine cards and smoke readings, and does clearings.

Willie:

My mother was the type of woman who worried about her family. Even after all of us grew and married, she still worried about us. Last September 2006, our Mom was rushed to the hospital by my brother. When later checked on her in bed, her breathing had almost stopped. She was placed on a ventilator, and for three months she battled to get off the machine.

Throughout her battle she always had a smile on her face, as to say, "Don't worry about me; I will be okay."

On December 21, 2006, our Mom passed away. When she passed she had a smile on her face.

The next day my sister went to the hospital to collect her things from the room. They had already packed them in a box, and were waiting at the front desk for her. As my sister picked up the box, she could sense something behind her, so she turned but saw no one there. The nurse, who was at the desk, started to walk with my sister to the elevator. When they got to the elevator, a picture on the wall in front of the elevator fell and broke.

As everyone was looking at the broken picture on the floor, the elevator started opening and closing as to say, "Hurry up, and leave this place!"

My sister got on the elevator and pushed the button to go down to the lobby. Then when the door opened and she got out, something told her to look around. And there standing in the elevator was my mother dressed in a white robe. She was smiling, and healthy.

My sister got the feeling that she was telling all of us, "Don't worry about me. I'm fine."

My sister came home and told us what happened. We all believed her because we were brought up to believe in God and God's angels. I believe Mom was allowed to come back and show us that she was fine and that she was in no more pain. She wanted us to be happy and not to worry about her. I know she's one of God's angels now and that she's happy.

White-Robed EMT

James White, Lexington

I travel to Louisville to visit my daughter. On September 24, 2007, I drove my truck with a friend as passenger near Interstate 64 and Hurstbourne Lane. We came out of the Red Carpet Inn, and started to cross into Hurstbourne, when a truck came off the Interstate ramp going 60 miles per hour. His vehicle smashed into my truck right on the driver's side, my side.

When I looked around, I saw blood over the inside of my truck. I thought I was dead. My passenger was able to get out on the other side. Suddenly, I looked up to see a young lady next to me. She had climbed in on the passenger side.

She said, "My name is Mary Freeman. I'm an EMT. I'm going to hold your head back here to keep you from moving and getting hurt." She put her hand around my neck to help hold it straight. I looked up at her and I saw the most beautiful glow around her. The glow filled up the inside of my truck.

She had what looked like a white evening gown, and her hair was medium to light brown. Her hands were very soft and gentle. She had deep blue eyes – a beautiful face with no makeup. There was a glow all around her.

I asked her, "Are you an angel?"

And she just looked down at me and smiled.

Then I saw a fireman who said, "Your head is stiff and I'm going to put a protective collar on your neck now."

I asked him, "Where is the pretty young lady who was here?"

He answered, "There is nobody here but me helping."

Well, I had been slammed into the driver's side door, which left me with contusions, abrasions, cuts, and bruises. The inside of my jaw was dislocated, my hip was out, my lungs were pushed against my rib cage, and my heart was bruised. They told me that, with the collision I had, I should have had multiple breaks in my bones. The other driver had only a sprained wrist and bruised shoulder. There was no alcohol involved for either of us.

They took me to the trauma center at the University Hospital. I was in trauma care for six hours, where my death seemed imminent. My EKG went flat twice. The doctors spoke to my daughter, telling her that they were losing me. They asked her about any instructions in the event of my death.

She told them, "Do whatever it takes to keep my dad alive."

I was released three days later. I know the accident was a wake-up call for me. I'm supposed to keep an eye on what God wants me to do for Him. From all the things I've been through during the last six months, I feel that it's all part of God's plan. I need to stay on track; he has something that he needs for me to do. I'm here now to be part of the plan.

Guarding the Door to the Afterlife
Rose Campbell

My father and mother decided that my father's last days with cancer would be lived out at home. I took a more active role with trying to help Mom out during these months and was with Dad a lot. As his time grew closer, he began to see and talk to different people. One person whom he would talk to a lot was his sister, who passed many years earlier. Mom and I both knew this.

However, one day when I was there at his bedside he told me something he didn't want my mother to know. He said that the night before he was sleeping. He suddenly awoke to see an angel standing at the foot of his bed. He asked the angel if it was time to go. The man – the angel had the form of a male – said to him that it was not for him to say, that he was sent only to keep "The Door" open so that when Dad was ready he could walk through much more easily.

Dad said he then told the angel, "I'm not leaving until the house is paid off and you shouldn't have to hang around for another couple of weeks holding a door open that wasn't going to be used."

The angel replied, "There is no hurry. It will be as it is given from God."

He left, fading from view. Dad did not want my mother to know about his conversation with the angel, for he feared she would break down, so I held my counsel.

About two weeks later when I arrived to my parent's home, Dad sent Mom to the store. As soon as we heard the car leave, he told me the angel had returned and assured Dad he was still standing guard over The Door.

Dad said he told the angel, "I'm not going until after the third of the month. That's when the social security check comes to pay off the last house payment."

He told the man he could go elsewhere until the third.

Dad said the angel replied, "It's no chore. It is my privilege, and I will wait. Again...poof...the man, according to Dad, whooshed up and out the through the transom over the living room door.

One and half weeks later my father sent my mother to the post office and told her if the check was in to go directly to the bank and pay off the house. She did this and returned about noon. At 2:00 PM she laid down to take a nap on a cot in the same room as Dad. She felt that all things were fine enough for her to get some rest in case the night wasn't so good. She awakened at 3:30 PM to the sound of a man's voice, and thinking my father needed something, went to him only to find him gone, with a semi-smile upon his face.

In a few days time I told her of Dad's story.

She then told me, "Then that must have been the angel's voice I heard! I knew it didn't sound like your father, but no one else was there. I figured he was just telling me he could wait a little longer for me to get to him."

She recalled the words "wait" and "later". It all made great sense in light of the conversation between Dad and the angel. I'd like to think that with his goal accomplished Dad decided it was time to go and let the "Man" get on with waiting for someone else.

Angel Driver

A client of mine was driving with her daughter in their car, when they ran off the road. They landed in some snow and part way down an embankment. The daughter tried and tried to back the car up the embankment but it was stuck. Some folks had stopped on the roadway above and someone yelled down that a tow truck had been called. The daughter got out and climbed the hill to speak to the folks above. My client looked up to the other side of the embankment and saw a young man, sitting in the snow with only a shirt and pants on.

As she was thinking this was odd the young man jumped the ravine and came up to the car. He opened the door and said to her could he try to free her? She nodded and he climbed in.

Her next words were this, "He got behind the wheel, and put the car in gear. That car rose up and out of that ravine like it was on dry payment. I would swear it floated up that hill!

She said she was so stunned that she couldn't think of anything to say as he climbed out of the car.

When her daughter came running up and asked how she got the car up from the ravine, she told her it had been a young man who did it. She turned to thank him and he was nowhere to be found!

She said, "It was less than a minute. I swear to you, he was an angel, the real kind but I didn't see any wings!"

This woman says she will go to her grave knowing she had been sitting in a car with an angel, the real kind.

Drowning Girl Rescued

Lois Madden, New Richmond, Ohio

My family is from the Somerset, Kentucky area. Growing up as a child in Cincinnati, Ohio, we often went to visit my grandma and my uncle and his family on Tick Ridge. It was during one of these trips that I had a near drowning experience.

We loved boating on Lake Cumberland, and often visited General Burnside Park and went swimming in that lake. It was during one of our swimming excursions at General Burnside that I had a lifesaving angelic intervention.

I wasn't a swimmer as a kid, but I was never afraid of being in the water. I finally learned to swim as a teenager in gym class. As a young child, my dad loved throwing me high in the air and catching me on the way down. One of my Great-Aunts recently told me it used to scare the wits out of her when Dad threw me in the air like that. *I loved it!* I distinctly remember being scared and enjoying it all at the same time-I felt like I was flying-pretty cool for a young kid!

Dad often took me to the deep part of the lake where he'd toss me in the air and catch me. However, this particular time he didn't catch me. Of course, I fell into the water fully expecting him to retrieve me, but he didn't. I remember sinking very slowly. I felt calm and peaceful, almost like I wanted to drift into sleep. I wasn't the least bit scared and I wasn't struggling. At some point I remember wondering why it was taking Dad so long to pull me out of the water. *Where was he?*

About this time I became aware of a light source. It was very bright under the water. I felt really tired when, very gently, I felt myself being lifted out of the water. I was aware of a presence but I didn't see anyone. Help had come at last. My next memory is that of waking up on the beach surrounded by my family. There were a lot of questions and confusion about what had happened out in the water. I sensed that Dad really couldn't explain.

I remember him saying that he'd tried getting me when I fell in the water, but that he'd found me floating on the waters surface; he hadn't lifted me out of the water. I can't say with certainty what happened that day. However, I do believe with all my heart and soul that a guardian angel intervened on my behalf, saving me from certain death by drowning.

Angel Brings Gift of Song

Sometimes the divine brings gifts that arrive in a powerful way. Before Paul began his life as a follower of Jesus, he was struck down by the awesome force of God. Some people go through a crisis of body, mind or spirit before they earn God's gift. In this story, a humble housecleaner was blown over by a mighty wind, when an angel brought the gift of song to her and her newly formed Christian Ministry of Unity and Oneness.

Pam Hadesty of New Port Richey, Florida, is a friend of my friend Jan, who lives in Louisville, Kentucky. Just a few days after I determined I wanted to find more angel stories for my book, Jan heard Pam's amazing tale, and I called Jan the day after that, to say hello. Pam called me that same day to tell the story in her own words. The Spirit can work very quickly.

Pam:

This story is very true. I would take a lie detector test, because it happened in just this way. Three years ago, in 2004, my husband and friend Mary Lou and I started our ministry. We wanted music to go with the spoken ministry, and Mary Lou asked my husband Mark to write some new songs. It was then eight years since Mark wrote music, and a few additional months went by when I was at Mary Lou's house.

As I stood in front of one of the windows, I sensed someone walking up behind me. I thought, *maybe Mark drove over and he's trying to surprise me.* I started to grin, and felt that someone leaning down toward my left ear. Mark is six feet and four inches tall. But then a massive sound blew into that ear, knocking me to my knees. I managed to grab the counter as I went down.

When I got up, I turned around to see who was there – there was nobody. I felt chills go through my body, and I ran upstairs to tell Mary Lou what happened.

She said, "God's just opened you up to something, but I don't know what it's about."

A week later, as I cleaned a house, I was intrigued to hear an inner voice start to sing. A wonderful song came to me then, with both melody and words. I immediately called my own home phone number, and sang the tune into my answering machine. When I got home, I told my husband to be sure and not erase that message!

The amazing thing about this experience is that I am the least likely person to write a song. I never really cared that much about music up until that time. I can't sit still long enough to write a song. But as I tell the story, other people clearly see that a messenger opened me up to receive beautiful songs. I have constantly heard that voice since then. I have a tape recorder and after I sing the song, I give it to Mark to write out the chords. Mark is a fabulous musician, but in 1996, he had six strokes and his whole right side was paralyzed. But he plays with one hand. The songs given to us have been the only music we use in our services.

I've received eighty songs, and I'm still hearing new music. Mark and I have made three CDs and we're working on several more. The angels sing to me, and everybody enjoys the music. Everything we need to fulfill the ministry was brought to us. People from around the world find our website and call to talk about our music ministry. The message in both our ministry and music is that God loves you, and positive thinking. And what is interesting is that the content of

Pam and Mark Hadesty

the song has, over time, spiritually ascended. The words are a higher expression of God's peace.

Mary Lou also had an experience of God's grace. She was not a speaker, until something happened. She was sitting on the couch in her den, when she saw lips floating over the air toward her. She thought *yes I'm awake, I'm not dreaming*. The vision didn't scare her. The lips floated over to her, and into her body. Since then she has easily been a wonderful speaker for our ministry.

Angel Trucker
Fred Reaves

A former client from Hopkinsville, Kentucky told me a story about his daughter. His daughter was on her way from school one Friday afternoon. I think she went to Western Kentucky University. She had a blowout and ran off the side of the road. Not only did it destroy the tire, but it also destroyed the wheel of her Toyota car.

She was on the side of the road and not long after a truck came by. The driver came back around and asked her if she needed help. She said, "Yes, I had a blowout and it destroyed my tire and wheel."

He said, 'Let's put on your spare." But for some reason she didn't have a spare tire.

He said, "Well, let me see what I can do."

He went to his truck, which was full of tires and came back with a tire she needed and the <u>exact wheel</u> for the car she was driving. He changed the tire for her, put on the wheel and put the old one in her trunk.

She asked, "How can I pay you?"

He said, "Call so and so at this company and tell them I helped you out. He'll figure out what the bill is." It was something like "Jones Tires" in Podunk, Kentucky.

She got home and told her Dad about it. He called and said, "My daughter had a blowout and destroyed her wheel. One of your guys came by and fixed it for her. We want to pay you for it."

He said, "I don't have any 'guys' that are one the road.'"

So the Father tried to explain, "Well, the truck looked like this and so on. The guy said to call you and you'd have a bill ready."

"No. I don't have anybody who is on the road that's fixed a tire. I wouldn't have anybody over there anyway. We don't do that. We're a tire store. I truly don't know what you're talking about."

They never found this trucker. They never found who he was. Her Dad was a sheriff's deputy at the time in Hopkinsville. So he's pretty thorough. He was intent on finding this trucker to pay him for helping out his daughter. He did an investigation to track down the helper and he never found him. He did not exist. It was a mystery what was never solved. If there are angels, maybe that's what that was. Those things make you pause and think.

Angel at the Circus

Judy Mullins

I once took a picture of what I call an angel at the circus. This was taken three or four years ago at a Barnum & Bailey circus in Cincinnati. At the time, all I was attempting to do was to take a picture of two guys on the balancing wheel, for lack of a better word. I'm not sure what this performance event is called but they stand upright on a wheel, one on each end and go spinning around & around.

There was nothing in the viewfinder but the two circus performers. I took the picture with a digital camera. Needless to say, I was amazed to see a

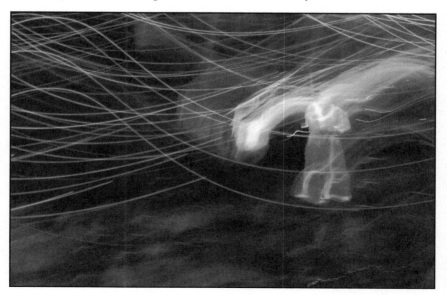

lady in a chiffon dress, with no feet that also appeared to have wings. I sent a letter to the circus telling them about this picture but got no reply. I didn't send the actual picture, because I was afraid they wouldn't give me credit for it. Maybe they were afraid my picture would be bad publicity too.

I don't really know if it is a spirit or angel or even if it's a lady versus a man. When I enlarged the picture, the person seems to have masculine features and the legs look muscular. I call it an angel for the sake of people who don't believe in ghosts, but do believe in angels.

There is nothing in the picture that looks anything like what I had the camera pointed at. I had three adult witnesses with me. They all agreed that they saw nothing the entire night that looked anything like this image.

About the Author

Thomas Freese is a writer, storyteller and author. He currently lives in Louisville, Kentucky. Thomas Freese is also a counselor and expressive therapist.

Thomas wrote over 130 articles, since 1999, for Lexington's *Chevy Chaser*, *Southsider*, and *W. Weekly* Magazines, www.chevychaser.com. His monthly feature is called "Day Trips", and highlights fun and intriguing local travel destinations. Thomas employs his own photographic talents in his articles and books. He illustrated another author's book, Shirley Hayden-Whitley's *Sometimes Life Ain't Sweet You Know*, (1994). His first book, *Shaker Ghost Stories from Pleasant Hill, KY*, was published in 2005. He followed *Shaker Ghosts* with two sets of fiction ghost stories, *Fog Swirler and 11 Other Ghost Stories*, (2006), and *Strange and Wonderful Things* (2008). A book of Civil War ghost stories which he co-wrote with Bryan Bush is titled *Haunted Battlefields of the South* and will be published in 2010. Besides ghostly tales, he will publish in 2010, *How to Make Southwest Jewelry in Wood*

Thomas Freese entertains audiences as a storyteller. He tells tales in libraries, story festivals, museums, and bookstores, using animated voices from his collection of accents and characters. He plays guitar and harmonica, creating wonderful original songs, such as "Whatja Gonna Do With a Silly Kitty?", "All in My Head", "Porquois Song", "Lost Shoe Blues", "Stuffed Animal" and more. His story programs include Porquois Tales, Ghost Stories, Silly Tales and Songs, World Folktales, Fairy Tales, Winter Tales, Origami Stories, and the Desert Southwest.

His webpage is *www.ThomasLFreese.com*.

Shaker Ghost Stories From Pleasant Hill, KY

by Thomas Freese

Shaker Ghost Stories is a collection of true experiences from the visitors to and employees at Shakertown, Pleasant Hill, Kentucky. Pleasant Hill has been 200 years in existence, and is one of the restored Shaker villages in the Eastern United States. The Shakers, or United Society of Believers in Christ's Second Appearing, worked diligently to create a Zion, or heaven on earth. Their founder, Mother Ann, encouraged them to put their "hands to work and hearts to God". While the Pleasant Hill Shakers have passed on, their legacy of spiritual devotion and material prosperity remains. The Shaker village is a peaceful place to visit and learn about Shaker life, to enjoy singing and overnight stays. Those who come find a spiritual touchstone in walking the land, hearing Shaker music, and marveling at their craftsmanship.

Some of those who work or visit there have discovered that some Shaker spirits have perhaps returned to Pleasant Hill. The collection of odd occurrences reported in Shaker Ghost Stories include mysterious singing, phantom footsteps, appearances and disappearances of Shaker-looking people, invisible helping hands, and the sights and sounds of work and worship continuing at odd hours. The Shaker spirits seem to act much in character with their original dispositions – demonstrating faith, fervor, and a guardianship of their homes and land.

Traveling east in 1990, Thomas Freese visited friends, looking to relocate from New Mexico. Thomas was intrigued by Shakertown and the lives and accomplishments of the Shakers. He moved to Lexington the following year, and in 1996 became one of the Pleasant Hill Singers. While learning and performing Shaker music, he heard his new friends often speak of their "Shaker experiences", occasional and unusual happenings. Boosted by their encouragement, he spent the summer of 1998 taking notes and collecting accounts of the Shaker Ghost Stories. While returning for performances and singers' retreats, Thomas continued to collect Shaker ghost stories up until the publication of his book in 2005.

The chapters include an introduction, The Shakers at Pleasant Hill, "Are There Any Ghosts Around Here?", A Whirlwind, Women in White, The Mystery of Holy Sinai's Plain, and The Shaker Experience.

Bill Bright, a former Pleasant Hill employee, tells of an amazing experience.

"It was in the winter of 1996, and Dixie and I were working in the village. She noticed that the candles from a candlelight performance were still in the windows of the Meeting House. Dixie decided that they needed to be put away, so we stopped in there. I helped gather up the candles, and Dixie went to put them in the closet."

"Since I was a bit bored, I walked over to a spot between the two front doors to sing a little. I was next to a gap in the wall benches, facing the back wall. I started to sing sets of three, descending notes (triads). Since I had spent plenty of time in high school band, I figured that it'd be a neat exercise to try the acoustics in the large room of the Meeting House."

"As I was singing, something appeared in the middle of the benches to my right, on the sister's side. For lack of a better explanation, it looked like a human form, very similar to the special effect done in Star Trek when they beam up somebody. It seemed to rise up from the floor to my height. At that point, the hair on the right side of my body stood on end, while the left side was not affected. I immediately got cold chills, like I had just walked into a meat locker. I just wanted to get out of there. I left the building immediately, quickly enough to make Dixie come out after me."

"She asked me, 'What's wrong?' "

"I told her what had happened, and she suggested that I talk to Randy Folger, the music director. When I saw Randy, I told him about the experience, and he simply asked me if I knew what I had been doing. At that point I had no idea. Then Randy asked me to sing as I had been singing in the Meeting House. After I sang for him, Randy explained to me that I had unwittingly been singing the "Angel Shout". The "Angel Shout" was a set of notes that were sung like: "Lo...lo...lo..." and were sung in descending thirds. The "Angel Shout" was supposed to call the Shakers to meeting."

"Today I have no reservations about going into the Meeting House, but I will not try my experiment again!" (Pages 34-35, *Shaker Ghost Stories from Pleasant Hill, KY.*)

Shaker Ghost Stories from Pleasant Hill, KY, by Thomas Freese. Published August 2005 by AuthorHouse, ISBN # 1420850725, 36 B&W photos, 136 pages, Retail: $13.95

Fog Swirler and 11 Other Ghost Stories
by Thomas Freese

Fog Swirler is the second of a series of ghost story books. *Fog Swirler* is "fiction that falls not far from fact." Having heard over a hundred true mystery and ghost stories, Thomas Freese combines some of these classic elements with his creative imagination, and puts them into form in classic storyteller fashion.

The title story, Fog Swirler, tells of a woman who crosses paths with the bad boys in town. When they try to burn down her house, she turns to nature and summons help from the river fog. Sum of the Parts, his second story, springboards from a true tale of 'resurrectionist' Simon Kracht. In nineteenth century Louisville, Simon robbed fresh graves to provide the University of Louisville medical students with bodies for dissection. Thomas's story, Sum of the Parts, tells what might have happened in the dry well filled with discarded body parts.

Other story titles include: Dare Gone Bad, Final Arrangements, Road Cut, Sunspots, Mexican Vacation, and more. In Strawberry Picking, a young man takes advantage of the empty homes when nearly everyone is out picking strawberries. He tries to rob one home too many. In Hotbox, two boys find that their errant baseball has knocked out an unusual stuffing from the scarecrow in their playfield. Ghost Dog is both scary and tender, as the ghost of a murdered woman and her dog work with a sensitive boy to locate her body. Here is a short segment from Ghost Dog:

> *When spring came, Charlie went to his favorite private spot; at least this was one secret that Max had not found. Charlie cleared away the fallen branches that had snapped off during winter. The warm spring sunlight shone through a high gap in the woods above his hideout, and he saw something stand out, something not brown or gray or green. It was a heart-shaped locket, sort of a tarnished golden color. He pried it open and there was a curl of pretty red hair, fine and long. At that moment, Charlie got the feeling that he wasn't alone. He looked up at the entrance, expecting to see the Captain, or the young woman who had visited a few times last fall. There was no one there.*
>
> *But as he held the locket, he heard, faintly, the woman's voice, and she said, "You will find me." He realized again that someone, something was there with him, not at the entrance, but farther back in the hidden copse of green bushes. And then, he saw him. Below the curved and fallen log, in a little spot just big enough, there was a dog. The dog must have crawled in to escape the coyotes, or had smelled the traces of food that Charlie sometimes brought to his fort. He seemed friendly, but sort of sad. Charlie looked in his eyes and knew he was a stray dog without a home.*

Fog Swirler and 11 Other Ghost Stories by Thomas Freese. Published August 2006 by AuthorHouse, ISBN # 1425950868, 129 pages, 5 pen & ink illustrations, Retail: $14.95.

Strange and Wonderful Things: a Collection of Ghost Stories with Special Appearances by Witches and Other Bizarre Creatures

by Thomas Freese

This third in a series of five ghost story books by author Thomas Freese features a wonderfully crafted variety of mysteries. Nine tales are set in Kentucky, two are placed out west and one is located somewhere in Vietnam; all display the enchanting storyteller's voice that Thomas Freese gives in his performances as well as what readers of his previous two books enjoyed (*Shaker Ghost Stories* and *Fog Swirler*).

Perfect for nighttime fare, reading to children or adding to your ghostly library, *Strange and Wonderful Things* shows off the author's skill in creating surprise endings and karmic circumstances. For example, in "The Closet", we read about a young girl's haunted home in Old Louisville. She discovers an invisible playmate, who warns her of more sinister spirits whose portal is a spooky closet in her bedroom. "Car Rider" artfully combines several stories within a story and demonstrates Mr. Freese's experience from twelve years living in the desert Southwest. "The Witch's Rake" layers several moral lessons while ending in a gruesome event for two naughty sisters. On the other hand, in "The Healing Child" and in the title story, the spirits act in a benign and compassionate manner. "Moving Graves" and "Perfect Work Record" are set in counties close to Louisville. They each illustrate the power of ghosts to affect the world despite the death of the person's physical form. Mistreated animals somehow create a force for their own defense in "Dust Bunnies". "Whispers" concerns a gossipy woman who travels to Lourdes and receives an unwanted miracle. "Namphuong" tells the story of a woman who uses the help of a witch to find her true love. "Ornaments" provides a warning against using mojo and magic to trap others. "Happy Campers", set in a California summer camp, is a classic tale of the interaction between a young man and other teenage ghosts.

Strange and Wonderful Things, is suitable for children and adults and will provide many readers with suspense, ghostly intrigue, life lessons and pleasurable entertainment.

Strange and Wonderful Things by Thomas Freese. Published 2008 by PublishAmerica, ISBN # 1-60563-974-5, 144 pages, 15 illustrations, Retail $24.95.

Book & Online Bibliography

A Book of Angels: Reflections on Angels Past and Present, and True Stories of How They Touch Our Lives by Sophy Burnham, 1990, Ballantine Books, New York, NY, ISBN # 9780345361578.

Abernathy, Diane, St. Johns Wort, http://www.juniperandsage.com/herbs_adv_stjohnswort.php.

Adobe Angels: The Ghosts of Santa Fe and Taos by Antonio R. Garcez, 1995, Red Rabbit Press, Santa Fe, NM, ISBN # 0-9634029-3-5.

American Airlines Flight #965 crash near Buga, Colombia on December 20, 1995, http://lw.bna.com/lw/19990629/984739.htm.

American Indian Myths and Legends edited by Richard Erdoes and Alfonso Ortiz, 1984, Random House Inc., New York, NY, ISBN # 0-394-74018-1.

Angel Letters by Sophy Burnham, 1991, Ballantine Books, New York, NY, ISBN # 0-345-37342-1.

Apparitions: An Archetypal Approach to Death, Dreams and Ghosts by Aniela Jaffe, 1978, Spring Publications, Inc., University of Dallas, TX, ISBN 0-88214-500-2.

Originally published as *Geistererscheinungen und Vorzeichen*, Rascher Verlag, Zurich, 1957, and in English translation, *Apparitions and Precognition – A study from the Viewpoint of C.C. Jung's Analytical Psychology*, University Books, New Hyde Park, NY, 1963.

Best True Ghost Stories by Hans Holzer, 1983, Prentice Hall, New York, NY, ISBN # 0130719366. Quote from page 26.

British Folktales by Katherine Briggs, 1970, Pantheon Books, New York, NY, ISBN # 0-394-73993-0.

Campfire Stories…Things That Go Bump in the Night, by William Forgey, 1985, The Globe Pequot Press, Guilford, CT, ISBN # 0-934802-23-8.

Cassell's Dictionary of Superstitions by David Pickering, 1995, Sterling Publishing Company, New York, NY, ISBN # 0-304-36561-0.

Children of the Dome: Twenty-eight True Stories of Survival and Hope After the Loss of a Child by Rosemary Smith, 1999, Pathfinder Publishing of California, Oxnard, CA, ISBN # 0934793-78-6.

Civil War Ghosts and Legends by Nancy Roberts, 1992, University of South Carolina & Barnes and Noble Books, New York, NY, ISBN # 0-76070-366-3.

Creative Storytelling: Choosing, Inventing, and Sharing Tales for Children by Jack Maguire, 1985, Yellow Moon Press, Cambridge, MA, ISBN # 0-938756-35-4.

Dennis, Michael, Website: http://www.mikethepsychic.com/.

Do Dead People Watch You Shower? And Other Questions You've Been All But Dying to Ask a Medium, by Concetta Bertoldi, 2007, Harper Paperbacks, New York, NY, ISBN # 978-0061351228.

Don't Call Them Ghosts: The Spirit Children of the Fontaine Manse. A True Story, by Kathleen McConnell, 2004, Llewellyn Publications, Woodbury, MN, ISBN # 0-7387-0533-0.

Enchantment of the Faerie Realm: Communicate with Nature Spirits and Elementals by Ted Andrews, 1993, Llewellyn Publications, Woodbury, MN, ISBN # 0-87542-002-8.

Encyclopedia of Urban Legends by Jan Harold Brunvand, 2001, W.W. Norton and Company, New York, NY, ISBN # 0-393-32358-7.

Ghost Hunting in Kentucky and Beyond by Patti Starr, 2002, McClanahan Publishing House, Kuttawa, KY, ISBN # 0-913383-84-8.

Ghosts Across Kentucky by Lynwood Montell, 2000, The University Press of Kentucky, Lexington, KY, ISBN # 0-8131-9007-X.

Ghosts and Haunts from the Appalachian Foothills: Stories and Legends by James V. Burchill, Linda J. Crider, Peggy Kendrick, Marcia Wright Bonner, 1993, Rutledge Hill Press, Nashville, TN, ISBN # 1-55853-253-6.

Ghosts of Old Louisville by David Domine: True Stories of Hauntings in America's Largest Victorian Neighborhood. 2005, McClanahan Publishing House, Kuttawa, KY, ISBN # 0-913383-91-0.

Ghost Stories of Indiana by Edrick Thay, 2001, Ghost House Books, Edmonton, Canada, ISBN # 1-894877-06-03.

Haunts to Hookers by Joe Ford, 1980, McDowell Publications, Utica, KY.

In Search of Ghosts: Haunted Places in the Delaware Valley by Elizabeth P. Hoffman, 1992, Camino Books Inc., Philadelphia, PA, ISBN # 0-940159-14-7.

Irish Ghosts compiled by J. Aeneas Corcoran, 2002, Geddes and Grosset, New Lanark, Scotland, ISBN # 1-84205-205-5.

Jackie Tales: The Magic of Creating Stories and the Art of Telling Them by Jackie Torrence, 1998, Avon Books Inc., New York, NY, ISBN # 0-380-97582-3.

La Llorona, The Weeping Woman, An Hispanic Legend told in Spanish and English, by Joe Hayes, 2004, Cinco Puntos Press, El Paso, TX, ISBN # 0-938317-39-3.

Lamplight Tales by Roberta Simpson Brown, 2004, PublishAmerica, Baltimore, MD, ISBN # 1-4137-5524-0.

Louisville Ghost Hunters, www.louisvilleghs.com.

Magnes, Debbie, www.kycenterforselfgrowth.com.

Maudie and the Green Children by Adrian Mitchell, 1996, Tradewind Books Ltd., ISBN # 1-896580-06-8.

Mostly Ghostly: Eight Spooky Tales to Chill Your Bones, adapted by Steven Zorn, 1991, Courage Books, Philadelphia, PA, ISBN # 1-56138-033-4.

Nature Spirits and What They Say: Interviews with Verena Stael von Holstein edited by Wolfgang Weirauch, 2003, Floris Books, Edinburgh, Scotland, ISBN # 0-86315-462-X.

New Beginning Ministries, Pamela and Mark Hadesty & Mary Lou Houllis, http://www.newbeginningministries.com/.

Offbeat Kentuckians: Legends to Lunatics by Keven McQueen, 2001, McClanahan Publishing House, Kuttawa, KY, ISBN # 0-913383-80-5.

Past Masters: The History and Hauntings of Destrehan Plantation by Madeline Levatino, 1991, Levatino & Barraco, New Orleans, LA, ISBN # 0-9630144-6-3.

Peace Tales: World Folktales to Talk About by Margaret Read McDonald, 1992, Linnet Books, Hamden, CT, ISBN # 0-208-02329-1.

Phantoms of Old Louisville: Ghostly Tales from America's Most Haunted Neighborhood by David Domine, 2006, McClanahan Publishing House, Kuttawa, KY, ISBN # 978-0913383957

Real Ghosts, Restless Spirits, and Haunted Places by Brad Steiger, 2003, Visible Ink Press, Canton, MI, ISBN # 1-57859-146-5.

Queen of the Cold-Blooded Tales by Roberta Simpson Brown, 1993, August House Publishers, Little Rock, AR, ISBN # 0-87483-408-2.

Scary 2: More Stories That Will Make You Scream, Edited by Peter Haining, 2002, Barnes & Noble Books, NY, NY, ISBN # 0-7607-3762-2.

Staying Well With Guided Imagery: How to Harness the Power of Your Imagination for Health and Healing by Belleruth Naparstek, 1994, Warner Books, New York, NY, ISBN # 0-446-67134-7.

Stories You Won't Believe by Lonnie E. Brown, 2007, PublishAmerica, Baltimore, MD, ISBN # 1-4241-8812-1.

Storymaking in Education and Therapy by Alida Gersie and Nancy King, 1990, Jessica Kingsley Publishers, London, England, ISBN # 1-85302-520-8.

Storytelling Folklore Sourcebook by Norma J. Livo and Sandra A. Rietz, 1991, Libraries Unlimited, Inc., Englewood, CO, ISBN # 0-87287-601-2.

Tales of Witchcraft and the Supernatural in the Pecos Valley by Nasario Garcia, 1999, Western Edge Press, Santa Fe, NM, ISBN # 1-889921-03-3.

That Dark and Bloody River: Chronicles of the Ohio River Valley by Allan W. Eckert, 1995, Bantam Books, NY, NY, ISBN # 0-553-37865-1.

The Bell Witch: the Full Account, by Pat Fitzhugh, 2000, The Armand Press, http://www.bellwitch.org/home.htm, ISBN # 97051560X.

The Findhorn Garden by the Findhorn Community, 1975, Harper and Row, Publishers, New York, NY, ISBN # 0-06-011249-2.

The Ghost and I: Scary Stories for Participatory Telling edited by Jennifer Justice, 1992, Yellow Moon Press, Cambridge, MA, ISBN # 0-938756-37-0.

The Ghosts of Charleston by Edward B. Macy and Julian T. Buxton III, 2001, Beaufort Books, New York, NY, ISBN # 0-8253-0505-5.

The Lady In Gray and Other Stories: A Collection of Tales by Lindsey Wilson College Upward Bound students and staff, edited by Rudy Thomas, 2006, ISBN # 978-1-84728-198-2.

The Moral Compass: Stories for a Life's Journey edited by William J. Bennett, 1995, Simon & Schuster, New York, NY, ISBN # 0-684-80313-5.

The Spirited and Haunting History of West Point, KY by Clara J. Toles & Faith S. Stewart, AuthorHouse, Bloomington, IN, 2007, ISBN # 978-1-4343-1275-4.

The Telltale Lilac Bush and Other West Virginia Ghost Tales by Ruth Ann Musick, 1965, The University Press of Kentucky, Lexington, KY, ISBN # 0-8131-0136-0.

The Walking Trees and Other Scary Stories by Roberta Simpson Brown, 2007, August House Publishers, Little Rock, AR, ISBN # 0-87483-143-1.

The Unabridged Devil's Dictionary by Ambrose Bierce, 2002, University of Georgia Press, ISBN # 978-0820324012.

Too Good to be True: the Colossal Book of Urban Legends by Jan Harold Brunvand, 1999, W. W. Norton and Company, New York, NY, ISBN # 0-393-04734-2.

Twilight Dwellers of Colorado: Ghosts, Ghouls, & Goblins by MaryJoy Martin, 1985, Pruett Publishing Company, Boulder, CO, ISBN # 0-87108-686-7.

Wagging Tails, Swishing Tails, Fluffy Tails and Other Tales by Judy Fuson, 2003, AuthorHouse (then 1st Books Library), Bloomington, IN, ISBN # 1-4033-8266-2.

Western Ghosts: Haunting, Spine-Chilling Stories from the American West, (The American Ghosts Series), Edited by Frank D. McSherry, Jr., Charles G. Waugh and Martin H. Greenberg, 1990, Rutledge Hill Press, Nashville, TN, ISBN # 1-55853-069-X.

Willie Windwalker, http://www.myspace.com/crystalchief55.

World Folktales: A Treasury of Over Sixty of the World's Best-Loved Folktales, by Atelia Clarkson and Gilbert B. Cross, 1980, Charles Scribner's Sons, New York, NY, ISBN # 0-684-17763-3.

Story Collection Notes

Someone Who is Not There Author recollection from experience in late 1960's, St. Louis, MO.

Old Man on Gravestone, Flapping Curtains with no Breeze interview with Joan Freese voice recorded on 8-2-2006 in Chesterfield, MO.

Weird Photos photo taken by author of the Hawkins-Kirby House in Warsaw, KY, Gallatin Co., 10-29-2005.

General's Cabin visits by author on 7-22 & 23-2005, also 5-18 & 19-2006, Lee County, KY.

The Evil Ones Draw Nigh story as told by A.H., circa 1995, Nicholasville, KY, briefly mentioned in the Oct. 2001 Chevy Chaser Magazine.

Good Knight 8-12-2007 site visit and interview with Kathy Nash, 9-26-2007 group visit ghost hunting, (Jean Adams, Roberta Simpson Brown, Lonnie Brown, Robert Parker), Shelby County, KY.

The Ghosts of La Grange interview with Barbara Manley Edds of La Grange, two ghost tour visits on 10-19-2007 & 10-9-2008, email from 8-15-2008 and voice recorded interview at Borders Café Hurstbourne on 8-19-2008.

With the Eyes of a Child contributed by Jennifer Beasley, Louisville, KY, told to Expressive Therapies graduate students and submitted via email 10-4-2005, updated version received 6-26-2007.

Harbeson House on location interview with Larry Johnson, Flemingsburg, KY, part of an article for the Chevy Chaser Magazine.

Hospital Ghost submitted by Grace, Jefferson, IN, via email, 1-4-2006.

Nighttime Warnings submitted by (name withheld) female by email, 8-20-2007.

Deceased House Owner Still Around phone interview with Sarah Thomas, Lincoln County, KY, 8-15-2007, Louisville, KY.

Family Ghost, Car Accident, Cursed White Mink Stole, Miss Sally the Witch, Nightly Visitor, Impression of a Murder 8-9-2007 phone interview and submitted emails with Cindy Savey, Richmond, KY.

Bell Witch Cave 8-8-2001 location visit, research, and originally published in full account as a Day Trip, "The Bell Witch Cave", October, 2001.

The Ghosts of Charit Creek initial voice-recorded interview with A.H. in Hyden, Leslie Co., KY, in March 2000 and also phone interview with ranger 8-22-2007.

Two's Company interview with Jane H., 9-10-1999, 9-13-1999 and published in the October 1999 Chevy Chaser Magazine.

Historic Haunts research on locations and at the Lexington Library 9-14 &15-1999, 9-21-1999.

Lexington Ghosts interview with M. & B.L., September, 1999.

Hurricane Hall contributed by Mary Mackin-Salazar of Lexington, KY, transcribed from hand-written letter of 5-27-2008.

Restless Door...and more, Restless Door, Gold Tooth, Help from Beyond the Grave 8-9-2007 phone interview with (name withheld) female, Franklin Co., KY, and submitted email.

The Homestead trip to location on 8-25 & 8-26-2005, voice-recorded interview 8-26-2005 with Joanne Hobbs, part of article used from Chevy Chaser Day Trip, Nov. 2005.

Haunted American Castle location visit, (7-13-2002), research and interview with Nick Fantetti, also story appeared in the October 2002 Chevy Chaser Day Trip. A story from online posting was contributed by Lady Donna Jean, with permission for original Chevy Chaser article.

The Doctor is In but They Wish He Was Out initial interview E. H.-C. and J. D., 3-25-2001, and location visit with voice-recording interview, 6-20-2007.

Waverly Hills Sanitarium location tour 8-29-2003 with the Louisville Ghost Hunting Society and interview with Keith Age, online research, previously published in the October 2003 Day Trips, Chevy Chaser Magazine.

Photo of a Ghost Nurse voice-recorded interview with Ashley Campbell, Blackacre State Nature Preserve, Louisville, KY, 3-21-2009.

The Return of Waverly voice-recorded interview with Kevin Milburn, Louisville, 3-28-2009.

Shadow People submitted via email by Roberta Simpson Brown, 3-29-2009.

Ghost Next Door, Anonymous, Louisville, told to author at a New Year's Eve Party, 2008/2009 and submitted in writing via email 1-8-2009.

Tales from the Mountains, Little Boy Ghost, My Last Halloween, Ghost in Clear Fork, WV transcribed letters and phone interview 9-12-2007 with Sabrina Blackburn and Mary Bentley, Ashland, KY.

Historical and Hysterical – the Culbertson Mansion 8-23-2006 location visit and interview with Joellen Bye, previously published in the October 2003 Day Trips, Chevy Chaser Magazine.

Ghost Tour Guide in Off Hours email submission 6-26-2007 by Robert Parker, author of *Haunted Louisville*.

First Sighting of a Ghost, Odd Happenings, on site voice recorded interview with Pam, Danny, and Janna Downs, New Albany, Indiana, 8-23-2006.

After Death She Came to Talk, Our House Ghost, & A Big Wind notes from phone interview with Bonnie Casto on 1-27-2009.

Power Tools in Heaven, voice-recorded interview with Jean Romano, in Louisville, KY, 10-4-2005.

House Built Over Indian Battleground Author remembrance of stories shared by college roommate, R.J. N., Jr., St. Louis, MO, 1979.

Double Trouble & Scared by the Dead interviews with Beth Wilder fall 2008 and submitted in writing.

Living with Ghosts voice-recorded interview with Andrea Yussman at Borders, Louisville, KY 6-29-2007, also 7-6-2007.

Lost Camper, phone interview with Eruma Taylor, of Harrodsburg, KY, on 7-11-2007.

Meeting House Bed and Breakfast initial interview on location 6-1-2007, Frankfort, KY, and phone interview 9-6-2007 with Rose Burke.

House Ghosts initial voice-recorded interview at Louisville location with Becky, 6-1-2006, and email submission 8-10-2007.

Haunted Quaker Church & Murder Victim in Courthouse told by Fred Reaves, Henderson, KY, from a voice-recorded phone interview at Barnes and Noble, Evansville, IN, 3-16-2008.

Disappearing Old Woman, Invisible Lady, Call to Heaven, Destiny Calls, voice recorded interview with D.M. at Borders, Hurstbourne Parkway, Louisville, KY, on 8-22-2008.

Mysterious Wavy Light email submission by Pat Sisson, Nashville, TN, on 6-27-2007 with corrections 8-10-2007.

Family Spirits, interview with Bridget Larmour, Lexington, 9-10-1999 and published in the October 1999 Chevy Chaser Magazine.

Four Stories of Spiritual Battle, Angel of the Lords Visits, Preach or Die, Witness to Amazing Powers, Casting out Spirits of Disease and Death voice-recorded interview in Boonville, IN, on 3-18-2006 with Don Seaman.

White Horse, Foggy Night & Deceased Resident Still Calls "Yoo-hoo", interview with Lahna Harris, Louisville, KY, and email submission, 6-26-2007 & 12-6-2008.

Visions and Spirits 8-18-2007 submitted by email from (name changed) female in the Evansville, IN, area.

Bright Light Figures visit 10-7-1999, also 6-10-2006, phone interview & submitted email from Carol Cassedy.

My Haunted Cabin & Spirits Visited Me, on site voice recorded interview at the Mullins Cabin, Grant County, KY, with Judy Mullins on 11-26-2008.

Protective Family Spirit, Cross Image in the Mirror, Healer's Story, Finished with Cancer, on site voice recorded interview with Claudia Thurman, Sonora, KY, on 2-4-2008.

Turn Around, Woman's Counsel, Seeing Back in Time, Bad Spirit Energy initial voice-recorded interview with Normandi Ellis, 9-17-2006 in Berea, KY, emailed corrections from notes received 9-1-2007.

Ghost Cat voice recorded interview on location with anonymous, Louisville, KY, 7-9-2007.

Girl with a Watering Can & Dad's Spirit in Our Home, Anonymous, Louisville, KY, voice recorded interview on 9-26-2007.

Civil War Spirits, Stormy Spirit, Grandpa's Icy Visit, Mam's Lasting Gift, contributed by Lois Madden

The Message contributed by Jennifer Jones, Northern KY, initial contact 7-5-2007 at storytelling venue, submitted by email 7-11-2007.

My Nanny the Witch, Papaw on the Hill, Runaway Ghost in Car, Dead Baby Ghosts in Well, Dead Man with Axe, voice recorded interview with Lisa Renee Myers on 3-30-2008 in Louisville.

God Wears Shiny New Pajamas first heard at Kentucky Storytelling Association Board Members retreat in Bethlehem, IN, at the Storytellers Riverhouse B & B, related by Cynthia Changaris. The story is originally from Linda Moore, Charleston, SC. Phone interview done on 8-18-2007 with email corrections 8-22-2007.

Jesus is Holding Your Baby voice recorded interview with Ashley Campbell, Louisville, KY, 3-22-2009.

Gift of God, group of stories voice-recorded phone interview with Dorothy Kress, Cross Plains, TN, 9-22-2007.

My Angel was a Good Ol' Boy recounted by Author.

Baby Angels submitted by email from Janet Marlin 12-4-2007.

Guardian Angel submitted by email from Virginia Gilpin 12-5-2007.

Mystery Lady submitted by email from Michael Dennis, Cincinnati, OH, 12-4-2007. Contact Michael at mike@mikethepsychic.com.

Twice Saved from Death initial phone interview with Ann Richer, 12-4-2007 & emails submitted.

Mosh Pit Angel, Brooke Raby, Lexington, KY, told to author on 10-1-2008 and submitted via email on 10-19-2008.

Angelic Intervention, Deena Madison.

Cat Angel phone interview with Debbie Magnes, Louisville, KY, 12-5-2007

Family Angels, Little Cripple Angel, Angelic Children phone interviews and email submissions (2007) from author Roberta Simpson Brown, Middletown, KY. Roberta is the author of *The Walking Trees and other Scary Stories, The Queen of the Cold-Blooded Tales, Scared in School, Lamplight Tales.*

Dad's Visitor submitted by email from El Wanda Horsley 12-12-2007.

Flooded Car, Dog Daze, interview and email submission from Jackie Atchison, Louisville, KY, 12-18-2007.

Lord Giveth and the Lord Taketh Away (Scattered Undies), voice-recorded interview with author Cora Seaman, in Boonville, IN, on 3-18-2006.

My Angel Smells like Vanilla, Claudia Thurman.

Camouflage Angel phone interview, 6-26-2007, with Pam Ford, Auburn, KY, with email submission, 8-8-2007.

An Angel's Warning Call submitted by email from Charles Nave, 12-21-2007.

I'm an Angel phone interview, 6-26-2007, with Jan Carter, Louisville, KY, with email submission, 12-5-2007.

The Quilt and the Angel, story told to group by Oleeda Bolton on July 22 at the Southwest Regional Library, and submitted via email 8-27-2008.

Angel's Voice 8-18-2007 submitted by email from (name changed) female in the Evansville, IN, area. Story edited via email 9-4-2007.

Invisible Protector, interview with Lahna Harris, Louisville, KY, and email submission, 6-26-2007.

Ruthie's Angels, Nanna Heard Angel Music, Ginger my Angel Dog interview and email submission from Jackie Atchison, Louisville, KY, 12-5-2007.

Swirling Pillar of Light, voice-recorded phone interview with Dorothy Kress, Cross Plains, TN, 12-6-2007.

Spinning Tires submitted by email from Diana Szerletich, 12-10-2007.

Angels on the Lookout, contributed by Glynnis Whitwer, 12-27-2007.

Flames of Light, Flames of Love, My Guardian Angel Damien submitted by email from Dale Epley, 12-10-2007, with corrections 12-13-2007.

Floating White Feathers submitted by email from Kim Owens, 12-12-2007.

Mom's an Angel Now submitted by email from Willie Windwalker, 12-3-2007.

White-robed EMT, phone interview and email submission from James White, Lexington, KY, 12-10-2007.

Guarding the Door to the Afterlife, Angel Driver submitted by email from Rose Campbell, 12-12-2007.

Drowning Girl Rescued, Lois Madden.

Angel Brings Gift of Song, phone interview with Pam Hadesty, New Port Richey, FL, with email editing, 12-3-2007.

Angel Trucker, Fred Reaves.

Angel at the Circus, Judy Mullins.